Critical Humanism

In loving memory of my dear brother,
Geoff Plummer (1942–2020)

Critical Humanism

A Manifesto for the Twenty-First Century

Ken Plummer

polity

First published in 2021 by Polity Press

Polity Press
65 Bridge Street
Cambridge CB2 1UR, UK

Polity Press
101 Station Landing
Suite 300
Medford, MA 02155, USA

ISBN-13: 978-1-5095-2794-6
ISBN-13: 978-1-5095-2795-3(pb)

A catalogue record for this book is available from the British Library.

Library of Congress Cataloging-in-Publication Data
Names: Plummer, Kenneth, author.
Title: Critical humanism : a manifesto for the 21st century / Ken Plummer.
Description: Cambridge, UK ; Medford, MA : Polity Press, 2021. | Includes
    bibliographical references and index. | Summary: "A passionate defence
    of human value and human potential"-- Provided by publisher.
Identifiers: LCCN 2021006115 (print) | LCCN 2021006116 (ebook) | ISBN
    9781509527946 (hardback) | ISBN 9781509527953 (paperback) | ISBN
    9781509527960 (pdf) | ISBN 9781509527984 (epub)
Subjects: LCSH: Humanity. | Humanism--Social aspects. | Human beings.
Classification: LCC BJ1533.H9 P58 2021 (print) | LCC BJ1533.H9 (ebook) |
    DDC 179.7--dc23
LC record available at https://lccn.loc.gov/2021006115
LC ebook record available at https://lccn.loc.gov/2021006116

Typeset in 10.5 on 12 pt Sabon
by Fakenham Prepress Solutions, Fakenham, Norfolk NR21 8NL
Printed and bound in Great Britain by CPI Group (UK) Ltd, Croydon

For further information on Polity, visit our website:
politybooks.com

Contents

Boxes, Tables and Figures

Boxes

Tables

Figures

Acknowledgements

My special thanks to Jonathan Skerrett, who has been my advising editor for the past three books. I have had some really good editors over quite some time, starting with Peter Hopkins at Routledge one very drunken lunch back in 1972; Jonathan has been wonderfully supportive, critically shrewd and very patient. I also thank Karina Jákupsdóttir for always being there to help bring this book into fruition. Sarah Dancy revised a very messy text into a much clearer one and I am very grateful. Thanks too to Evie Deavall (production) and Michael Solomons (index).

Nowadays, most of my intellectual debts go back a long way and most of my teachers, sadly, are dead. My earliest tutors (and colleagues), Stanley Cohen, Mary McIntosh and Jock Young, among others, taught me not only a passion for doing academic things that personally matter, but also showed me that intellectual life can be fun and enjoyable. John Gagnon and Bill Simon were dear friends as well as extraordinary thinkers. Michael Schofield was there with my very earliest worries. I remember them all with deep fondness.

A few people have been regular supports and I thank them dearly: Molly Andrews, Neli Demireva, Carlos Gigoux, Miriam Glucksmann, Mark Harvey, Phil Jakes, George Kolanckiewicz, Travis Kong, Harvey Molotch, Ewa Morawaska, Lydia Morris, Peter Nardi, David Paternotte, Colin Samson, Steve Smith, Arlene Stein, Jeremy Tambling,

Pauline Tambling, Paul Thompson, Jeffrey Weeks and Glenn Wharton. I especially thank Rob Stones for years of engaged discussion and for a critical but sympathetic early reading of this work. And I thank Daniel Nehring for all his detailed, critical and generous comments on a final draft of the book. This has not been an easy book to write, but I hope it can make a small and timely contribution to a never-ending debate.

Sadly, although my Gay Liberation Front days were a critical turning point in my life, I have never been quite the activist I would have liked to have been. But I have always admired those who are. Any proceeds from this book will be donated to Amnesty International.

Finally, I dedicate this book to my dear brother Geoff, who died as I was completing it, after many years of cheerful illness. I am very thankful for my family of 'Plummers': Ethel, Len, Steph, Jon and Tony, Chris and Lorraine, Abigail and Emily. Most of all, I fear I could do very little without the perpetual kindness, support and love of my life-long partner and 'bestest friend', Everard Longland. We have had a long and wonderful journey together.

Wivenhoe, November 2020

Imaginations: Only Connect

Only Connect. Tell the Stories.
Connect the machine to the action
And the action to the person.
Connect the person to the other,
And the other to the self.
Connect the self to the body,
And the body to the mind.
Connect the mind to the senses,
And the senses to the community.
Connect the community to the country,
And the country to the world.
Connect the world to the earth,
And the earth to the sky.
Connect the sky to the cosmos,
And the cosmos back to humanity.

Connect the particular to the general,
And the unique to the universal.
Connect the public to the personal,
And the personal to the political.
Connect the present to the past,
And the past to the future.
Connect the media to the reality,
And the reality to the truth.
Connect the knowing to the doing,
And the doing to the values.
Connect the generations to our dreams:
Of love and kindness and care.
Connect creativity to dignity and hope,
To a politics of better worlds for all.
Connect to rights and justice and flourishing.
Hear the Stories. Only Connect.

Introduction

What do we live for, if it is not to make life less difficult for each other?

George Eliot, *Middlemarch* (1871)

The year was 2007. I had been 'born again': a new human person, reconnected, full of life, energy and joy. I now had a new liver placed gently inside my body – donated by a seventeen-year-old girl, killed tragically in an accident. At any other time in history my life would have surely come to a fatal end. But in 2007, I was able to have a liver transplant. Over many years, I had developed chronic, fatal liver disease. The only way out now was full-blown transplant surgery. This saved my life. Recently invented, the transplant process brought together the altruism of the donor, the skills of the surgeon, the care of the nurses, the practical endeavours of hospital staff, the love of friends, partner and family, the intellectual brilliance of scientists – a full assemblage of humanity at work. Balancing on the edge of death for three and a half years and experiencing a successful transplant most surely wants to make you celebrate the wonders of being uniquely alive, connected to the world and being complexly human.[1]

And yet. Even as I was slowly being returned to my fragile wider planetary home, this very world looked like it could do with its own transplant! It was 2008: just seven years after the atrocity of the 9/11 New York twin tower slaughtering, we now had to face the enormous greed and corruption of the financial crash – casino capitalism – and its dishonest aftermath. Today as I write, in 2020, we confront a quite different order of crisis: a twenty-first-century plague, Covid-19, which has shaken everybody's life and the very social structures in which we live.[2] A new generational world experience is happening all around, like it or not.

Even as I recognize much of the extraordinary progress made in some parts of the world, I can also clearly see a world in woe, a much-mutilated humanity. We live in the chaotic flow of liquid modernity, a time of extraordinary volatility and change where life and the future have been rendered unsafe, insecure and at risk.[3] The recent dominance of the West is now firmly in decline, and a new pluriversal world order is in the making.[4] This is also an order with a tangible sense of the extreme harm we are doing to our environment. We build megacities of pollution in the middle of deserts. We cut down large swathes of forests all round the world, destroying both wildlife and the air we breathe. We elect leaders full of self-pride and little concern for global humanity. We fail to prepare ourselves adequately for a world in which a long line of antici-pated catastrophes and disasters (the Anthropocene and the Precipice) is lining up for us. We tip endless muck into the oceans and rivers, so life cannot survive. We turn all of human sensitivity and life into a deluge of digital dehumanization. And wherever we look – if we do look – we can see a morass of inequality: the rich and their unqualified 'greediness' doing so much more damage than the poor, who are forced to suffer so much. The deep structural divides over men and women, different ethnicities and sexualities, and more, are embedded in deep levels of violence. An unbearable suffering stalks the world in many places. Myanmar's generals preside over the brutal ethnic cleansing of the Rohingya population; Syria's President al-Assad wages bloody war, bombing civilians and targeting hospitals; and in Yemen, the Saudi-led coalition has killed and wounded thousands of civilians, bringing an entire country to the brink of famine.

Here is our cruel world of winners who get more and losers who get less. A world where women continue to be downgraded. A world where the humanity of some groups who are ethnically, sexually or bodily different is denied. And despite years of accelerating warnings, a world in which many people live in full-blown and much-celebrated, irresponsible, cruel and violent ignorance. We dwell in what might be called anti-humanity: a deep disconnection from being human as we engage in mass dehumanization, mass expulsions, mass digitalism and mass extinctions. Much of the pluriversal world lives in deep ignorance of the complexity (and often the suffering) of the rest of the world. And everywhere, Covid-19 has not made living any easier. So many people suffer; so many have been seriously let down by the human world in which they live.

From Humanism to Critical Humanism

So here we are. As agentic human beings we face the muddles, failures and tragedies of our world: some certainly more than others. How can our human world, one we have been building so artfully over the millennia, remain such a flawed place? Over the years we can see the uneven march of progress in the sphere of the technical. But in the ethical and human sphere, we linger behind. Advances in our 'inner humanities' do not match our scientific and technological awareness. Nearly 100 years ago – only three or four generations – there was the most atrocious Holocaust. Science and power were put to use with the vilest of thoughts. Today, despite our ritualistic posturing 'lest we forget', many in the world are no longer even aware of it. Indeed, what have we learnt since then? In writing this book, I found for a while that the Holocaust overwhelmed me as a serious preoccupation (as it probably should in every human life at some time). How can it be that after all these thousands of years of so-called humanity we had learnt nothing and were capable of such cruel atrocities, often in the divisive language of humanity and nonhumanity? Humanity is in a mess. Why still write about a moribund humanism?

My interest in a sociological humanist stance goes back to the modern foundational works of William James, George Herbert Mead, Jane Addams and Herbert Blumer.[5] As a young gay man in the 1960s, then outlawed, stigmatized and apparently nonhuman, my earliest research on gay culture told me that the best way to understand the world was to be pragmatic: to get close to life as lived in its rich complexity and to listen to the diverse stories of unique human lives. Too much social science is done at a great distance from the lived human experience and its joys and pains. More: sociology should not just get done for its own sake. It needed to aim for social goals, social purpose, emancipation, connection and amelioration. Some forty years ago I wrote my first set of humanist claims, about using human stories to understand life, in the hope that we could move on. Today, many social scientists have long left humanism behind, if they ever even countenanced it. The worlds of big data, post-theory and academic capitalism have arrived.

There are very good reasons why some of my colleagues in the academic and political worlds have been critical of humanism. Political scientist Anne Phillips summarizes the objections well:

> Humanism has come under attack from a number of directions in recent decades: for its essentialism of human nature; its tendency to read the course of human history as the steady progress towards realising the potential implicit in that nature; its misguided confidence in the powers of science and reason; its celebration of an autonomous self-determining subject; and so on and on.[6]

I have much sympathy with such critiques. There are many very good reasons to attack. But there are also many good reasons to defend and develop.

Critics argue that the very idea of humanism has become Westernized. It has led to the abuse and monstrosities of colonialism, slavery, femicide, class oppression, racism and exploitations of all kinds: ultimately, to genocides of the races. And they are indeed right. Yet, today we live in a world where anti-humanity is still rife. I will argue, somewhat ironically, that we now need the highly charged and contested term 'humanity' (or some equivalent) more than ever before: to help defend us and to give our lives, work and play some coherence, connection and common purpose. To act in the world for a more connected world. We need to find a fallible universality out of our precarious particularity. And I ask: what else is there? At its fragile core, the invented idea of humanity has to suggest a collective social nature of being human that is connected, relational, valued. Ours is an embodied narrative species and a connective humanity. Through language and stories, we can act to share common good things with each other: creativity, love, kindness, hope perhaps. We can find a shared solidarity in caring for one another. There may even be a possible common worth, respect, even 'dignity', to be valued across our species. And there is a putative mode of feeling for our human interconnectedness with other species, life forms and even planets. To live well with other people, animals and things in the deep multiverse is surely a laudable goal. Maybe, too, our world can now come to thrive on inter-dependent differences, be deeply pluralistic, learn from our connectivity. As times change and new debates appear, these all seem worthwhile aims for our different kinds of experience and activity in life. (Box 0.1 suggests a basic working set of terminologies, open to debate and change.) Ultimately, key questions become: *How are we to live cooperatively with our diverse yet common humanity, not rendering it divisive or dehumanizing? How can we best live together with our differences?*

Most versions of humanism, of which this is one, are ultimately engaged with a human search for meaning. They usually tell a specific story of what it means to be human. In the Renaissance and Enlightenment of the West, a strong and unified storyline emerged. Here I take the stance of a critical humanist who appreciates this, but immediately sees how damaging this idea has been for much of the wider pluriversal world. We have to move beyond this to see the very ideas of humanity and humanism as themselves fragile: multiple and shifting over lives, time and place. Different humanisms bring contested claims about what it means to be human. These change over history as different (usually powerful) groups make different claims. Critical humanism engages with (and tells the stories of) the perpetual narrative reconstructions and conflicts over what it means to be human. Ultimately it does this with the goal of building on these contested under-standings to find pathways into better futures and worlds. Critical humanism is an emerging project to remake sense of

Box 0.1: Defining humanity

The languages of both humanism and humanity are contested and muddled. That said, in this book I use certain key words to mean certain things while certainly acknowledging all these words need debating.[7]

The term *human species* (*homo sapiens*) is fairly straight-forward. We are a biological species (*hominin*) and part of the evolutionary classification of domains of life. We make up about 0.01 per cent of life on earth,[8] taking a small place in the grand encyclopaedia of living things. *Humankind* is a collective word to depict our bio-geo-historical existence.

The idea of *human beings* (or even *persons*)[9] builds on the above but suggests the ways in which we differ from other animals. These terms bring a range of *descriptive formal properties* open for discussion. This includes (i) we are embodied with feelings and elaborate brains and cognitions; (ii) we are animals aware of our vulnerability; (iii) we develop language, consciousness, symbolic communications, we tell stories and create selves; (iv) we live in worlds of values, becoming moral animals; (v) we are agentic animals who act in the world; (vi) we have emergent potentials, capacities, capabilities; and (vii) we are creative animals. We could add more. These are only formal features of being human. The controversies start when we talk about their *substantive content*. What kinds of bodies, selves, vulnerabilities, values, capabilities? Some ideas – rights, dignity, equalities – are perpetually controversial because they straddle the descriptive formal and the evaluative substantive.

Humanities refers to the study of all things human – especially its arts, literature, languages, music, poetics.

Humanity is a more recent and more muddled idea. It can be taken (i) as a collective descriptive word for the entirety of human life. But it can also suggest (ii) a collective *evaluative* word for human life, often implying those who show human sympathy with others. Often these two get muddled. (An emerging idea, (iii), is that we are actually all 'little gods', albeit little gods who shit! But we can leave that controversy to one side for the moment. See pp. 84–5.)

Finally, *humanism* itself has many meanings. Here I use it to signify all ideas that try to understand what it means to be human and to find ways of enhancing our being in the world.

all this. Even as it will raise many problems, it enables us to ask questions about what kind of human world we want to live in, what kind of person we want to be in that world, and how it needs to be transformed.

The Book and Manifesto Ahead: A Politics of Humanity

I have written this book to help re-energize an interest in humanism. I examine how we are dehumanizing the world (through damage, division and atrocity) and how we might reconnect and humanize it (through narrative, values and creativity). I identify many humanist practices at work across the world, from dialogue and cosmopolitanism to creativity and 'generational hope', and aim to give them a rudimentary coherence. An opening section explains why I use the term 'critical humanism'; I outline its key claims and challenges (as a project, an agenda, a narrative). The middle core of the book looks first at the failings of humanity and then goes in pursuit of its successes. The closing (and final) part makes a direct link to a politics and education of humanity, suggesting things that could be done to make a connective world for all. I illustrate the importance of cultivating a generational hope and building on a multiplicity of existing world projects that work to make the planet a better place for all.

This had to be a short book so there is much ground I have not covered. That said, there is a website (**kenplummer. com/criticalhumanism**) with substantial guides to readings, websites and other material concerning critical humanism.

As I write, Covid-19 has arrived; wildlife is in serious decline; the world is literally and metaphorically ablaze. The global hazards so long predicted are becoming the stuff of everyday life. So much suffering in the world and the widespread failure of many key institutions. So much unnecessary suffering for so many, wrought often by so few. We could do so much better as a species. (And I could do so much better as a person.) Very many have had such thoughts before me. Why have we not put our enormous learning into better practice? I make the claim here that we need 'humanity' as a narrative to guide us, a literacy to learn with and a tool to act with. Human beings can be creative. They can create a common empathic and dialogic world of human connections. They can build a world that will flourish over the generations by creating strong, caring, just and loving institutions so we can live well, if fragilely, with each other and our differences. But still, I sometimes ask myself: am I just a foolish dreamer?

PART I
Rethinking the World: Connecting Humanity

Critical humanism:

- a *narrative* that provides changing, connective, critical and contested stories of how we become human in the universe;
- a *dialogue* between contrasting and contested meanings about what it is to be human in the universe;
- a *project* that aims to repair the damaged world and cultivate its flourishing;
- a *connection* between life and earth, people and communities, societies and the world: and the cosmos beyond;
- an *imagination* that thinks like a planet, 'only connects' and creates a generational hope;
- an *imaginary* that builds grounded projects for a better world for all;
- a *politics* of humanity that works for positive transformations of the world in a multitude of ways;
- a *theory* to make sense of all the above.

1
Critical Humanism

The status of human is something we claim and enact rather
than something we uncover.
Anne Phillips, *The Politics of the Human* (2015), p. 131

Humanism and humanity have fallen on hard times. They need
to be reimagined and reconnected. As Anne Phillips points out,
our human status must be enacted, not simply discovered. Three
or four generations ago, their death was being firmly announced
by European philosophers.[1] More recently, a posthuman era
has been ushered in. This 'ending' of humanism happens
periodically; the sociologist Marcus Morgan nicely calls it 'the
phoenix of humanism'.[2] Humanism has its fates, fatalities and
foes; yet it rises back up again and again. Humanity seems to
keep calling us. At its best, as John Dewey once remarked, it is
'an expansion, not a contraction, of human life, an expansion
in which nature and the science of nature are made the willing
servants of human good'.[3] Each generation finds its new
responses. This book is one such response.

Critical Humanism as a Project

Critical humanism suggests a fallible, worldwide, contested
narrative about the collective, connecting and changing ways

of being 'human'. Just what this 'human' signifies is itself a long tale: of searching for the meanings of vulnerable life in a precarious plural world. The very idea of 'humanity' becomes a debated and contested one.

Critical humanism becomes a project shaped by many controversies. It highlights the plurality of our lives and humanisms, the connectivity and contingency of life and the narrativity of humanity. It argues for a humanism that is truly worldwide and not just an argument for some narrow, culture-bound version. It can learn from a wide range of different humanisms that have existed. And all this leads to the thorny problem of universalism and essentialism, a problem that haunts all discussions of humanism. As such, it is clear that a deep tension arises between the various claims for the *generalities* of a universal humanity in a world where lives are also and always lived in context-specific *particularities*, a 'radical contextuality'.[4]

Critical humanism, then, is an open project not a closed theory. It is an ever-changing endeavour to rethink and remake a narrative of a world humanity. Different groups have struggled throughout history over just what it means to be a human being in a fragile universe. The task now is to connect: to imagine 'like a world' and build a rich planetary agenda of diverse and multiple critical projects that bring us together to re-create a better world for all. Box 1.1 sets out the basic agenda, which is then pursued in the rest of the book. By the final chapter, it will have somehow transformed itself into a political manifesto.

Humanist Sociology and Critical Humanism

To be clear at the outset, critical humanism is not new. It draws on a range of past humanisms, especially a flexible humanist sociology, but takes it further. A humanist sociology is one that builds on pragmatism. It recognizes and appreciates the value of every grounded, down-to-earth and uniquely different active human life. It listens to their stories and search for meaning. It appreciates the significance of their vulnerability, suffering and joy in life; aims at building a

Box 1.1: Connecting humanity: the critical humanist project

Critical humanism suggests an opening eight-point agenda to get us going. I explore all these in the chapters that follow.

1. *Critical humanism* What is this thing called 'critical humanism'? Why do we need it? Where is it heading? What are its challenges?
2. *Damaged humanity* How have we come to construct such a mutilated, disconnected world? How might we repair it?
3. *Divided humanity* Why is humanity so divided? How can we learn to live well together with our amazing and vast array of differences?
4. *Traumatized humanity* How can we make sense of the atrocities of our past? Why have we treated each other so badly and with such cruelty? How can we build narratives and institutions of reconciliation, justice, truth and accountability with one another?
5. *Narrative humanity* How has humanity been assembled through narrative? We have become the distinctive, even distinguished, storytelling animal. So how can we cultivate stories that will encourage a better future, a flourishing world? Can there be a narrative of worldwide connection?
6. *A valuing humanity* How have we built a long and distinguished history of human values? We have become the distinctively 'moral animal' that dwells in a culture with 'values for living'. Can there be worldwide values that will bring us together?
7. *Transformative humanity* What kind of futures do we want? We have become the creative creatures: we bring new things into the world. Can we create ways of making a better future that will connect all peoples, life and the earth?
8. *A politics of humanity* How can we act in the world to bring about change? How can we use creative political actions to bridge the local and the universal? And reconnect us all to earth, life, world and the cosmos. Can we create a globalization of better worlds for all?

Critical humanism establishes a politics of humanity. It asks (a) How can we reduce the human harm and hazards in the world, especially for the vulnerable, exploited and marginal? (b) How can we connect lives to the continuity and richness of the earth we live on? (c) How can we build creative and flourishing human worlds for all?

We look for *harm reduction, connectivity, flourishing*.

sympathetic human knowledge; connects to wider structural, historical issues; provides a conversation about human values; suggests transformations that aim to make better worlds; and confronts an emancipatory politics head on.[5] It has many kindred spirits.[6] Nowadays, this has to be a global argument not a local one: after all, although Bangladesh, Brazil, China, India, Indonesia, Mexico, Nigeria, Pakistan and Russia rank as the largest and most populated countries in the world, they typically get little mention in the many works on humanism. It is part of the movement to de-Westernize, decolonize and repolarize the world. A new and important idea here is that of the pluriversal world: there are many 'worlds of worlds' living alongside one another. Ours is a plural world.[7]

Critical humanism becomes both a worldly project of human connectivity and a global narrative that expands on this. It claims a critical stance by appreciating that humanity and humanism act as a narrative that shifts over time and space, bringing about historically grounded 'projects' as humans go in search of meaning. It can never be a pure universal constant. But it will most surely show slender threads of 'fallible continuities' – ways of making broad but tentative connections. There is no fixed meaning of humanism or humanity: they operate as a narrative that draws from a widely held pragmatic view of the workability, yet fallibility, of the everyday world.[8]

The idea of humanism is not always seen in quite this way. (More commonly it is seen as a fixed universal linked to some version of human nature.) But I think this more critical, long narrative view is helpful: it shows how the very idea of humanity and humanism, indeed the words themselves, signifies changing historical understandings developed in different contexts by different groups. What is claimed to be human at one moment in history may not be so claimed at another, even if slender threads hold them together. Our narratives are multiple in form, producing claims that are contested by (usually political) groupings. In all this, I draw from both classical humanism and a humanist sociology, but move beyond them.

Ultimately, I argue that the narrative of humanity is a changing, multilayered and plural idea. It introduces a value struggle over what it means to be a human being. Always diverse, it recognizes the need for a cooperative mutuality that will connect us all in the sharing of a universal planet. Some kind of 'common ground' has to be found to create visions of life and a future. We need some kind of global human imagination, practice, aesthetics, ethics and politics to go with it. 'We' (and by this I mean, rather immodestly, you, me and the whole damned human world) have to move through our differences. We have to find some of the things we can agree on. And this is a key theme of this book. Critical humanism seeks a narrative for the betterment of a global humanity, in all its rich connected diversity, by enhancing the world for all in each generation. This just might be a commonality worth trying for. We need here to think and talk, a little, like a planet.

The critical humanist imagination moves from a unique, but limited, little human being towards a vision of a collective way of 'living with difference' – of all being valued and connected to a wider planetary world. It moves back and forth between the biological and the cosmic, the local and the global, from personal sufferings to political transformation. It is grounded in a paradox: while it recognizes just how fragile, contested and divided our humanity is, it also challenges us to ask how we human beings can build a world of shared common humanity that enables us all to flourish and live well with each other and our differences.

The Plurality and Hybridity of Humanisms, Humanity and the World

And so, let's see humanity at its most expansive and generous. Humanism suggests a theory and practice of what it means to be human and to live a vibrant human life in an infinite pluriverse of time and space. But there is never just the one way: humanism appreciates the rich diversities of humanity in an ever-changing world, and the way in which human beings struggle to make sense of their lives, ultimately building worlds that intermingle with one another, with animals and with other things. A little while back, the sociologist Alfred McClung Lee, a much-ignored champion of a humanistic sociology, saw humanism emerging everywhere throughout history:

> Humanism has figured in a wide range of religious, political and academic movements. As such it has been identified with atheism, capitalism, classicism, communism, democracy, egalitarianism, populism, nationalism, positivism, pragmatism, relativism, science, scientism, socialism, statism, symbolic interactionism, and supernaturalism, including versions of ancient paganisms, Hinduism, Buddhism, Judaism, Roman Catholicism, Protestantism and Mohammedanism. It has also been rationalized as being opposed to each of these. It has served as an ingredient in movement against each. And these terms do not at all suggest all of humanism's ideological and social associations.[9]

This listing is not exhaustive: how could it be? There are many practitioners who make very particular claims: for example, Mahatma Gandhi's *nonviolent, pacifist humanism*, Franz Fanon's *new humanism*, Edward Said's *democratic worldly humanism*, Marcus Morgan's *pragmatic humanism*, Martha C. Nussbaum's *'cosmopolitan-cultivation-capabilities' humanism*, Paul Gilroy's *antiracist planetary humanism*, Jeffrey Weeks's *radical humanism*, Judith Butler's *mortalist humanism*, Cornel West's *prophetic humanism of love*, William E. Connolly's *entangled planetary humanism*, Roberto Unger's *new religious pragmatic humanism* – and many more.

To take just one major example. Edward W. Said was one of the world's leading cultural critics of the late twentieth century. His work *Orientalism* spearheaded the postcolonial movement and decolonization. He argued for a position that many claim is anti-humanist. But this is not so. From his earliest works to his very last, he remained a staunch, if critical, humanist. As he famously said: 'Humanism is the only ... I would go as far as to say the final resistance we have against the inhuman practices and injustices that disfigure human history.'[10] Working with this is a wide array of humanisms in the making that highlight the struggles of a range of human peoples: indigenous, disabled, colonized, racialized, gendered, queered. This curious listing seems endless. Diverse humanisms provide a deep flow of rich thinking.[11]

Debating Humanism: Learning from Controversies

With all this, why might another humanism be needed? Here I discuss some controversies of recent developments in humanist thinking. I claim that a great deal can be learnt from these arguments, but we need to make connections and move further.

Humanism as Western Enlightenment

I start straightforwardly: with the widely accepted claim that humanism is a Western phenomenon and derives from the Enlightenment. This view has been promoted over the last 250 years; it is pervasive in the academy and the West, and its most prominent, popular proponent these days is the cognitive psychologist Steven Pinker.[12] For Pinker, humanism begins with the ancient Greeks, is rediscovered in Renaissance Florence, and accelerates with the science and rationality of the Enlightenment. It claims to be the harbinger of unmistakeable essential human progress. And such ideas have been widely influential. But they flag just one form of humanism bound up with one narrow 'Western' context. It is better to call it just that: 'Western Enlightenment Humanism'. It should not be allowed to completely overwrite the rich diversity of earlier and wider claims for thought about humanity across world history. If followed, it can indeed become part of the much wider dominance and hegemony that male Western thinking has been busy claiming for itself over the past 500 years or so (a view recently claimed as narcissistic in the extreme[13]). It seems, rather perilously, to have claimed to be the only serious thought in the world! Creating a monologic world, it has denied the rich reality of a 'world of many worlds', a 'plural world'.

For some time, a number of major intellectual and political movements have been trying to bring this 'rest of the world' back into our thinking. We need a world humanism, not a Western humanism. As ideas of globalization have accelerated, we have been made to think about the processes and interconnectedness of the world's nations. More strongly, key ideas around colonization and postcolonization have brought us to see the divide between the global North and the global South, the East and the West, the poor and the rich. Starting perhaps with Gandhi and Franz Fanon, these ideas developed especially in the works of Edward Said. They are now advanced in the writings of Gurminder K. Bhambra, Raewyn Connell, Arturo Escobar, Marisol de la Cadena, Boaventura de Sousa Santos, Bernd Reiter and many others, in a major critique of colonized, metropolitan, Western-centric thought.[14] These works suggest there exists a vitality of intellectual and creative humanity across history and cultures that has been ignored or stunted. Providing a much greater awareness of a diverse human world and its 'ecologies of knowledge', they raise the ways different ideas are bound up with diverse local cultures and social conditions. Where, for example, do Africa, Asia and Latin America fit into this Enlightenment account? Where are China, Russia and India in this story?

From this, we start to see the role of power, ideology and hegemony in understandings of the Enlightenment. 'Knowledges' of many of the world's countries – like the countries themselves – have been colonized. Spanish sociologist Boaventura de Sousa Santos notably talks about the 'waste of experience' and a world knowledge (epistemology) where so much has been excluded through 'blindness' and 'absences'.[15] A wide rich mosaic of diverse cultures all over the world, a pluriverse, gets excluded by Western thought. The lush richness of world humankind gets denied, lost or betrayed.

Humanism as secularism

A second debate is closely linked and also Western. In this, humanism is a secular, rational critique of religion. This is a little odd given that such luminaries as the Pope, the Archbishop of Canterbury and several Chief Rabbis also proclaim humanism. Nevertheless, since the Enlightenment, many humanists have argued for the Death of God. An age of secularization is arriving whereby rationality, objectivity and truth will come to reign, old mythologies and fables of religions past will ebb and flow away, and science will come to 'lighten the burden of human existence'.[16] 'Humanism' becomes the term for rational progress in the world. For much of the twentieth century, Western intellectuals generally envisioned religion's demise in this new world.[17] And the idea of humanism became almost synonymous with atheism or nonbelief.

Such arguments have been widely promoted by public atheists: notably, in works like Richard Dawkins's bestselling *The God Delusion*, Sam Harris's *The Moral Landscape*, Christopher Hitchens's *God Is Not Great*[18] and the works of many others, such as Daniel C. Dennett and A. C. Grayling. Most contemporary organizations for humanism, for example Humanists UK and Humanist International, take this view. It is a stance also taken in the important *Wiley Blackwell Handbook of Humanism* (2015).[19] And in some accounts, these claims go much further. If there is a God, then it is indeed the human being, humanity itself, that is this God: *Homo Deus*. In his bestselling work, the Israeli Yuval Noah Harari sees modern humanism as 'the worship of man': 'On the verge of becoming a God, poised to acquire not only eternal youth but also the divine oblivion on creation and destruction.'[20] Likewise, as the physicist Brian Cox has said: 'We are the Cosmos made conscious and life is the means by which the universe understands itself.'[21]

Widespread as this view may be in scientific communities and some Western countries (though certainly not in the United States), the secular claim remains a minority view.[22] There may well be major countries where religious storytelling has become much less significant[23] (atheism attracts around 14 per cent of the world, mainly in Western Europe and the Nordic countries). Yet the power of religion is still growing in many countries across the world. Christianity remains the largest world religion, with around 2.4 billion adherents (and growing). The Islamic world expects a 70 per cent growth between 2015 and 2060. Far from the secular world that was once predicted, a post-secular age has arrived.[24]

In examining this, sociologist Ulrich Beck has suggested that religion in the twenty-first century now has two faces.[25] One face takes a decided turn towards fundamentalism:

there is only one story, one God, one truth. It has led to a proliferation of devastating major armed conflicts and global violence. In the Middle East between Shi'ite and Sunni, and a global Jihad; in the Israeli–Palestinian conflict; in the Syrian civil war between ISIS, Kurdish forces, the Assad government and others; in the wars in Afghanistan and Iraq, all raising issues of religious extremism. There are also Buddhist revolts in Asia: for example, Sri Lanka, Mongolia and Myanmar, where the Arakan Rohingya Salvation Army (ARSA) attacked the Muslim Rohingya community, creating a large refugee group. And lesbian and gays are under attack in many countries from fundamentalist Muslims, Christians and Jews.[26] Fundamentalism is absolute and seeks to destroy any whiff of plurality, including humanity, through devastating violence.

More hopefully, a second 'religious' route is outlined by Beck. It is a more open, plural and tolerant vision. This response takes a more humane and cosmopolitan narrative, encouraging people to live together with their differences. It draws on past religious works and more recent arguments of people like Mohandas Gandhi, Thich Nhat Hanh, Martin Luther King and the Dalai Lama to work towards creating interfaith communities, listening to others and searching for basic common values. In 1993, the celebrated theologian Hans Küng drew on the key principles of the world's major religions to build 'a global ethic'.[27] This was based on a declaration made at the Parliament of the World's Religions in 1993 by more than 200 leaders from forty or more different faith traditions; it claimed four essential affirmations/commitments as shared principles essential to a global ethic:

- commitment to a culture of nonviolence and respect for life;
- commitment to a culture of solidarity and a just economic order;
- commitment to a culture of tolerance and a life of truthfulness;
- commitment to a culture of equal rights and partnership between men and women.

Here is an indicator of visions to grow. Today we can find a major mission for a common discourse across civilizations and religions alongside the development of this interfaith dialogue.[28] We find it evidenced in works like the Dalai Lama's *Beyond Religion*, Daisaku Ikeda's *A New Humanism* and Felix Unger and Daisaku Ikeda's *The Humanist Principle*.[29]

Beck argues that religions need to become civilized if the world is to survive. The absolutist and totalitarian narrative of religion will feed into populism and encourage both hatred and violence. It makes humanity very unsettled. It threatens its extinction. The other open response suggests the need to practise values like the capacity for peace and global justice rather than totalitarianism and violence.[30] These contrasting capacities can be found throughout the history of religion. Religions of love and religions of hate provide two contrasting unresolved tensions over being human. It is in the hands of the latter to destroy the world.

Humanism as rationality and science

Science has long searched for a rational and objectively 'true' account of what it is to be a human being in a wider universe. From Chinese and Arabic Islamic science, through Leonardo, Galileo and Newton to Hubble and Hawkins, the gradual growth of scientific ideas about the human species has told us much. And advances have rapidly accelerated in recent years. Quantum revolutions, biomolecular revolutions and digital revolutions bring key issues for humanity. A biomolecular revolution, for example, raises issues of designer babies, cloning, gene editing, the extension of life and the problems of eugenics. A digital revolution brings widespread surveillance, data selves, fake imaging and an algorithmic social order. Space science develops plans for sustainable living in outer space. Overall, science is now assembling a very detailed mapping of just what it might mean to be a member of the human species in a future universe of infinite time-space. It is at work everywhere enhancing and challenging what we know about humanity. But wondrous as it is, problems surely come with it.

Charles Darwin's influential work (even if still rejected by significant numbers of the world's population[31]) sets the major evolutionary frame of thinking for science around the emergence of humanity and the universe. His work has been central not only in understanding the evolution of the human species, but also in showing how it connects to all other life forms. We are understanding more and more about our complex relationship with earth and sea, life and animals – no longer can we see ourselves as the supreme or exceptional life form.

Consider just a few recent achievements. Geology, palae-ontology and architectural history have mapped out the phases of our historical existence. The study of rock forma-tions from the distant past shows the rise and collapse of different civilizations and helps create an awareness of just how short our own human existence here has been. We now understand something of the history of world catastrophes: there have been five great extinctions on this planet; an Ice Age preceded us. And this has enabled us to designate more clearly the epochs in which we live: the Holocene (coming after the Ice Age) and the Anthropocene, a recently designated era which demonstrates how we have played an active role in destroying our universe. And all this has led to the suggestion of a potential coming of a sixth extinction.[32]

Biotechnology has also played a key role in redefining humanity. These technologies invade the body and being of humans, working to reconstitute what previously existed. Here we have a world of organ transplants, test-tube babies, altered foetuses, human genomics and gene editing, cryonics, slow ageing – and the Human Genome Project. We can now trace our personal DNA.[33]

Likewise, astrophysics, astrobiology and planetary science now provide 'objective' photomapping of the vast and infinite planetary worlds in which humanity dwells. With Google Maps, we have become the little animal that can map out our positions in an advanced world of astronomical objects (such as planets and stars) and cosmic time. As Brian Cox says: 'The Sun is one star amongst 400 hundred billion in the Milky Way Galaxy, itself just one galaxy amongst 350 billion in the observable universe.'[34] Meanwhile the futurist physicist Michio Kaku charts our futures to live sustainability in this outer space.[35]

Our little human being now enters a world full of deep, disturbing facts about the pluriverse. We are able to look at ourselves reflected back from the moon. And we can even, if we have the money, make plans to travel to it! We can sense that the whole planet on which we live is just a small part of the infinity of time and space: and our own species is but the tiniest of species, both significant and insignificant. Insignificant in that we are the merest of blips in cosmic time and space; significant in that we are the only animal we know that has the necessary consciousness to explore this multiverse. We have become a global humanity, a cosmic human species. And we can reflect on it.[36]

Finally, there is the rise of AI (artificial intelligence) and 'Humanity 2.0'.[37] Already, we start to see the emergence of a robotic life, one that is radically transforming health, transport, work, governance and war. We are only at the beginning of this latest stage of human life, which may well lead to a super intelligence and 'singularity': the machine that will take over our lives, helping create a serious risk to our humanity and our existence. Extraordinarily big claims are being made for this. Mildly, it forecasts the 'enhancement of humanity' as never before; more extravagantly, we face the 'the end of the human species'. At the very least, we may enter a world where the human being is significantly devalued.

The dark side of science

Science has clearly brought great advances to humanity, enabling us to live in ways that have hitherto been inconceivable. But it has not been without its troubled side. The algorithmic world is colonizing human life. Most blatantly, it has brought into being the most destructive forms of technology that humankind has ever known: the science needed for the Holocaust, the bombs on Hiroshima, cyberwar and now drone bombing. More: it has also brought into being a string of anti-human ideologies advancing beliefs that some human beings are subhuman. We find this in the early eugenics and race genetics of the nineteenth century, some of which are still at work in current times.[38] And as we look forward to a new age of surveillance capitalism and robotic superintelligence, we may find a new super elite emerging, killing off the uniqueness of the clever, fleshy, passionate, big brains of human beings as we currently know them to be.

With all this, we see the need for a new kind of ethics and politics of life itself. A critical science, a critical digitalism. The very nature of what it is to exist as a human being is being radically transformed by these genetic, biological, neurological and technological interventions. Whatever human nature might have been, it is certainly now open to radical transformation. We are witnessing a new 'emergent form of life'.[39] Science on its own, then, can be a very dangerous thing. It needs a constant ethical, political and, above all, human counterstory to move it in humane directions.

Humanism as humanitarianism

In their important work, *A Passion for Society*, Iain Wilkinson and Arthur Kleinman argue that 'humanitarian culture has made a vital contribution to the cultivation of modern social consciousness'.[40] They call for social science to make key commitments to understand the centrality of repairing human suffering in social life. Since time immemorial, human suffering and vulnerability have been cast as central features of being human. Most religions put suffering at their very core, claiming the significance of dealing with this through caring, benevolence, beneficence, hospitality and 'love'. The very human act of looking after others shows this most clearly. Throughout history, we have been concerned with doing good, cultivating human compassion and being kind – seen in the early historical example of the Hippocratic Oath. It recurs frequently in any discussion of the Golden Rule (see p. 141). Its modern history arrives with antislavery movements. Very much alive today, it has become a kind of duty for many – helping the sick, doing no harm, caring for others.

As society rolls on, benevolence, care and human amelioration have spread beyond the religious and medical concerns of churches to more and more human institutions. We now see this humanitarian movement at work in education, social work and the caring profession; in the rise of welfare states; in legislation around factory acts; in the rise of philanthropy and charity; in the gift relationships of blood and transplant donations; in the peace movement; in international aid; and as the bedrock of ethical anthropology and sociology. Through this, we sense a picture of humanity gradually emerging as a history of empathy and generosity, care and kindness, and even altruism.[41]

And yet, all of this brings problems. As literary critic Lionel Trilling once strikingly remarked: 'Some paradox in our nature leads us, once we have made our fellowmen the objects of our enlightened interest, to go on to make them the objects of our pity, then of our wisdom, ultimately of our coercion.'[42] There are paradoxes and problems with benevolence. To take one example: Tony Vaux had had more than twenty years' experience as one of Oxfam's leading emergency programme coordinators. It took him through Kosovo, Ethiopia, Sudan, Mozambique, Afghanistan, Somalia, Bosnia and Rwanda – all key emergency sites at the end of the twentieth century. The title of his book, *The Selfish Altruist*, suggests the irony of his work:

> Looking at situations such as the famine in Ethiopia we may conclude that humanitarianism … has not always been as altruistic as it should. Ideological prejudices clouded judgement of aid workers in Ethiopia and they did not see the imminence of famine. Aid workers in Sudan battled against the war mentality but overlooked the marginalisation of women. In Mozambique an obsession with white South African power deafened us to the roar of our own power. In Afghanistan personal and organisational interests masqueraded as principle. In Somalia we were too self-righteous about good intentions and did not listen enough. In the post-communist world, we could not rationally limit our response. In Rwanda we hid from the fallibility of our own humanity. And in Kosovo, we let our human concern be swept away on a political tide.[43]

Worse still, contemporary humanitarianism, in its rush to help those in distressed conflict situations, often find themselves perpetuating or amplifying wars – creating a kind of cosmopolitan dystopia.[44] Didier Fassin's important study, *Humanitarian Reason: A Moral History of the Present*, clarifies all this; he takes us to the intellectual hub of this issue. Writing as a physician social scientist, a critical thinker who works in the field (sometimes for Médecins Sans Frontières (MSF)), Fassin notes:

A remarkable paradox deserves our attention here. On the one hand, moral sentiments are focused mainly on the poorest, most unfortunate, most vulnerable individuals: the politics of compassion is a politics of inequality. On the other hand, the condition of possibility of moral sentiments is generally the recognition of others as fellows: the politics of compassion is a politics of solidarity. This tension between inequality and solidarity, between a relation of dominance and a relation of assistance is constitutive of all humanitarian governance.[45]

Here we see that paradoxes run deep: between self-interest and altruism, dominance and assistance, care and regulation, kindness and violence. There is a political hierarchy within the workings behind humanitarianism. All is not quite as wonderful with humanitarianism as might initially seem to be the case.

Humanism as rights

Much humanism has developed ideas around the rights of human beings. In modern times, these are embodied in purest form in the Universal Declaration of Human Rights (UDHR; originating in Paris at the United Nations General Assembly meeting in December 1948).[46] The document asserts:

recognition of the inherent dignity and of the equal and inalienable rights of all members of the human family is the foundation of freedom, justice and peace in the world ... [D]isregard and contempt for human rights have resulted in barbarous acts which have outraged the conscience of mankind, and the advent of a world in which human beings shall enjoy freedom of speech and belief and freedom from fear and want has been proclaimed as the highest aspiration of the common people.

Here, core notions of equality, justice, freedom, peace, dignity and rights are all brought centre stage in a document that haunts all major contemporary humanist thought and writing. In one clear sense, this movement for 'rights' can be seen as a tremendous success; it has established a universal language that has gradually moved across the world over the past half century. And there is much evidence of a sort of success: a 'justice cascade'.[47] The world has become infused with a human rights culture, some even claiming that it has radically changed the nature of our human world. With the idea of rights, humanity has been given a major common language, an equality of dignity for all. And it has provided a strategy for political change that has already had far-reaching consequences for the lives of many peoples all around the world.[48] Given that the document was only introduced seventy years ago, it has achieved much, and for a wide variety of groups. Box 1.2 suggests a little of this.

Despite considerable achievements in a very short period of time, human rights are under attack from many directions. First, some major countries (including Russia and China) have in practice shown little interest or regard for human rights (they also take little interest in the United Nations or use it for their own ends). Most recently, the USA, under President Donald Trump, stopped using the language of rights; Trump publicly expressed his dislike of the UN on a number of occasions, even withdrawing from the World Health Organization (WHO). But there have also been many schisms and factions within the UN, leading to blocks of voting against rights. For example, although there has been considerable action for women's world rights, there have also been alliances between Catholic and Muslim countries to prevent advances on certain issues (like health and reproductive rights). Likewise, gay and lesbian issues are on the agenda, as are protocols from the Yogyakarta Principles; but religious alliance (between Muslims and Christians) have again prevented any advance in this area.

Many academics have also highlighted human rights failures. Samuel Moyn claims that human rights campaigns have deflected attention from world inequalities; Philip Cunliffe suggests they have led to a cosmopolitan dystopia; and Stephen Hopgood suggests: 'We are on the verge of the imminent decay of the Global Human Rights Regime.'[51] But most seriously, human rights are seen as a Western invention, another form of colonialism, forcing many countries once more to fall in line with Western ideals. This means that, for example, although the struggles faced by non-Western women are different from those of Western women, they are

Box 1.2: An expanding concern over human rights

Debates on 'rights' have expanded from individual rights to collective rights;[49] and this has meant the gradual inclusion of different groups and people into the official world orbit of what it means to be human, alongside the monitoring of their progress. Full of controversy, they are still not always fully recognized in practice.[50]

Children In 1946, UNICEF was established; in 1959, the Declaration of the Rights of the Child; in 1989, Convention on the Rights of the Child.

Women International Year of Women, 1975; Decade of Women, 1976–85. The Beijing Platform for Action, adopted at the 1995 Fourth World Conference on Women, included 'the elimination of all forms of violence against women' as a key objective. The Beijing Declaration and Platform for Action at the 23rd special session of the UN General Assembly, 2000. The creation of UN Women, and the monitoring of their progress in the world: https://www.un.org/en/chronicle/article/brief-survey-womens-rights.

Ethnic persons In 1969, the UN International Convention on the Elimination of all forms of Racial Discrimination: https://www.ohchr.org/EN/Issues/Discrimination/Pages/discrimination_racial.aspx.

Disabled persons In 2006, the UN Convention on the Rights of Persons with Disabilities (CRPDS) was adopted, to eliminate disability discrimination round the world (that is, for roughly 1 million people, 15 per cent of the world's population): https://www.ohchr.org/EN/Issues/Discrimination/Pages/discrimination_disabilities.aspx.

Refugees The 1951 Refugee Convention: https://www.unhcr.org/uk/1951-refugee-convention.html. And its 1967 Protocol, which defines the rights and duties of refugees.

Indigenous persons In 2007, the UN adopts the Declaration on the Rights of Indigenous Peoples (UNDRIP): https://www.ohchr.org/EN/Issues/Discrimination/Pages/discrimination_indigenous.aspx. Publication of a major report, *State of the World's Indigenous Peoples* (4 vols, 2009–19). Survival International formed in 1969.

Lesbian, gay, bisexual, transgender persons In 2011, Human Rights Council and Resolutions on Sexual Orientation and Gender Identity: https://www.ohchr.org/EN/Issues/Discrimination/Pages/LGBT.aspx. The Yogyakarta Principles, originally launched in 2007 (UNHRC).

being colonized by Western rights feminism. Likewise, the Western way of being gay, lesbian and queer is being universalized. Specific cultural differences and problems of being a woman or gay become undermined as the world is shaped by the ideals of Western feminists and queers. In addition, indigenous peoples have not, until very recently, been recognized as having rights.[52]

So it is a complex problem. As rights are argued for, so traditional Western modes are established. As rights are critiqued, so they become undermined. And with this, so too the quest for humanity. Critical humanism recognizes the failings of rights theory and work, but claims that human rights have only been taken seriously for a couple of generations. There are many future battles to be fought for the strong and vital future of human rights.

Humanism as dignity

Closely intertwined with ideas of rights are ideas of equality and dignity. Dignity has featured in discussions of humanity over the centuries. Most religions and discussions of 'human nature' will at some point raise the issue of human dignity. Closely linked to ideas of honour, dignity involves the right of all people to be equally recognized, respected and given worth as human beings. It is a claim that can be found in Cicero; it is developed in much religious writing; it gets its humanist flourishing from the 24-year-old Pico della Mirandola in his *Oration on the Dignity of Man* (1486); it is central to Kant's belief in human agency; and, as we have seen, it has been embedded in most of the fundamental human rights documents since the 1940s: 'All human beings are born free and equal in dignity and rights.' Versions of dignity can be found across cultures, originating as a term for those with elevated status from China to Persia, who required respectful treatment, but trickling down from this bourgeois use to the masses.

That said, the idea has many critics. Schopenhauer once called it 'the shibboleth of all perplexed and empty-headed moralists', and Nietzsche dismissed it rapidly. These days, it is seen as a relic of essentialist thinking – giving the human a kind of essence. It has gone out of fashion in much thinking, and at its very best is seen as (yet another) contested concept.

Still, we should not be too dismissive too quickly. Dignity shows signs of widespread use today and is undoubtedly central to much thinking about justice and rights. It is also bound up with the value of a human self. It suggests that each individual has the right to be valued and treated well, including the idea of equality of peoples. People are vulnerable and need security from others; they need to be valued. That said, they are often failed by society, in which systems of rank, privilege and status are created that devalue vast swathes of people. Life becomes a struggle for honour and esteem.[53] So, as we will see in detail later, the very term 'dignity' can also be used divisively: to carve out the dignified and non-dignified, doing terrible things in the process.

Two contemporary thinkers are worth noting here: Christian Smith and Martha C. Nussbaum. Realist sociologist Christian Smith writes from a position often called personalism, claiming that the person and their agency form the prime locus of human studies. He is worth quoting, as he represents one major contemporary stance:

> Dignity inheres in the emergent constitution of human personhood ... It is inalienable. It cannot be thought or wished away ... [It is] an inherent worth of immeasurable value that is deserving of certain morally appropriate responses. Dignity makes persons innately precious and inviolable ... The ontology of personhood makes it morally true that persons are creatures worthy of being treated with respect, justice, and love.[54]

This is an unusually strong stance. Smith puts dignity at the very heart of his scientific account of what it means to be human. For him, the idea cannot be contested: he takes a strong essentialist line.

Likewise, philosopher Martha C. Nussbaum – indisputably one of the most prolific and central philosophers of humanity[55] – weaves her many wide-ranging and influential discussions around the connectedness of human capabilities, human rights, cosmopolitanism and dignity. She does not use the language of essentialism, but it is clear she accords major worth to the idea of human dignity. At the very least, all this means that the idea of dignity should at least be a part of the vocabulary of a critical humanism.

Humanism as transhumanism

The most well-known contemporary debate about humanity is that it is being enhanced and changed out of all recognition by new technologies. This becomes the challenge of transhumanism. Western Enlightenment ideas (and often secular humanism) evolve to show how new digital technologies, artificial intelligence, space travel, etc. are leading to a new humanity. We are becoming a supercharged, superintelligent, machine-based techno-animal. Transhumanism becomes 'an intensification of humanism'.[56] It leads to better health and a longer life, enhances our capacities, and increases our control over minds and bodies. We have already become quantified, data selves.[57] But we have further to go: the machine (and singularity) will take over (and probably rightly so!). At its tipping point, we face superintelligence: machines will move far beyond the level of the existing human being. Today's humanity will be superseded by the hyperintelligence of transhumanism.

Humanism abolished: the posthuman

A final illustrative debate takes all this to an extreme conclusion. Looking disdainfully at humanism (as well as 'humanitarianism', 'rights' and even 'transhumanism'), this debate aims to deconstruct these notions and come up with a real alternative. It suggests a posthuman, as opposed to a humancentric, worldview.[58] This argument stretches back to the nineteenth century with Nietzsche and Spinoza. It moves forward in the context of two world wars and the Holocaust, with landmark debates between, first, Cassirer, Heidegger, Sartre, Barthes and Adorno, and, later, Foucault, Levinas and more: all, ironically, white European men. Ultimately, it pronounces on the 'death of man'. It turns active human action and language into discourse performance and text;

active human consciousness into a language of human subjectivity. It claims that too much damage has been done in the name of humanism: the very idea has been used to divide groups, and has brought suffering and cruelty to the world in its own name. It was most flagrantly revealed in the horrors of the Holocaust. Here, humanity was used by Nazis and fascists as a weapon to mark out the human from the nonhuman, the civilized from the barbarian, the grand colonizer from the pathetic colonized. Gradually (under the influence of largely male French theory), it morphs itself into the posthuman, against humanity and a sense of universal man. At its most flagrant, humanism is about man not woman. As a major proponent Rosi Braidotti says: 'Universal "Man" ... is implicitly assumed to be masculine, white, urbanized, speaking a standard language, heterosexually inscribed in a reproductive unit, and a full citizen in a recognised polity' (I might add able-bodied, too). As she wryly asks: 'How non-representative can you get?'[59] More: it ignores animals and other forms of life. Here we have a humanism of elite and dominant groups working as a dangerous and exclusionary ideology.

In this argument, the central modern strategy of humanism is exposed as that of essentialism and racialization. It makes the nonhuman out to be a racialized being, the other. Exemplified in the appalling examples of indigenous peoples, slavery, the Jew and the Holocaust, it can also be found in the worldwide exploitation of lands and people through colonization. Here, large populations of the world have been subordinated (often slaughtered) by the invasion and rule of other (mostly European) countries. It was exemplified in the rise of scientific racism. And right now, often in the name of 'humanitarian exceptionalism', conflicts like those in Afghanistan have been waged, creating new dystopias.[60] With seeming good reason, this is a growing argument that wants to abandon any kind of humancentric view of the world.

And it has a wide range of followers in a very broad range of activities. A work like Braidotti and Hlavajova's *Posthuman Glossary* shows an extraordinary cacophony of new voices making new claims for the future, with an explosion of exciting new ideas from 'Blue Humanities' (Steve Mentz) and 'Ecohorror' (Christy Tidwell) to 'Gaga Feminism'

(Jack Halberstam) and 'Necropolitics' (Christine Quinan). There is much of great interest in such detailed studies.[61]

That said, critical humanism cannot agree with any position whose ultimate conclusion is to announce the death of humanity and the human. I call this *the fallacy of the end times*. Once we announce the death of man, and the arrival of the posthuman, *we are gone*. There is little, maybe nothing, more to say about us. We have wished and written ourselves away. We are not here. End of Story. And these accounts ultimately do pronounce, even celebrate, this end of humanity.

Again, a critical humanist can agree with some of this posthuman analysis. But it argues that posthumanism throws away the baby with the bathwater. Despite its many earlier sins, maybe now we have reached a key time when we can learn to think of the wide interconnectedness of humanity with all life, all things – with the world and the cosmos.

Moving Humanism On: The Dynamics of Diverse Thought

Let's be clear. Debates can move ideas along, even as they disagree with each other. The world of ideas is a magnificently grand, agonistic and open one. Western Enlightenment humanism has undoubtedly advanced humanist thinking in important ways, demonstrating the importance of rationality and the strong idea of human amelioration. Secular humanism has been a vital corrective to the dogmatic, schismatic, irrational, religious conflict that is doing the world no good at all. Rights thinking has weaknesses but a strong future. Transhumanism has shown how human beings are making great strides both in understanding the universe and in enhancing its workings. And posthumanisms have surely shown us just how flawed many past versions of 'the human' have been, as well as introducing us to a scintillating array of new ideas and complexities. It is certainly true that many past humanisms have dehumanized large groups of people: women, migrants, indigenous peoples, ethnic groups and 'queers' amongst them. It is certainly time for a change.

Critical humanism does not arise in opposition to these stances: it works to learn from them and tries to work with them. It recognizes that ideas about humanity are always wide open to disagreement. Through these conflicts, we move on.

- We move beyond an exclusive focus on the rationality of Enlightenment thought, to incorporate affect, feelings and bodies: the world is not simply a rational, progressive order.
- We move beyond a Western humanism to a global humanism. The monocultural ideas and structures of the dominant, colonizing and totalizing 'male' West need to be transcended by the multiplicities of world cultures, intersectional ties and the plural planet. It recognizes a pluriversal humanity, and the wide relational world of differences.
- We move beyond the religious and secular divide. Ultimately, we are on a journey to perpetually expand all our horizons of thinking about and experiencing the world in many directions.
- We move beyond the idea that science knows all the answers. Yes, science is making great strides in the advance of knowledge. But we need to be cautious of its overreach – it can become a dangerous divisive weapon. Debates about science must always be infused with debates about values.
- We move beyond an uncritical claim for human rights. It is not all good news. It has achieved much, but it has failed too. The same holds for ideas of dignity. As potentially key values for humanity, they need to work in conjunction with a world of other values, especially those of inequality, justice and care.
- We move beyond the idea that enhancing, modifying and developing the human endlessly and excessively (so that it no longer exists) is necessarily a good thing. We have to be cautious about human beings being 'enhanced out of existence'!
- We move beyond the 'othering' of some humans as nonhumans: from essentialized views of women, race, sexual difference and disability. We have to widen the circle of heterogenous humanity. And we must resist the

use of 'humanism' as a tool for discrimination, exclusion and the extermination of groups we see as *less than human*.
* We move beyond any narrow and exclusive definitions of what it means to be human; we can always be a little *more than human*, too. But we always need to keep some version of a fragile existential core of 'being human', so that we can still see, appreciate and talk about the problems of our own human existence.

Each debate is of value. I simply start to disagree with them when and if they turn into unitary dogmas against the human person or start restrictive thinking about what the idea of being human means. They then become the enemies of a more reflective and critical humanist thinking. Both Enlightenment thinking and secular thinking can bring about the possibility, for example, of excluding most of the contemporary world.

As I sit here writing this, I cannot help but see myself as a little human animal precariously doing what little human animals do: puzzling. In this, I join an infinite chorus of billions before me, with many more – I hope – to come. I am a rational, emotional, embodied world species, not a robot, a monster or a God. I share a history, a story, even an identity: that of a human being, a person. I am interconnected with the earth, animals, relationships, community, country, world and cosmos that I live within. As such, I am very unhappy to pronounce on my own death and that of my species. I am decidedly against the move around restricting our view of humanity or abolishing the very idea. Indeed, the danger might be that some ideas – of posthumanity, the critique of rights – may come to act as a self-fulfilling prophecy, hastening our own very demise. Humanity has to strive to keep connecting, to stay wide open.

That said, this attitude of multiplicity and openness is not what many people traditionally see as humanism. It is usually given a dogmatic Western, often secular, twist. The focus has tended to be on the autonomous rational human agent, the unencumbered self: man (or should I perhaps say, white heterosexual men). Although, over the millennia, what it means to be human has clearly taken very many forms – from Buddhist humanisms to Islamic humanisms to African humanisms – it is Western humanisms that have come to dominate thinking. Critical humanism has to go beyond such narrow views, taking seriously the idea that we are a planetary animal living in a world of many worlds.

Many humanisms of the past were only able to take seriously the world in which they belonged: the West, the Asian, the Christian, the Muslim, the male and more. Speaking for *the* world, they only considered *a* world. It is only fairly recently in our history that we have been able to see the planet as a world and to map through narratives the rich diversity of lands, cultures and hybrid ways of being in it. Now, with Google Maps, it is so easy to sense this. And so we start to tell the stories of an emergent, hybrid, worldly humanity. The time has now come to see the rich diversities across the world and their deep interconnections.

The Call of Humanity: Only Connect

> Only connect! That was the whole of her sermon. Only connect the prose and the passion, and both will be exalted, and human love will be seen at its height. Live in fragments no longer.[62]

'Only connect!' This was E. M. Forster's famous pronouncement in his novel *Howards End*. What does it mean? In current times the very word, 'connect', has been taken over by digitalism. We speak of *the culture of connectivity* to indicate a world of platforms and the coding of human life.[63] Much contemporary writing talks about 'connectivity' being through digitalism and machines. But this, most emphatically, is not what Forster meant. And nor do I. I want to reclaim the word to talk about human life, not digital life. Surely, if there is one idea that connects us all, it is that of 'humanity'. It can help us 'live [our lives] in fragments no longer'. It helps us bring together our fragile animality and the wider worlds of interconnected 'other people', 'other species' and 'other things', dwelling in time, space and the cosmos. Over and over again in the worldwide concern about Covid-19, the idea of humanity was been evoked to 'bring us together' and to make us conscious of our interdependence in the world and planet. Not to hear humanity's call to 'come together' presents us with a clear and present danger.

Critical humanism sensitizes us to humanity as a narrative that can help bring things together. We can find many and various ways of achieving this connectedness[64] linking the personal and political, time and space, mind and body. To give one illustration: the influential sociologist C. W. Mills argues for an important connection between the personal and the public: we need to bridge personal sufferings (and inner life) and public problems (and outer structural social problems). While personal suffering (a Rohingya refugee or a racial attack, for example) is endured as an intensely subjective experience, often in isolation, it ultimately needs to be connected to a wider (historical) environment. (There are more than 900,000 Rohingya living in camps in southeast Bangladesh; the Black Lives Matter movement arose to show that race attacks by the police are not isolated incidents; and there is, in the USA, a 400-year-old history of deep racism.)[65]

The connective spirals of humanity

A broad sense of connection can be depicted as a spiral of weaving and widening circles of a web of domain of life:

1. *Bio-earth.* We are intimately bound up with the bio-earth, the earthly commons, as a planetary ecological biological species. We are necessarily interconnected through our own bodies (and all their microbes) with all other things and forms of life on earth in time and space. As *Homo sapiens*, we bring our distinctively developed big brains, bipedal bodies, long postbirth dependency and upright postures to the grand march of animal life that has evolved over the earth's millennia. We have become 'the human species', living around 200,000 years on Planet Earth, spanning something like 600 generations (see Chapter 5). Right now, we can count nearly 8 billion individual human animals on earth (estimated to reach 11,200 billion by 2100).[66] Each of us may be uniquely individual; but we make up only about 0.01 per cent of life on the planet. And

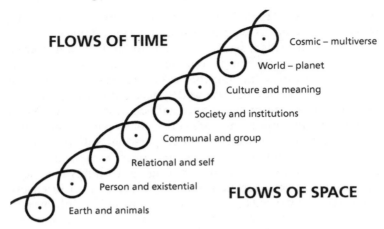

FLOWS OF TIME

Cosmic – multiverse

World – planet

Culture and meaning

Society and institutions

Communal and group

Relational and self

Person and existential   **FLOWS OF SPACE**

Earth and animals

Figure 1.1: The connective spiral of humanity

we have only been here for a very short time. We can never stand alone as a species, but live within a deep ecology encompassing the earth, other people, other life, things and the cosmos. There is a deep interdependence of all. It is dangerous to break this connection. As we will see, many of the problems we now face may well flow from the fact that we have in recent centuries been slowly breaking this bond with a wider universe of which we are an irrevocable part.

2. *Existential human beings* (persons). We are emergent, embodied creatures bridging inner agency with outer lives. Collectively, we are creatively engaged in symbolic human activities, self-reflexive and permanently unfinished. We are the vulnerable, biographical creatures of body, feeling and reflective consciousness. We are born, we suffer, we face ambivalence and contingency, and we die. We may even have an afterlife. And each life brings its own distinctively different and unique life story. Humanism then becomes its grounded project: to tell its story. Narratives are collectively developed with others, refined and distorted, persistently contested, and reshaped generation by generation. All the time, they pump meaning into life. We seem to be the only vulnerable life form on a fragile earth that is consciously aware of this. Suffering, and our responses to

it, are key. A connecting humanity brings a major reflexivity and awareness to all these issues.

3. *Interpersonal.* We interact and relate to each other in families, friendships, networks. More: human life is intersubjective. People can never really be alone. We 'do things together', 'living in the minds of others', in 'circles of others' (see Chapter 3). Human 'persons' develop actions that are grounded in complex language and symbols, capable of engaging with a startling creativity: writing literature, composing music, engaging in Olympics, doing science, sending people to the moon. No other planetary life that we know of at present can quite do this. Humans are creative beings who connect to others in relationships.

4. *Communal.* We bond, sharing life together in a wide range of communities. We are the bonding group animal who lives with others in close social proximity (like many of our ancestors, especially apes); and we do this through bounded and bonded families, groups, communities and local social worlds. We clash and we cooperate; these bonds provide the direct canopies of meaning, sentiment and solidarity in our lives. We are the belonging animal. But the ability to connect with others in communities also brings the potential to not connect.[67]

5. *Societal.* We are the human life that flows through societies and their tribes, civilizations and nations. Our challenge is to create social institutions and practices that enable the flourishing of production and work (economy), reproduction and socialization (education, family, religion), communication (language and media) and security and welfare (governance). And through these we achieve practical things like food distribution, transportation, housing and good health, all interconnected with one another. *We connect to each other through societies.*

6. *Cultural.* We are the animal who weaves complex 'ways of living' – bringing values and stories – across the world. We are the linguistic, symbolic, manipulating, communicative, cultural animal. Ultimately, we are also the animal that creates symbolic cultures, ways of living, that are necessarily messy and murky. These bring issues of values and power relations. Establishing relations of symmetry and asymmetry, power expands or concentrates the degree of

freedom and control exerted over lives. All life might be guided and shaped by certain rules; and many animals have a sort of sensitivity to other life. But only humans invent elaborate cultural frames of values; only they can develop ethical and normative orders organized through legal and power relations. Our cultures become sites of struggle over value and emancipation – of what it means to lead the good (or bad) life. We are elaborate linguistic animals capable of manipulating symbols in complex ways to produce historically based value systems. But cultures usually also have material foundations. We connect to others through these cultures.

7. *Worldly*. We are the animal that finds other tribes and creatures living on the earth. We look to become a worldly animal as humanity becomes globalized. We get to know these other strangers living in other parts of the world. A cosmopolitan attitude is in the making. We have to live with each other. There is life beyond the little world we live in.

8. *Cosmic*. And finally, we are a planetary animal connected to the cosmic universe or multiverse. We are a lunar, cosmic animal. A hallmark of our being human in the world is that we look up to the heavens and down to the oceans and can see our insignificance in the vastness of the cosmic order. Excitingly, in many ways hard to fathom, we are connected with this vastness of planetary things. These days, with the help of satellites, we can just click on Google Maps to see and sense our close interconnectedness.

There is more than all this. Very significantly, we become, each one of us, a uniquely different human being. Remarkable to behold, like all life, the billions of us are each distinctly different from one another and connect to one another in uniquely different ways. A distinctively different and unique life story can be told by each and every life. *Humans alone develop a personal and heightened self-aware consciousness of these unique differences.* This can become the basis for tensions as well as conflicts. But also surprise and amazement. Consider your own life: even as it remains enmeshed in connections, nobody can ever live a life quite like you. Ever.

Living in Connection and Complexity

Taking our spiralling human connections seriously is no easy task, especially in a digital age. Critical humanism sees 'connection' as a pragmatic tool for living life. 'Humanity' here becomes the narrative that binds us together through our habitats and pursuits, from the bio-organic to the cosmic. It is through our stories of collective living that we come to sense our togetherness with others, our creativities, our limits. It is through these stories that we can come to sense possible human coherence. We start to see things that might just hold us all together: maybe a common humanity, a solidarity of common projects. Once we start making these narrative connections, we recognize something about *who* we are, *where* we came from and, indeed, *why* we are. All this is at the core of learning about becoming human. Religion is often at the heart of this storytelling. But in the twenty-first century we need more: a wider literacy and pedagogy of hope. New ideas appear across the generations. And older ideas that have recently been heavily critiqued and become unfashionable – like progress, dignity, rights, universal values – can be brought back, reconsidered and reconnected. The world is not a closed place, but a perpetual series of challenges to 'only connect'. It will be wise to return to humanity and humanism. But this time round, we must do all this with a cautious, careful and critical eye.

PART II
Dehumanizing the World: Disconnecting Humanity

Man was made for Joy and Woe
And when this we rightly know
Through the world we safely go
Joy and woe are woven fine ...
                    William Blake, *Auguries of Innocence* (1863)

Definitions:
To dehumanize: to make less than human
To damage: to harm and impair functioning
To disconnect: to break connections
To divide: to separate, to create barriers and walls

PART II

Dehumanizing the World:
Disconnecting Humanity

2
Damaging Humanity

Humanity is facing an unprecedented crisis ... climate change, the mass destruction of species and the rapid acceleration of inequality are merely its most acute manifestations ... [T]he current moment is proof of a civilizational crisis.

Arturo Escobar, *Pluriversal Politics* (2020), p. 121

The Columbian anthropologist Arturo Escobar senses that human life is in trouble. And he is not alone. Many claim that we now live in a very disconnected world. Indeed, one in ten of the world population born around 1900 were slaughtered through war or genocide. (In the Great War alone: 8.5 million dead, 21 million wounded.)[1] At the same time, at least 20 million people died from plague. The leading German philosopher and sociologist Jürgen Habermas looked back to remark:

[The twentieth century] 'invented' the gas chambers, total war, state-sponsored genocide and extermination camps, brainwashing, state security apparatuses, and the panoptic surveillance of entire populations. The twentieth century 'generated' more victims, more dead soldiers, more murdered civilians, more displaced minorities, more torture, more dead from cold, from hunger, from maltreatment, more political prisoners and refugees, than could ever have been imagined. The phenomena of violence and barbarism mark the distinctive signature of the age.[2]

As we see from Escobar's remarks above, the twenty-first century, so far, is really not faring much better. Many have documented these horrors of the never-ending dark side of humanity, and the Great Abyss that has developed between continents, especially the global North and global South, the East and the West. From the earliest groups and civilizations right up to the latest events of this century, there is a long history of bloodshed, rage and suffering brought about by colonialism, exclusion, femicide, genocide, homophobia and sexual fear, racism and racial hatred, rape, slavery, torture, tyranny, wars, violence, poverty, and the rest. Billions of lives have been born and then dehumanized, rendered 'less than human'. We 'demean, enslave and exterminate others'.[3] Lives on Planet Earth have been lived recklessly. We have made the world a place that is unfit for a lot of people to live in. And it may be becoming more so. As I write, the world is confronting a major global pandemic of Covid-19, which is causing deep and long-term damage. It is changing everything.[4]

In this chapter, I give a very brief report on the state of this disconnected, dehumanized world *circa* 2020. As Covid-19 advances, so many of these problems are becoming greatly exacerbated.

Suffering in a Mutilated Covid-19 World[5]

Bare humanity

I start with the worlds in which human beings can scarcely exist at all. Call it 'bare humanity'.[6] In 2019, about one in ten (736 million) of the world's population were living in extreme poverty. They barely survived, with little food, housing, water or security, living at the most basic level. More: some 135 million people across fifty-three countries experienced acute hunger, 785 million people had no clean water near their homes and 2 billion people did not have a decent toilet.[7] The incidence of disease and frequency of violence is high. Some 80 million people were 'displaced'. Life is precarious, especially amongst those 'locked out' from civil society, and from work. Many countries are disproportionately mentioned in this respect over and over again: Yemen, South Sudan, DRC, Syria, North Nigeria. And life is becoming disproportionately harder in these areas under the rule of Covid-19.

Degraded environments, deranged worlds

We are seriously damaging our environment. Welcome to the age of the Anthropocene: climate inequalities and injustice, climate refugees, climate war, 'environmental grief', existential crisis, a climate leviathan, a sixth extinction and, for some, a 'Requiem for a Species'.[8] Nearly a century ago, in 1928, Gandhi said of industrial capitalism: 'God forbid that India should ever take to industrialism after the manner of the West. ... If an entire population of 300 million took to similar exploitation, it would strip the world bare like locusts.' Asked if he would like to see the same standard of living for Indians as for the English, he replied: 'It took Britain half the resources of the planet to achieve this prosperity. How many planets will a country like India require?'[9] And now his fears have come true. Modern capitalism has generated an extreme environmental emergency: the most serious problem facing humanity in the twenty-first century.

Increasingly, we face catastrophically precarious conditions: we cannot breathe the air, drink the water, or live with other planetary life. Big business, governments and human beings have felt free to actively ravage their environments over the past two centuries, creating worldwide environmental injustice. Nature itself – the earth, the sky, the seas, plant and animal life – has been degraded, disordered, deranged. We humans have been destroying the world in which we live. Planet Earth and the people who live on it are in jeopardy. Species have become endangered: 1 million species are threatened with extinction.[10] We have created seriously unequal, deranged worlds of *air pollution, carbon damage, climate refugees, climate warming, coral reef destruction, deforestation, destructive food chains, dying oceans, endangered species, energy crises, famine, flooding, heat deaths and heat waves, ice-cap melting, over-consumption, plagues of warming and food contamination, plastic pollution, poor land use, population crises, rising seas, transport trouble, urban slums, waste expansion, water shortage, wildfires, zoonotic disease.*

David Wallace-Wells has documented all this in his wonderfully readable *The Uninhabitable Earth.* He says: 'Global warming has improbably compressed into two generations the entire story of human civilization.'[11] This crisis was foreseen by 98 per cent of scientists; very few disagree. An almost unthinkable world may be coming our way (see Box 2.1). Richer countries are causing the most damage, while

---

Box 2.1: Eight ways to destroy the planet over a few hundred years

1. We expand the population - from 800 *million* in 1750 to around 8 *billion* now.
2. We heat up the globe – through emitting gases like carbon dioxide, methane and nitrous oxide – trapping heat and leading to climate change.
3. We destroy natural habits of life – through deforestation, ocean acidification, mass food production, creation of megacities and mass transportation – resulting in pollution of land, sea, rivers, coral reefs and air. We destroy indigenous cultures and biodiversity.
4. We ravage the seas, earth and ice caps, extracting vital minerals and valuables.
5. We build mass food systems that overfish the seas, poison the lands and mechanize animal life and its slaughtering.
6. We create indestructible commodities (from plastics to cruise liners to space junk) creating mass waste that litters and damages the skies, the earth and the seas for generations to come.
7. We fight military, chemical, biological, nuclear and mega-wars – damaging mass life and creating vast waste lands of mines, wreckage and poisons.
8. We engage in a never-ending growth as if the world and life know no limits.

Ultimately, we fall out of harmony with the world: we fail to connect.
(On all this, see: Earth.org; Ecowatch; Environmental-Watch.com; World Wildlife Fund (wwf.com); UN Biodiversity Reports; UN World Urbanization Prospects etc.)

---

poorer countries are already showing signs of being most damaged. But it is a global crisis that affects everyone, even as some remain blind to it. Some claim the damage has already gone too far and we are already at the 'end'. Others give us a decade or two to make effective change. There is much to be done; the pressing question is just why our governments are acting so slowly. There is a need for action – now and for the long term. We need, as environmental scholar and activist Vandana Shiva claims, an 'Earth Democracy'. As I write, China is going Green, and Extinction Rebellion is challenging the destruction of our world. *Critical humanism seeks a new world of environmental care and justice.*[12]

Destructive technologies, digital threats

People make machines to help in the wellbeing of humanity. Yet it is these very same machines that sometimes destroy just what it means to be a creative, thinking, feeling human being. Much has been written about the ways in which our humanity came under attack with industrialization and its 'Dark Satanic Mills'. Each of the four key early transformations – of mining, cotton mills, steam engines and factories – brought with them a simultaneous advance in the regress of humanity. The human suffering caused by industrialization is well documented in the great writings of the time: Engels's *The Condition of the Working Class in England*, Disraeli's *Sybil*, Charles Kingsley's *Alton Locke*, Elizabeth Gaskell's *North and South*, and many of Dickens's novels. The story is now very well known. But that was then, and this is now.

Today, we can certainly see this industrial destruction still taking place, in the sweatshops of the world, in mines, in fracking, in hard labour, in trafficking of all kinds. But a new form of serious danger has emerged. Technology is rendering more and more lives digital and robotic. We are being 'colonized' by data, living under the Law of the Algorithm.[13] Once again, who would choose not to live with the very many stunning benefits this brings? And yet, just as industrial technology destroyed the natural environment and introduced stultifying problems of dehumanizing life for vast numbers, so too does this new hi-tech, robotic world. *Digitalism brings a strong potential to destroy our humanity.* Just what is digitalism and AI doing to our humanity? Where are the pitfalls and what can be done about them? Can we create a set of values that will enable us to live well alongside the digital? An immediate challenge is to rescue us from both the digital techno experts and the market business folk, who often have less interest in the human problems that emerge around what they are creating: extreme surveillance, the loss of human autonomy (and dignity) and the breakdown of democratic communications that become unregulated and cannot be trusted.

Here is the making of a world of inhumane and abusive humanity, threatening relations for many: from abuse and dumbing down, to drone assassination, to cyberwar. Many now confront a shocking new world of online abuse, bullying, fear, violence, cruelty, crime, hacking, scams, corruption, fake imaging, sexual exploitation and trafficking, which the old systems of policing and regulation seem incapable of handling. At the same time, we see the creation of yet more layers of new digital inequalities and human divides. At its most extreme, we already see a world where robots are taking over and the threat that we humans will vanish. While digitalism can certainly make humanity function more smoothly, it can also greatly weaken it. So here is another major dilemma that needs urgent critical examination and action. We are facing the coming *deep digitalization and mediatization of humanity.*

In all of this, I am regularly reminded of Goethe's celebrated tale of the Sorcerer's Apprentice: a tale of human powers getting out of control. Little digital skills and technologies produce a monster that is increasingly running amok. And just as the rise of capitalist technology in the nineteenth century led to a raft of critical literature, railing against the horrors of the machine age, so too the current world of digitalism and robotics has brought on a prolific and widely mounted attack, with titles like *New Dark Age* (James Bridle), *The Age of Surveillance Capitalism* (Shoshana Zuboff), *Ten Arguments for Deleting Your Social Media Accounts Right Now* (Jaron Lanier), *The Internet is Not the Answer* (Andrew Keen), *Automating Inequality* (Virginia Eubanks), *Weapons of Math Destruction* (Cathy O'Neil), *The Twittering Machine* (Richard Seymour), *Algorithms of Oppression* (Safiya Umoja Noble), *Zucked: Waking Up to the Facebook Catastrophe* (Roger

McNamee), *Anti-Social Media: How Facebook Disconnects Us and Undermines Democracy* (Siva Vaidhyanathan). They all, in their various ways, see the possibility of the end of humanity as we know it. They are not usually Luddites, but careful thinkers who foretell the real dangers of the digital life.

From such writings, we start to sense that digitalism and AI bring the potential to destroy humanity as we have known it for the past few thousand years. Our very sense of time, space – and being human – is being reworked. As human face-to-face communication declines in significance, so impersonal networking grows in importance. Friends are measured by Facebook contacts not intimacy. Time is reordered so we now live perpetually with our own digital world that makes instant demands on us; all the world becomes immediately urgent, speedy and overwhelming. Oh, for the chance to wander and dream! Likewise, the private and the public worlds are now reconfigured with the distinct possibility that all of our life is maintained and monitored by others: a ubiquitous surveillance society far worse than anything Orwell or Huxley ever dreamt of. And yet, even as we become more and more aware of how our distinctive human life is now being directly and ubiquitously monitored by companies, organizations and states, we seem to carry on regardless. Here is the new world of global positioning system (GPS); here comes satellite monitoring; look out for synthetic imaging; welcome to the drones. Here is a world of facial recognitions, the personal digitalization of body and self, genetic screening devices, a personal robot who records our every wish – and more. Here is a world of 'data selves' rather than human selves. The algorithm is colonizing our lives.

Shoshana Zuboff's *The Age of Surveillance Capitalism* is one handbook (and a very big handbook at well over 600 pages) that warns of the dangers of this new digital world, which the author sees as very widespread and very threatening, and which she fears could grow out of our control unless we do something quickly to stop it.[14] And the Chinese social credit system, involving mass surveillance, developed in 2013, is intended to record our social reputation, which, as result, becomes standardized. Here is Big Brother Data.

We are only at the start of this new system, and I wonder just how far the downsides of digitalism will spread. A key question is posed: 'How are we to look after each other in a digital world?'[15] Serious interventions are needed to ensure that our valuable techno world can keep us as caring and compassionate human beings. As we will see later, critical humanism suggests *the development of a compassionate digitalism and digital citizenship*.

Dehumanized economies, crisis capitalism

Human beings always create their own economic systems. These are given neither by God nor by nature. Indeed, one of the central tasks for the human species is to evolve ways for dealing with their means of existence: of finding shelter, food, warmth and security; of creation and exchange; of reproducing a humane social life. There are many systems that can do this. Anthropologist Marshall Sahlins, in his book *Stone Age Economics*, suggests that the original 'affluent society' may have evolved with the early hunter-gatherers, with people living healthy and fulfilled lives. As he provocatively remarks, 'the amount of hunger increases relatively and absolutely with the evolution of culture'.[16] And so we find an ongoing controversy about our past and the nature of economics.

Although there can be many economic forms, capitalism has emerged as the dominant world economic system of the early twenty-first-century world. The great transformation of societies into modern capitalist economies started during the eighteenth century and introduced certain values that would eventually prove inimical to being human.[17] Starting in small ways, capitalism has turned the whole of humanity into a world of markets, money, profit, competition, GDP and perpetual growth, consumption and commodities, and ceaseless streaming advertising and promotion. It has made the central value of human life commercial and commodified; it has given 'us' our central concerns with economic growth and making wealth. Other human values (see Chapter 6) have been pushed aside.

As this happened, economies were created in which many people cannot find decent work, where conditions of great inequality exist, often offering only bare subsistence, and where life is perpetually driven by competition, greed and ambitious success. It becomes a world where people are 'losers' or 'winners' according to their economic status. Within this declining neoliberal capitalist world, life became dehumanized for very large numbers of people. Its central value (following economist Friedrich Hayek and others) was freedom – but this is very far from being a straightforward idea. We are engulfed by markets, immersed in a consumption and promotional culture driven by money and processes of financialization. We are hardly 'free'. Human relations become subject to the commodification of everything. Driven by the desire for endless and unlimited growth, human life in all its aspects becomes a cashable, business-like, money-based affair. This is true not just for food and housing, as has been the case for some time, but also for the air we breathe and the water we drink and wash in.

Humanizing economics

In recent times, many have argued that modern economics is seriously failing, and a raft of new ideas have been proposed as to how things should be changed. In *Caring Democracy*, feminist political scientist Joan C. Tronto argues for interspersing social care with the economy; in *What Money Can't Buy*, philosopher Michael Sandel famously suggests that there should be moral limits to a market economy; and social theorist Andrew Sayer discusses *Why We Can't Afford the Rich*.[18] Along with others, these scholars seek wide-ranging alternatives to the market economy, ones that have generally given a higher priority to human values. They look for a wider and deeper change that usually gives a prime focus to people: a human economics 'fit for people' (see Table 8.2). A few examples include:

- Humanist economics, which aims to make an 'economy fit for all people'.
- Green, environmental, low-growth economics, which gives a key focus to the environment and its preservation.[19]
- Value-based economics – those that explicitly acknowledge market values as limited and suggest alternatives.[20]
- Majority economics – that is, economics of the 99 per cent – which focuses on the welfare of the majority rather than the 1 per cent who gain most from the capitalist system.

- Feminist economics, which identifies key issues that are faced by women in a largely male economic order. This includes the recognition of an economics based on care.
- Doughnut economics, which focuses on 'humanity's long-term goals' – 'a social foundation of well-being that no one should fall below, and an ecological ceiling of planetary pressure we should not go beyond'.[21]
- Participatory economics, which aims to build an economy based on 'solidarity, diversity, equity and self-management'.[22]

Here is a world where economies focus on humans: they will be centred on the majority of people and concerned with wider issues like social justice, care, the environment and wellbeing. *Critical humanism looks for a human economy organized with people and human values in mind.*

Unequal humanity, immiserating inequalities

Sociologist Göran Therborn has commented that inequality is 'a violation of human dignity; it is a denial of the possibility for everybody's human capabilities to develop ... a general plague on human societies'.[23] Throughout history, social inequalities have reduced human opportunities. Inequalities are linked to changes in birth and death rates; to shorter, more stressful lives; to a stunting of physical growth linked to poor diet and poor health; to reduced literacy levels and restricted life opportunities in education and work; to poverty and poor housing; to a greater likelihood of dangerous work, anxiety, stress and violence; and to less access to the digital world. And across all of these are key differences in gender, class, ethnicity and nation.[24] Recent evidence also suggests that Covid-19 has amplified the impacts of inequalities both between countries and within countries.

It is those who hold power who actually create their worlds, and they often have scant regard for the lives of others. They build their wealth and status privileges out of feudal servitude, slavery, forced mining, colonial extraction, indigenous looting, exploitative labour, corporate corruption and religious hierarchy. While only a few people live with these extreme privileges, often accompanied by a privileged sense of entitlement to demean others (the 1 per cent), for vast swathes

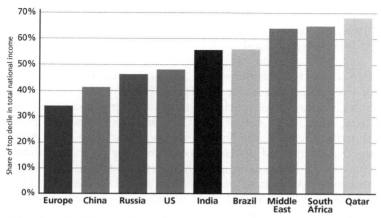

Figure 2.1: Global inequality regimes, 2018
Source: Thomas Piketty, *Capital and Ideology* (Harvard University Press, 2020), p. 650[25]

of the population the world is diminished (the 99 per cent).[26] The world becomes divided into 'winners' who gain more and more, and a vast number of 'losers' who get less and less. Figure 2.1 suggests how this works round the world. Such inequalities can make life precarious and bitter. Inequalities of wealth are notably growing worldwide, linked to austerity, globalization, deregulation, regressive tax policies, technology and the emasculation of trade unions. In 2020, Oxfam estimated that the world's 2,153 billionaires had more wealth than the 4.6 billion people who make up 60 per cent of the planet's population. The twenty-two richest men in the world had more wealth than all the women in Africa.[27] To linger on this statement is to see an extraordinarily unequal humanity.

Why has it been so hard to solve this problem after so many centuries? How can we accept the brutalization of so many lives in order that so few can live luxuriant lives? *Critical humanism looks out to minimize the inequalities of the world.*

Excluded humanities, disposable life

Large numbers of human beings (many just children) are being rejected and ejected from the mainstream of the world, facing formidable 'borders'[28] and pushed into vast waste-lands, corrosive institutions, abject ghettos. From refugees to prisoners, we find a disposable humanity. Here is:

Expulsion by environmental damage, destroying millions of lives across the more vulnerable parts of the world: with homelessness, poverty, death, famine, plague and serious life disruption. India, China, the USA, Ethiopia, Malawi, Haiti, Somalia, Vietnam, the Philippines and Zimbabwe are some of the most impacted. Twenty-two of the world's most polluted cities are in India, Gurugram being the most polluted. Many confront risky oceans such as Manila and Kiribati. Visually, all this is well illustrated in Ai Weiwei's *Human Flow* (2017), a film that documents environmental crisis. Here comes the tragedy of climate refugees.[29]

Expulsion by economic failure, bringing large numbers who confront the degradation of work, austerity, unemployment, poverty and slum cities. Having no wealth, property or land, little or no work, they lead harsh lives. Here come displaced workers and forced migrants.

Expulsion by political failure, resulting in large numbers being ejected by their state through war and conflict. Here are displaced people, migrants, refugees and the dispossessed. In 2019 some 79.5 million people (1 per cent of the world's population) were forcibly displaced. Some 68 per cent of refugees came from just four countries: Syria (6.6 million), Venezuela (2.7 million), Afghanistan (2.7 million), South Sudan (2.2 million) (85 per cent are 'hosted' in 'developing' countries). This global displacement is the crisis of our time; and the world has mainly shown a malign, inhuman response to it. Humanity has broken down here. As I write, Wikipedia lists more than 150 displaced camps, often housing some 50,000 or more people. Around 2.6 million live in refugee camps (often housing as many as 11,000 people). They live in the most dehumanized and degrading situations, usually cut off from visibility.

Expulsion by communication, bringing large numbers who live without modern media communications: about 4 billion people, half the world, live without the internet. And more:

many live with the limits of a very biased, minimal or even totalitarian mode of communication. And even with digitalism, people increasingly exist only within their own bubble – and all this as they also live in worlds of growing and intense surveillance.

Expulsion by prison, bringing some 10.7 million people who are physically cut off from the world through incarceration. The US alone has nearly 2.3 million prisoners (some 20 per cent of the global prison population); it has the highest prison rate in the world – with El Salvador coming second.[30]

Sociologist Saskia Sassen sees a new world order appearing, with an elite that live 'wonderful lives' while vast numbers are excluded to live non-lives. In *Expulsions: Brutality and Complexity in the Global Economy*, Sassen gives a telling report on the state of the world in the twenty-first century.[31] She provides a new way of seeing it, no longer through the lenses of countries and nations, but through the mobilities and exclusions of people. Critical humanism looks for a world *of inclusion, harmonizing and humanizing.*

Ignorant humanities and a post-truth world

We seem to live in a time when people have access to more and better forms of knowledge and education than at any time in our history. But they are also suffering from an overload and a crisis in knowing. We have entered a fragile, risky, complex world of unprecedented and uncharted digital, environmental, marketized and global cultural change which has put knowledge at risk. This has become an epistemological crisis and a Post-Truth Era.[32]

For most of history, whatever has passed as knowledge has been secure: local, practical, ethnocentric and monocultural, often inspired by religion. 'Reality' has been limited, often false, but seen to be relatively secure and unproblematic. We have lived in focused, restricted worlds with trust and faith and local ecologies of knowledge. But with the rise of modernity, postmodernity, neoliberalism, decolonization and globalization, all this has changed. Past worlds of (apparent) truth and trust across the world face rapid change and become more complicated, questioned and precarious. Human beings now live in more fluid and self-conscious worlds of knowledge, epistemology, wisdom, religion, truth and trust that rapidly come to be questioned and exposed to threat from many sides. Humanity becomes less trusting and more risky as we are confronted by a variety of challenges:

- The diversity of faiths, languages and cultures makes us aware of a 'plurality of truths', suggesting different truths being claimed in different worlds. There is no longer just the one world: there are many. The idea of 'multiple objective realities' is a difficult one. But it certainly questions all notions of 'faith' and 'knowledge'. It can lead us into problems of relativism, and force us to ask whether some human realities are truer than others. How can we live with this global clash between cultures and truth?
- A mediated reality leads us to dwell more and more in worlds of recorded music, film, 'news': worlds of mechanical and electronic reproduction. Layers of media take us further and further away from direct experiences of the world. We lose touch with humanity's interconnectedness with the 'natural things' of Planet Earth. And within this, the realities of digitalism and AI create worlds of the 'second self', robotic superintelligence, algorithms, virtual realities. Social media forces many of us to live in restricted 'bubbles' of ideas. A sheen of phantasm and fiction passes over all real and concrete life.
- A rapidly commoditized and marketed world shapes much of our thinking into a world of commercialized values. Our ideas and knowledge come to acquire a cash value. Increasingly, education is organized through market and metric values. Culture becomes entertainment.
- The worlds of experts and professionals are not taken seriously and are given little credibility.[33] For some, all knowledge has been flattened, expert knowledge is no longer to be trusted and governments now deploy 'strategic ignorance' to avoid liability. And this comes at the very time when ever more expert knowledge is needed as we make our way in a highly complex world, and at the very time when ever more knowledge seems to be accessible to us via the internet.

All of this starts to dramatically change 'the world we know' and the 'truths we can believe'. If we fail to understand more clearly the nature of mediated worlds, the ways in which privileged realities are made, and how power plays a critical role in the organization of our belief and knowledge, then we remain in a chaotic world without truth. In the modern world, human beings create self-centred worlds in which knowledge is restricted to limited groups, ignorance flourishes and truth is lacking or denied. Even many modern education systems fail abysmally as a result of restrictive and imperialistic agendas that do not look out to the wider world. They have often become victims of an academic capitalism and marketplace. We are the intelligent animal, capable of thinking critically and knowing about the world – all key to being human. But we often fail.

We need clear debates about science and knowledge, and the folly of letting mediated digital messaging pass as truths. *Critical humanism is aware of ignorance and its strategies but aims to pursue knowledge, truth wisdom and trust.*

Perpetuating violent humanities

Is violence declining or increasing? This controversy has been well voiced by Steven Pinker in *The Better Angels of Our Nature*.[34] Pinker draws on masses of data to claim there has been a long-term decline in violence. Throughout history, billions of people have been killed in wars all around the world: wars of religious conflict, of conquest, of ethnic cleansing, of colonial revolt, etc. Whatever one makes of this analysis, the reader can be left in no doubt about the prevalence of human violence and atrocity throughout much of human history. Yet even if it has decreased vis-à-vis the distant past, in the very recent period it seems to be widespread.

Today, violence remains a major presence. Not only in civil strife, wars and crimes, but also in terrorism, sexual violence, digital abuse and the threat of drone warfare; in many cultures, violence and aggression have become normalized in the media. There also remains the persistent threat of nuclear aggression.[35] Since 2006, the Global Peace Index (GPI) has been ranking some 160 countries around the world in terms of peacefulness and violence (covering 99 per cent of the global population). The 2020 Report found the world to be considerably less peaceful than it was at the inception of the GPI.[36] Since 2008, there has been a year-on-year deterioration in peacefulness. Afghanistan is the least peaceful country in the world, followed by Syria, Iraq, South Sudan and Yemen. All, except Yemen, have been ranked amongst the five least peaceful countries since at least 2015. The decline of peacefulness since the 2010s has been caused by a wide range of factors, including increased terrorist activity, the intensification of conflicts in the Middle East, rising regional tensions in Eastern Europe and Northeast Asia, and growing numbers of refugees. In all, 104 countries recorded increased levels of terrorist activity, while only 38 improved, and the total number of conflict deaths increased by 140 per cent between 2006 and 2020.[37] *Critical humanism advocates peace and nonviolence.*

The failing of human governance

As I write, in 2020, there is widespread concern about the failure of governance across the world. People are rejecting their 'old orders'. And government responses to Covid-19 seem to have been much more effective in Asia than in the West. A range of annual reports brings gloomy news. Humanity is under threat from four major tendencies: the fragility of governance, the rise of populism and authoritarianism, the decline of democracy and the rise of political digitalism.

At a most basic level there is now a Fragile States Index,[38] which aims to measure the vulnerability of states to conflict or collapse. It does this by looking at twelve risk indicators, including security, factionalized elites, group grievances, economic situation, human flight, state legitimacy, public services, human rights and rule of law, demographic pressures, refugees and internally displaced persons and external intervention. In 2019 it listed some 120 countries that were ranked according to risk: from 'Warning' to 'Very

High Alert'. Put bluntly, a lot of countries are in some sort of trouble. Most worrying (with very high alerts) are the Congo Democratic Republic (CDR), Syria, South Somalia, Sudan and the Yemen. Venezuela and Brazil tied for the title of the Most Worsened Country.[39]

But in addition to this, at least half the world is now manifestly authoritarian. More than 100 countries are run on an authoritarian model; some 50 are dictatorships. Amongst the largest nations, China has become 'democratic with Chinese characteristics'. In effect, this makes it home to high levels of restricted freedom (especially in the press), widespread bans on protests, deep surveillance, exclusions of minorities (the re-education and indoctrinating of Uyghurs and other Muslims since 2017) and a president (Xi Jinping) who will be in power until his death. Russia is de facto authoritarian, with Putin set to be president until 2036. In many countries, like North Korea, Sudan, Zimbabwe and Burma, there are severe restrictions of freedom. Indeed, the nongovernmental organization Reporters Without Borders talks of a deep and disturbing decline in media freedom around the world. And in a few countries, there may well be genocide: Myanmar, Syria, Sudan, Uganda, Ethiopia, for example. There is gross inequality, widespread corruption and a lack of free and fair elections.

Accompanying this is the growth of new, mainly right-wing, global 'populisms'. Populists with autocratic tendencies have won elections in the Philippines, Brazil and Mexico. Democratic institutions have been subverted in Hungary, Turkey and Poland. New populist movements make minority groups objects of hate: ethnic groups, refugees and immigrants, lesbians, gays and trans, and many others.[40]

All in all, by January 2020, only 430 million people in just twenty-two countries were living in something like a 'full democracy'. The Democracy Index[41] claimed that fifty-two countries were 'flawed', forty-five were 'hybrids' and fifty-four were directly 'authoritarian'. We live in a world of 'new demagogues'.[42] Even more dispiriting, a Pew Survey in 2019 found a worldwide discontent with democracy as a system.[43]

Democracy – with its commitments to freedom, equality and participation – is usually seen as the strongest political base for humanism, humanity and human flourishing

– focusing as it does on the free participation of all people in the political process. Any government that does not primarily use its power to work on behalf of the freedom, equality, dignity, security and flourishing of the diversity of all its peoples is likely to be inadequate, and also quite likely to be a dehumanizing, degrading, inhumane form of governance. Indeed, a central role of good governance is to assume a special responsibility to look after its weakest members. The very idea of global *humane governance* is, on the whole, a recent human creation.[44]

By this criterion, for most of human history, political institutions will have frequently failed. Certainly, the very long-term political wish for a democracy, even if much contested, has never been fully achieved. Instead, what we usually get are variants that have typically favoured small privileged and elite groupings that have used their populous as a source of taxation, as workers for their lands, as fodder for their battles. Ultimately, too, a central challenge for critical humanism includes not just the failures of state governance but also the need for a connectedness to a global governance. This has only become a possibility in our most recent history with the creation of organizations like the United Nations.

Finally, the emergence of new media-based sources of power are creating distortions and corruptions that are starting to unravel. Social media is now employed to mobilize and conduct politics. In an early phase, it looked as if digital technology would lead to an enhanced 'power for the people': new methods of petition signing, cyber activism, crowd funding, a new political blogosphere. But as this new world has unfolded, we find ourselves facing dangers such as *Platform Capitalism*, *Digital Demagogue* and *Democracy Hacked* (all titles of recent books).[45] The tweets of Donald Trump and his 'fake news', alongside the data scandal linked to the British consulting firm Cambridge Analytica, did much to disrupt smooth political processes. (In 2020, the *Washington Post* claimed that Donald Trump had lied 20,000 times during his time in the presidential office.[46]) *Critical humanism looks for a humane governance, one where all people matter.*

The everyday corruption of human life

Corruption involves abuses of authority and trust. It is widely found through acts of blackmail, bribery, cartels, 'dark money', digital misuse, extortion, fraud, nepotism and 'offshoring'. It is often extended to include abuses and harassments of various other kinds, including sexual. Corruption seems to be practised everywhere around the world and is often culturally condoned: by governments, business, law and the judiciary, educational institutions, trade unions and entertainment organizations – and even by 'good causes' like religion, health, environmentalism and humanitarianism. Indeed, it is the very pervasive nature of corruption that poisons relationships, generates fear and resentment, and centrally undermines trust. In some countries the overlap of corruption between organizations and the state is so pervasive that we speak of the *mafia state* (where organized crime directly links to the state, e.g. in Italy, Japan, Russia) or the *narco state* (where drug cartels are linked in with ruling groups, as in much of Latin America and parts of South America).

In the contemporary world, corruption seems widespread. We see it in the power of Russian oligarchs and the influence of a new transnationalism class (bureaucrats and politicians, corporate executives, media moguls).

Transparency International defines corruption as the 'abuse of entrusted power for private gain' and finds it everywhere. Its Corruption Perceptions Index measures corruption in a number of ways. One key measure constructs a scale from 100 (clean) to 0 (highly corrupt). On this basis, in 2020, two-thirds of countries scored below 50; and the average score was 43. The worst countries were Yugoslavia (16), Yemen (15), Syria (13), South Sudan (12) and Somali (9).[47] *Critical humanism fights corruption in all its forms.*

Disconnected humanities: a malaise in the world

So many people's everyday lives are spent in the midst of gross inequality, environmental degradation, digital abuse, economic exploitation, poverty, displacement and exclusion, troubled education, broken states, corruption, crime and ubiquitous violence. And then came a pandemic. It cannot be surprising that there are so many instances of troubled lives and mental health problems. Across the world, some 20 million people have schizophrenia and 264 million people face depression. Since the 1980s, suicide rates have increased by 60 per cent worldwide. And in many countries, happiness – measured by various scales – is in decline. *Critical humanism seeks good mental health, good thinking.*[48]

Living in a Post-Covid World

At the very moment when the Covid-19 pandemic emerged on Planet Earth in early 2020, the world was already facing crisis, chaos and regression. It was confronting a climate emergency, widening inequalities, a global crisis of displacement and refugees, 'democratic fatigue', digital surveillance and the rise of authoritarianism and autocracy, lush with corruption. Mental health problems were widespread. Instead of an open planetary world rich in diversity, openness and cosmopolitanism seeking to care for and connect with the planet, we witnessed the strengthening of closed nation-states and the rise of ethno-nationalism, along with border restrictions, greed and violence. We saw the rise of populist masses who were looking for their One and Only Way, rejecting the complex pluralities of global human life. The idea of human rights, which had achieved so much so rapidly, was increasingly being rejected. Global organizations were derided. A world of digital algorithms and big data posed as progress, while deepening the surveillance and regulation of life. The vast flow of human suffering, typified by the displaced and the refugee, was ignored. And all the time, a major ecological crisis – even a sixth extinction – seemed imminent. All kinds of catastrophic events were predicted. It is important to recall this context in which Covid-19 arrived. But, as we will see, it was also a time that saw the rise of global movements opposed to much of this. Their energy inspired. But will it be enough? Can most of us survive? We will need new visions, new stories, new actions. And this is one reason a new kind of humanism is needed.

Appendix: Monitoring the Mutilated World

Statistics do not tell the whole story and need to be approached critically.[49] But that said, we now have major resources from which we can monitor the state of the mutilated world (see Table 2.1).

Table 2.1: Monitoring the mutilated world

The damaged	*Key resources*
Bare Life	Global Health Observatory (https://www.who.int/data/gho) Global Hunger Index (https://www.globalhungerindex.org/pdf/en/2020.pdf) Food security Information Decent Water (https://www.wateraid.org/uk/)
Environment	UN Environmental Indicators (https://unstats.un.org/unsd/environment/indicators.htm)
Inequality	World Social Report (https://www.un.org/development/desa/dspd/world-social-report/2020-2.html) World Inequality Database (https://wid.world) World Rich Index (https://www.hurun.net/en-US/Info/Detail?num=LWAS8B997XUP) (https://en.wikipedia.org/wiki/The_World%27s_Billionaires) Forbes and *Sunday Times* rich lists
Digital	World Economic Forum: Wild Wide Web (https://reports.weforum.org/global-risks-report-2020/wild-wide-web/)
Exclusion	UNHCR: Internally Displaced People (https://www.unhcr.org/uk/internally-displaced-people.html) Internal Displacement Monitoring Centre (https://www.internal-displacement.org) Genocide Watch (https://www.genocidewatch.com) World Prison Brief (https://www.prisonstudies.org) Coalition Against Trafficking (https://catwinternational.org) Freedom from Torture (https://www.freedomfromtorture.org)
Ignorance	Freedom of the Press Index – Reporters without Borders (https://rsf.org/en/ranking) There are now many fact checking sites, many listed on Wikipedia, country by country. For an example, see Full Fact (https://fullfact.org)

The damaged	Key resources
Violence	Global Peace Index – Vision of Humanity (https://www.visionofhumanity.org/wp-content/uploads/2020/10/GPI_2020_web.pdf) Global Terrorism Index – Vision of Humanity (https://visionofhumanity.org/wp-content/uploads/2020/11/GTI-2020-web-1.pdf) ILGA State Sponsored Homophobia (https://ilga.org/state-sponsored-homophobia-report) Violence against Women: The Shadow Pandemic, 2020 (https://www.unwomen.org/en/news/stories/2020/4/statement-ed-phumzile-violence-against-women-during-pandemic)
Governance	Democracy Index (https://www.eiu.com/n/campaigns/democracy-index-2020/) Failed States Index (https://fragilestatesindex.org) Freedom House (https://freedomhouse.org/report/freedom-world/2021/democracy-under-siege) Human Rights Watch (https://www.hrw.org) International Centre for Transitional Justice (https://www.ictj.org)
Corruption	Rule of Law (World Justice) Index (https://worldjusticeproject.org/our-work/research-and-data/wjp-rule-law-index-2020) Transparency International and Corruption Index (https://www.transparency.org/en/countries/united-kingdom)
Malaise	World Happiness Report (https://worldhappiness.report/ed/2021/) Happy Planet Index (http://happyplanetindex.org) Global Mental Health (https://www.who.int/news-room/fact-sheets/detail/mental-disorders) Lancet Commission on Global Mental Health (https://www.thelancet.com/journals/lancet/article/PIIS0140-6736(18)31612-X/fulltext)
Catastrophe	Global Risk Report (https://www.weforum.org/reports/the-global-risks-report-2020) World Risk/Relief (https://reliefweb.int/sites/reliefweb.int/files/resources/WorldRiskReport-2020.pdf)
Human/ Sustainable Development	Sustainable Development Index (https://sdgindex.org/reports/sustainable-development-report-2020/) Human Development Index/Report (http://hdr.undp.org/en/2020-report)
See also	The New Humanitarian (https://www.thenewhumanitarian.org) New Internationalist (https://newint.org) Our world in data (https://ourworldindata.org)

3
Dividing Humanity

All peoples are different and it's natural that all think that its own way is best.

Herodotus, *Histories*, Bk 3, Ch. 38 (*c.* 430 BCE)

The poet Louis MacNeice once described the unique beauty of every snowflake as 'incorrigibly plural'.[1] And so it is with every human life: we live an 'incorrigible plurality' of lives. Each life takes on a magnificently unique identity from the life of others. This is a quite stunning fact of our humanity. Indeed, philosopher Hannah Arendt makes our human uniqueness the cornerstone of being human: 'Nobody is ever the same as anyone else who ever lived, lives or will live'; we all act in uniquely different ways from each other and dwell in uniquely different narratives.[2] And as we will come to see, it is this very difference that can be one of the scintillating joys of being human. But it can also be its downfall. Our differences are a double-edged sword: a paradox of humanity.

Critical humanism starts with human difference. How do we all differ and how can we come to live well with this? If we can appreciate human difference, our humanity will be enhanced. If we cannot, we may well dehumanize ourselves and others. We live life through these differences in our little human actions, creativities, stories, moralities, ways of being, identities, talking, feelings, sufferings, joys and passions. Empathy, compassion and dialogue will become our guiding tools for understanding such diversity. Cosmopolitanism and conviviality will be its key social forms. While our own lives matter, so too do the lives of others. And we have the capacity to share other lives and understand them. More: our collective lives are also always bound up with the wider biosphere of life. And this matters too. We live in a world not just of other different people, but also of animals and plant life, living things, all uniquely different, with human empathy as our central aid and decoder.

And all this leads to our paradox. The very idea of a difference comes with its opposite: a desire for some kind of common humanity, a unity that will hold us together. Yet as we seek a way of living with others, we stumble into worlds so different from ours that we often become estranged. 'These are not my people or my humanity', we say. And we face the possibility of turning the idea of humanity into a divisive weapon to categorize people, even exclude others. These are not my people: they may not even be human. From this it is but a short step to the long history of human cruelty, self-righteousness, inhumanity and dehumanization that grows out of a seemingly positive world of difference. In this chapter, I give a focus to this *paradox of humanity*.

Background: Circles of Connective Humanity

Here is a key puzzle: how do we move from our own unique, deeply held, ethnocentric worldview to a wider shared worldview of others and their plural cultures? Responses to this will differ widely across cultures; but in all of them we will find possibilities for a spiral of connections to be at work. The Western world develops a view of an inner self atomistically present within; the Eastern world sees a self that is collectively 'lost' in the outer world.[3] Our puzzle is to sense how a uniquely embodied human existential self meets a social world of others. Yet, as philosopher Emmanuel Levinas claims, 'the self is only possible through the recognition of the Other'.[4] For Levinas, the focus should always be on the Other. We can never be alone with a self. There is also always a conversation between ourselves and others. We ultimately see a move from a self-monologue to the Other and a potential mutual dialogue. We move from a conversation with self to a conversation with others: from an 'I' to a 'Thou', from a 'Me' to a 'We'; to a mutual recognition of others and their differences. We live with a potential for understanding the *standpoint of others*. And this raises a general practical problem for human beings: how do we cope with the array of meetings with these others, especially strangers? How are we to respond to them? Do we cooperate and share? Do we get into conflict? Do we absorb the strangers' world, extending it to ours? Is there a desire for mutual recognition?[5]

This is complicated. Two key ideas might help understand human connection: the centrality of empathy (sympathy and compassion are linked), and 'the circle of humanity'. The first looks at how we feel our way into the minds and hearts of others, how we develop mirror reflections acquiring sympathy, a feeling for others. In studies with monkeys, biologist Frans de Waal and others have found that empathy is not a uniquely human trait, even if it reaches more complex levels with humans.[6] A bedrock of human life is thus the development of mutuality and intersubjectivity (the interchange of thoughts and feelings between two people). We enter what philosopher Fonna Forman-Barzilai calls the 'circles of sympathy': 'Each of us is as it were entirely encompassed by many circles, some smaller, others larger.'[7] She draws on a range of formidable thinkers: Adam Smith, Ralph Waldo Emerson, W. E. H. Lecky, Albert Einstein, Gandhi and, most recently, Peter Singer. All suggest an imagery of life flowing through concentric circles. We become aware of ourselves and others, from the closest to the most distanced: intimate others, significant others, generalized others, abstract others, even enemy others. There can be an elaborate classification of these 'others'. The (somewhat over-simple) image shown in Figure 3.1 provides some sense of where I am moving.

This simple diagram encourages us to see life as a course of rippling, concentric flows encircling the human self: circles of others expanding or contracting. Expanding means inclusion: more people and life enter the circle. Contracting means exclusion: fewer people and life enter the circle. Life can be seen as a pulsating circle of connectivity perpetually rolling from a wide sweeping inclusion (call it humanity)

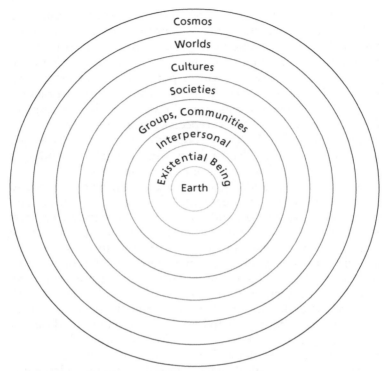

Figure 3.1: Circles of connective humanity

to a narrowing exclusion (call it less-humanity) – and back to inclusion. Along the way, we face differences, conflicts, dehumanization, enemies, resistances, tribalism, new identities, dialogue, civility, cooperation, cosmopolitanism and, maybe, even a common humanity. This is one way of seeing the journey that a life takes.[8]

From Difference to Division to Dehumanization

Our paradox of humanity is grounded in a flow of experience. Human differences can become human divisions. Divisions can be exaggerated and result in dehumanization. Life can become more segregated, antagonistic and polarized. Enemies are created. The struggle is then to see how we can resolve these conflicts – to bring people back together again, to create some sense of a common humanity, to live together well. The remainder of this chapter charts this flow.

On human difference

Just flip around the media: human difference is everywhere on show. Research from anthropologists, geneticists, historians, psychologists, palaeontologists, political scientists and sociologists makes this abundantly clear. Biodiversity can be a starting point. The much studied (and now easily accessible) DNA charts our genetic diversity as a unique structure, each one showing a long different evolutionary strand. We can now track our DNA back across our complex heritage through many generations and find our very varied ancestry.[9] We also now know a lot about the diversities in plants and animals and the very specialized locales in which they flourish.[10] In a similar way, certain modes of living and groups are able to flourish in various different locales and parts of the world. There is a geography of plural human life, a cartography; and a cultural anthropology of societies that documents a massive array of 'ways of living'. Evidence for this can be found in the great museums and digital libraries of the world. With a click of a digital finger, the enormous diversities within the human species can be rapidly found.[11] And such differences cannot be taken lightly. They resonate deeply with people and usually will not be open to easy change.

Very apparent is *linguistic diversity*. Most of us speak only one or two of a small number of languages; but in this century there are some 6,700 languages spoken across the world (down from 14,500 in 1500). Indonesia's population of 268 million spreads over thousands of islands, speaking several hundred languages. That said, conservative estimates suggest that more than half the world's languages will become extinct by 2100; and only twenty-three languages now account for half the world's population. But languages themselves result in a multitude of dialects and hybrid forms. Living languages are in perpetual change.[12]

Then there is *religious diversity*. The website Adherents. com suggests that there are currently more than 4,000 different religions in the world. And they all claim to be right! The top five – Buddhism, Christianity, Hinduism, Islam and Judaism – are all divided, fragmented and deeply conflictual. Throughout history, Gods and spirits have been created (or discovered) to create multiple meanings and rituals that give sense to different lives. With their core texts, leaders, prime rituals and ethical codes, they often reinforce difference and create social worlds closely connected to power.

There is also *tribal, indigenous diversity*. Currently, there are some 5,000 indigenous First Nations tribes around the world – the original inhabitants of parts of the earth: some 370 million people (6 per cent of the world's population) living in culturally different worlds (many are listed on Wikipedia's list of indigenous peoples).[13]

And there is *political diversity*. We move from ideas of 'tribes' to the very modern idea of nations: currently, there are around 200 states in the world. They act as political units to organize our differences. But within each state there usually exist great variations. Increasingly, we also have global – transnational – organizations, which cut across countries, mixing diversities across the globe.

I have only scraped the surface. We can find many more examples of diversity: of gender plurality, ethnic diversity and varied sexualities. And much of it runs very deep. Cultural variations are neither fixed nor settled nor uniform: we have hybrid cultures, mobile cultures, diasporic cultures. There is much more to say about this very wide pattern of cultural and historical diversity that marks humanity.[14]

On division and dehumanization

So difference is everywhere. And living with a human world stuffed full of variety, 'a world of many worlds', is not always going to be easy. It can lead to anxiety about the differences. We may fail to live easily with this enormous human diversity and start using the very language of humanity as a tool to divide the world up. We make some people 'less than human'; we dehumanize them.[15] The idea of 'human' now becomes a powerful sorting device, to distinguish between those who are really human (and hence positive and good) and those who are not.

It is here that the idea of the 'Other' (and 'Othering') arises. 'What is the nature of Othering's comfort, its allure, its power?' asks Toni Morrison in *The Origin of Others*.[16] This Other is depicted first as different, not-us (perhaps as a stranger or a foreigner); then as a lesser being, somewhat inferior – maybe barbaric, savage. And ultimately, it is claimed to be bad, a monster, evil. And so it is that some human beings become nonhuman. Ultimately, they are the objects of power, subjugation, hatred and oppression. The very idea of 'humanity' now becomes a strategy of exclusion. It drowns out other particular human-speaking subjects, voices, people. And along the way it introduces languages, strategies and methodologies that can, first, just disagree; then discriminate and exploit; go on to exclude, terrorize and torture; and finally savagely kill these other people who are different. It organizes deep structures of dehumanization. Here come the civilized and the uncivilized, the modern and the savage, the normal and the pathological. The cripples, the Dalit, the refugees, the Roma: the mad, the bad and the ugly.

Once we start thinking like this, we can soon see a shocking historical parade of people whose lives have been treated this way: humanity excluded by humanity. Lives have been marginalized, silenced, terrorized. Here are the billions of people who live largely brutalized, shamed, dishonoured and insecure lives. Often, they confront discrimination, exclusion and death. The tragedy here is that the very notion of humanity is being used negatively, as a weapon of attack. People quietly scream in fear 'Why am I not seen as human?' 'I am no longer human.' Cameroonian philosopher Achille Mbembe puzzles over this, asking who in the world can claim the right to live a life, and who is to be left to die.[17] This is a question that takes on an even more emphatic relevance as Covid-19 sweeps the world, and especially impacts the poorer communities within it.

We can find the horror of dehumanization at work everywhere. Racism is the most common institutional form of it: in the racialization of the world; in the colonization of many countries by ethnicity throughout history; in the caste system of the Hindus; in many mass displacements of peoples; in genocides, ethnic cleansing, ghettos, prisons, slavery and wars. But we find it elsewhere too, notably in gender. Feminist scholar Catharine A. MacKinnon, for example, can still ask of the twenty-first century: 'When will women become human? When?'[18] To this we can add the torture, abuse and killings across the world of lesbian, gay, bisexual and trans peoples.[19]

I will have more to say about all this in the next chapter.

Creating enemies

And so our human world becomes stuffed full of divisive, sectarian tribes in conflict. Why do we invent enemies, outsiders, monsters that are 'less than human'? Italian intellectual Umberto Eco puzzles over this and comments generally: 'Having an enemy is important not only to define our identity but also to provide us with an obstacle against which to measure our system of values and, in seeking to overcome it, to demonstrate our own worth. So when there is no enemy, we have to invent one.'[20]

This seemingly necessary creation of divisive and enemy worlds is complex, working on many levels, from the deeply psychological to the broadest historical-cultural. Many have studied it. For some, it is simply linked to our basic animality: like most animals, we simply show an instinctive fear of the unknown or of perceived danger. We fear what we do not know: people of a different body, ethnicity, nation, gender, sexuality or age disturb us. Perhaps this serves some kind of evolutionary function. Here, 'othering' can become a mode of projection (and protection). It is precipitated by a deep psychological threat: a form of scapegoating in which we project our own fears onto the other and render them the enemy, lush with hatred, anger and resentment.[21] A strong psychoanalytic link is often made here to fears and repressions of sexuality, aggression and status. Yet another argument suggests this 'othering' may be bound up with group loyalties: with belonging to groups that create 'insider identities' and stable attitudes and worldviews that are hard to change, while rejecting the lives and values of 'outsider groups'. Here, group belonging can bind us together. And closely linked to this is an explanation from anthropologists who suggest it grows from the elaborate working of cultural categorization around purity and taboos. Hence most known societies see the world as some kind of 'natural order' with binary boundaries that help to maintain a distinctive sense of the social order. 'Stuff' that falls outside this understanding becomes 'pathology'. Enemies mark out the symbolic boundaries of a group or society. And closely linked to this is the sociologist's explanation of the linkage between group boundaries and the formation of the self and identity.[22]

Bringing some of these themes together, we find a core *narrative of binary othering*. As we define our 'selves', create our own identities and bond with our own groups, so we create binary oppositions that we can come to see as the 'enemy', the 'other'. The 'ties that bind' become the 'ties that blind'. And this may be a cruel blindness: unable to see the worlds of others, we are condemned to create enemies.

This sweeping summary suggests that explanations of othering are multitiered: from the biological to the cultural. But all this has been very abstract. While there are many theoretical explanations, the focus ultimately has to move to the concrete case, real people and historically specific detail of their interests, fears and conflicts. To understand 'othering' always requires detailing the economic and power relations in the historical moment in which it happens: the real-life dynamics of war, slavery, colonialism, racism, migration. It is to power relations and history that we have ultimately to turn. It is only the detailed historical story that can deeply explain why it is that, at any time, one group of people are 'othered' and others are not. The history of racialized others in the US, for example, links to a wider historical system of massive slavery and economic exploitation.

In *Age of Anger*, Indian writer Pankaj Mishra looks at the tensions in Europe and Asia over the past 200 years.[23] He sees the breakdown of the old established orders and their legitimacy; the rise of new demagogues and authoritarian leaders involved in hatemongering against immigrants; and violence and terrorism stretching across vast swathes of land. It is the culmination of a long process. Here we find vast irrationalities and the rise of resentment, anger, hate. Just how has all this been working itself out in world history over the past 200 years?

There are many such studies. Norman Naimark, for example, has looked at five recent ethnic cleansings in Europe, from the Armenian genocide of 1915 and the expulsion of Greeks from Anatolia during the Greco-Turkish War of 1921–2, to Bosnia and Kosovo built on long-standing religious and ethnic hatreds.[24] I will be suggesting that the world is littered with this kind of traumatized humanity. A cycle of othering is linked to a simmering sense of *injustice*, a *fear* of difference, a *resentment* of others and a *hatred* of enemies.[25]

Resisting the Fault Lines of Hierarchical Humanity

The people we become hostile towards do not appear randomly on our horizons. They are structured by means of deep hierarchies and fault lines organized through well-embedded historical power relations. Most commonly, this involves relations of dominance and subordination linked to class, gender, ethnicity, sexuality, age, health and ability, and also religion, nation, environment and nature. These are the global fault lines of humanity and they cannot easily be wished away. These ideas (with long-hidden grounded histories) work to make visible not just difference, but *hierarchies of humanities and oppression*. They highlight many major forms of domination, not just one. They give voice and language to processes that may have haunted much of humanity. These days, we see these processes as issues of class and class consciousness, anti-racism and racialization, anti-Semitism and Islamophobia, sexism and patriarchy, generational ageism, homophobia and heterosexism, disableism and ableism, nationalism and postcolonialism. These are key 'new names' for the process of dehumanizing others. And they intersect with one another. Ubiquitous, deep and universal, they have a long, if hidden, history that runs alongside the structures of key social institutions.[26] Out of these have emerged a multitude of new 'tribes', global social movements and identity politics that help redefine what it means to be human in the contemporary world. Here we can find multiple struggles of everyday resistance throughout the world. Table 3.1 provides a schematic indication of all this.

Table 3.1: Hierarchies of humanity: the dehumanization of others

Ideologies: narratives of dehumanization	Fault lines: dominant structures	Subordination: dehumanized 'others'	Resistance: social movements
Class and class consciousness	economic divides	poor/rich; slave/free; Dalit/Brahmin	workers' movements
Racism and racialization	ethnic divides	black/white; colonized; indigenous/ 'advanced'	movements for indigenous peoples; colonized movements; antiracism movements
Sexism	gender divides (patriarchy)	man/woman; man-woman/trans	women's movement; gender movements
Ageism	age and generational divides	good age/bad age; young/older	youth movements; 'elderly' movements
Heterosexism, homophobia, transphobia	sexuality divides/ heterosexism	straight/gay; pervert/normal	gay, lesbian, transgender, queer movements
Ableism	health and disability divides	abled/disabled; healthy/sick	health movements; disability alliances
Fundamentalism, anti-Semitism, Islamophobia	religious divides	Christian/Jew; Hindu/Muslim; Protestant/ Catholic; Sunni/Shi'a/Sufi	multifaith movements; secular movements
Nationalism	national divides; tribal divides	my country/your country; colonized/ colonizer; citizen/migrant; home/refugee	local movements; indigenous movements; global movements; displaced peoples
Nature and environment	species divides; environmental divides	nature/culture; nature/ technology	environment movement; animal movement
and many others ...	systems of privilege/ division	insiders/outsiders	resistance movements

Resistances to division: the humanism of the subordinated other

Throughout history, subordinated voices struggle to tell their 'true' story. New critical stances can be taken towards dominant knowledge. This is also a way that emerging truth can be explored. Gradually, a 'standpoint' grounded in a group awareness (an identity and a belonging) of this subordination tries to become coherent and organized. A collective *humanism of the subordinated other* comes to be heard. And over long spans of time we have been gradually hearing this. Domination generates both a new form of embodied consciousness and a new self-identity.

Marxism explored the way a new potential for a class consciousness could emerge as classes came to identify themselves. Likewise, feminism found an epistemology of feminist standpoints as women struggled to find a new awareness of their oppressed situation. Slavery was slowly resisted and emancipated: the voice of the slave fitfully struggled to be heard, and continues to be so in its modern form as the Black Lives Matter and antiracism movement. Postcolonial repression brought us the subaltern standpoint and, ultimately, the movement for indigenous peoples and decolonization. In an influential work, Brazilian educator Paulo Freire looked for a 'pedagogy of the oppressed' as he examined colonized racism; while West Indian psychiatrist Frantz Fanon made his call for 'conscientization' (an emancipated consciousness) in outcast postcolonial groups.[27] Queer activists likewise developed a queer consciousness, arising to challenge the dominance of heteronormativity and establish new senses of sexual possibilities. A disability movement emerged to resist their mainstream mistreatment as they developed a language of 'abelism'. Indigenous tribal resistance movements emerge to fight development and the destruction of local cultures. And out of the awareness of the ecological rifts between Asia and the West, the North and the South, new pluralistic communities of resistance were born.[28]

Living Well Together: The Kindness of Strangers

As philosopher Richard Rorty pronounced:

> Progress on a world-historical scale consists in enlarging
> the range of people whom we think of as people like us.
> Barbarians, for example, get in as well as Greeks. Greeks get
> in as well as Jews. Women get in as well as men. Blacks get in
> as well as whites. Gays get in as well as straights.[29]

And so it is that a difference becomes a division; a division
leads to dehumanization, and an enemy. Enemies then
resist. And an agonistic world of lives in perpetual conflict
with others is created. Much of this book is concerned
with this very question. Throughout history and across
cultures, most societies have developed their own divisions
and enemies. And yet there are many historical situations
and locations where people with differences of all kinds
have lived well together in the past. It has been done. And
often. Classic examples include the Silk Road, where a
lucrative trade thrived across East and West for hundreds of
years; medieval Spain, where Muslims, Jews and Christians
created a culture of tolerance; and many big cities of the
past and today that became cosmopolitan, almost by
necessity, and thrive on a certain vitality that comes from
their differences.[30] We can indeed find examples of people
who assemble rich vibrant tapestries of diverse ways of
being in the world together as some kind of common
humanity. Yet for much of history, living with difference
and not creating division and dehumanization has been a
major challenge.

And so we return to a key question: *how can we best live
together with our differences?* Much of this book is concerned
with this very question. In a key study, *The Invention
of Humanity*, Dutch historian Siep Stuurman examines in
detail this problem of confronting our human differences
throughout a wide panoramic history. He poses the following
telling questions:

How and in what historical circumstances did cross-cultural humanity become thinkable? How could it happen that people came to see foreigners as fellow human beings or even as equals? How did they surmount the deeply ingrained ethnocentrism that was omnipresent at the dawn of human history? How did they arrive at the daring vision that all human beings on earth are basically alike and should be considered members of the overarching meta-community that was eventually denoted by the term *humanity*?

He also states:

Common humanity and equality are not primeval acts that patiently await discovery. We should, rather, conceive of them as inventions of novel and potentially disruptive ways of looking at human relationships. That all the people in the world constitute a single community is not an empirical fact. What it means is that people can be represented as members of the meta-community of an 'imagined humanity'.[31]

To provide evidence for his argument, Stuurman sets out on the very ambitious task of examining many significant texts throughout history (from the writings of Confucius to the Universal Declaration of Human Rights) asking how, from the dawn of established societies, the very idea of 'other societies' has been handled. Looking at a very wide range of encounters between strangers, he asks whether they meet each other with equanimity or with hostility. When travellers, traders or warriors meet other different people, what is to be done? Very often, they will confront extreme violence and fear, war and hostility. But there is evidence to suggest a gradual growth of cooperation, empathy and understanding, even sometimes a sense of immanent equality. We see the rise of what Stuurman calls the 'anthropological turn', by which he means how we look at 'the stranger in the eyes of others':

Haphazard enumerations of outlandish attributes of foreign cultures are transformed into environmentally grounded explications of functional patterns of culture. Uninformed ethnocentrism is supplanted by informed criticism. ... Observers of a foreign culture may seek to imagine how the foreigners look back at them, thus inverting the habitual hierarchy of the familiar and the foreign.[32]

Stuurman's book takes us through sweeping periods of history and wide-ranging writings that include the Islamic Koran, the works of the medieval Muslim scholar Ibn Khaldun; and others from more recent times: Haitian Antenor Firmin, Filipino José Rizal. Stuurman also goes right back to Homer, and to the histories of other societies produced by the first historian Herodotus. In all these accounts he is looking for – and usually finds – something of what has been called 'the kindness of strangers'. In all of them, he finds early signs of strangers being treated as fellow human beings: with hospitality and civility, with the possibility of care, including respect, recognition and dignity. There is indeed a history of our humanity.[33]

A Toolbox for Connection and Conviviality

Philosopher Martha C. Nussbaum suggests a conundrum:

> If our world is to be a decent world in the future, we must acknowledge right now that we are citizens of one interdependent world, held together by mutual fellowship as well as the pursuit of mutual advantage, by compassion as well as by self-interest, by a love of human dignity in all people, even when there is nothing we have to gain from cooperating with them. Or rather, even when what we have to gain is the biggest thing of all: participation in a just and morally decent world.[34]

How are we to act in the world so as to live well with others? The challenge of the paradox of humanity – of unity and difference, inclusion and exclusion – can be met in multiple ways. The struggles arise in finding ways to live well – convivially – with human differences. Here we can move from living well with different others in the particularities of everyday action towards the building of wider institutions that create a form of cosmopolitan living together. Right up front we start with the recognition of the physical presence of others: their faces, bodies, minds and personalities, and the mutuality (and disturbance) that can arise from this. We are in the presence of others. Bodies touch, faces gaze, multiple voices can be heard. Empathy, role-taking, human sympathy (even, sometimes, compassion) can be activated. Dialogues take place. A mutuality and conviviality may (or may not) be established. Circles of humanity may be expanded. A cosmopolitanism of openness, tolerance and living with others could be established. This is a kind of toolbox of ideas to help us live well with others.

At the heart of this paradox lies five elements. The first of these is human communication – *symbol, language and dialogue*. The words and symbols we use matter. They can wound and destroy, damage and degrade, and generate shame and guilt. And the idea of dialogue makes clear the fact that voices can speak and listen to one another responsively, openly, empathetically. Russian philosopher Mikhail Bakhtin has been a key guide here, focusing on great novels and showing the understanding that lies behind them.

> Life by its very nature is dialogic. To live means to participate in dialogue: to ask questions, to heed, to respond, to agree, and so forth. In this dialogue a person participates wholly and throughout his whole life: with his eyes, lips, hands, soul, spirit, with his whole body and deeds. He invests his entire self in discourse, and this discourse enters into the dialogic fabric of human life, into the world symposium.[35]

At our best, we are capable of digging deep to establish conversations with self and others. Here we can pay due respect, listen and take seriously multiple voices, trying our best to make sense of this, even when it disagrees with our stance. It is a fundamental attempt to create some kind of mutual agreement to live with each other well. It requires familiarizing ourselves with background issues of cultural difference, power and inequalities – of locating dialogic inequalities. Ultimately, there will be an 'unfinalizabilty' and open-endedness to such talk. Of course, this is a highly fragile and complicated process; but it is possible. And we now have to think long and hard about what is required for it to work. It requires that we *be attentive to other humans*. And this will never be easy. It does not mean we have to agree: only that we can get on a little, and hopefully agree on some things.[36]

Within this communication, *empathy and compassion* will come to play key roles. In Harper Lee's classic story *To Kill a Mockingbird* (1960) the lawyer Atticus Finch gives his daughter this warning: 'You never really understand a person until you consider things from his point of view, until you climb inside of his skin and walk around in it.'[37] In the strongest version of this, we develop *compassion*. For some, like religious writer Karen Armstrong, compassion is the central project of humanism. Her own work has led to a Charter of Compassion, and a Golden Rule: 'to look into our own hearts, discover what gives us pain, and then refuse, under any circumstance whatsoever, to inflict that pain on anybody else … It is an attitude of principled, consistent altruism.'[38] We can stretch this compassion across a wide array of situations, including the recent arrival of a widespread transnational literature and film that enables us to develop a wide-ranging appreciation of the different worlds of others.

Third, we move on to an *expanding of the circles of humanity* – extending our sense of dialogue and compassion by appreciating a wider and more varied range of 'others'. This branching out depends increasingly on some sense of common bonds that help to connect us. And here the very recognition of the idea of some kind of common humanity (bringing perhaps ideas of reciprocity, dignity and rights) helps towards the creation of human bonds. It is present in the worldwide creation of norms of hospitality and conviviality – where we build institutions of friendliness and kindness to strangers.[39]

All this might lead to the fostering of *a cosmopolitan ideal*, which, even if flawed,[40] helps us to envision a world consciousness and world activity where we can come together with a growing sensitivity to differences and how to live with them. For Diogenes, the idea of cosmopolitanism brought together *cosmos* (world, universe) and *polis* (local political community). For Kant, it brought world laws – and a principle of hospitality. There are intimations here of a world politics, coming together and bridging peoples of the world with a local, welcoming difference. Cosmopolitanism is a complex idea with many meanings: in the account of sociologist Robert Holton, more than 200 different types are listed, giving rise to numerous controversies. For British-Ghanaian philosopher, Kwame Anthony Appiah, it is a 'universal concern for legitimate difference'. And for sociologist Ulrich

Beck, it suggests a melange, where 'local, national, ethnic, religious *and* cosmopolitan cultures and traditions interpenetrate, interconnect and intermingle'.[41] I find it useful as a code term for highlighting the ways human beings learn to live with difference.

Finally, we reach the most problematic term in our toolbox – *a sense of common humanity*. The paradox of humanity suggests confronting differences and divisions, dehumanization and polarization, on the way to a wider understanding of what it means to be human. Indeed, one of the joys of using the word 'humanity' has to be that it brings the possibility of searching for unifying and harmonizing forces in the world. We human beings may find we have something in common – a universal – with one another after all: and this is often what we call humanity. But finding this is not easy. Whatever this may ultimately turn out to be, it suggests we might all share and belong to some kind of provisional common human universal world. (During the height of the Covid-19 crisis, the word 'humanity' was frequently evoked to flag the sentiment that 'we are all in this together'.)

Such universalism is fragile. And it takes two major forms. One is our *subjective*, phenomenological, personally sensed world of universals: the thought that human beings feel they are part of a similarly shared world, a common narrative of humanity. This sense does not arrive automatically or naturally when we meet 'strangers'; it has to be achieved and worked at (as we have seen above). A second sense of universals claims to be more *objective*. Certainly, long lists of such universals are regularly cited. In one book alone, *Human Universals*, anthropologist Donald E. Brown lists some 200 of them, ranging from 'abstraction in speech and thought' to 'weapons' and 'worldview'.[42] Despite the many suspicious critics, it is really not very hard to find a great many suggestive claims as to what the universals (essences) of a common humanity might look like. I already hinted at some of them in Chapter 1 – see Box 0.1.

In writing this book, I have sensed that several important features of being human are frequently suggested. The distinguished biologist Edmund O. Wilson, for example, argues: 'Creativity is the unique and defining trait of our species; and its ultimate goal, self-understanding;' while John

Hands, in *Cosmo Sapiens*, suggests that 'the one characteristic that distinguishes humans from all other species is reflective consciousness'.[43] These are not fixed traits, but capacities awaiting action. We are animals with potentials. We all have capacities to use language, create meanings, work with symbols and tell stories. This makes us self-conscious creatures who think about our being in the world. We are all vulnerable beings living in a fragile world. Yet we can also all act in the world (have agency): we can perform things and create things. We are social animals and like doing things together – even sharing things. We are the creative creatures who bring 'new things' into the world. And at some level, we need to be recognized for who we are – even accorded some kind of dignity, value. Much has been written about all these features.[44]

This is tricky ground. I am not claiming a fixed universal nature. But I am suggesting there are open-ended potentials for making us human. And they matter. And I am left wondering whether they make sense to you, as they do to me. It is some of these ideas that we will explore further in Part III of the book.

4
Traumatizing Humanity

> Human beings will never be delivered from evil. Our only hope is not to eradicate it definitively but to try and understand it, to contain and tame it, recognising that it is also present in us.
>
> Tzvetan Todorov, *Memory as a Remedy for Evil* (2010), p. 82

Tzvetan Todorov was one of the most prolific humanist writers of the twentieth century, documenting a world of atrocity and evil.[1] Humans act in the world to create an anti-humanity. A world where slavery, war, genocide, rape, racism, caste, femicide and colonization are routinely, in their times, normalized – leaving humanity ripped apart, disconnected, traumatized. The word 'atrocity' is derived from the Latin, meaning 'fierce' and 'cruel', and that is what this chapter is about. I try to confront the truly dark side of humanity, considering how we face the traumatic and violent past and 'settle accounts' with it. One meaning of the word evil is 'the denial of humanity'. This is our concern.[2]

Facing Humanity: Holocaust, Atrocity and Evil

A core, if agonizing, pathway to understanding humanity must come from scrutinizing the Holocaust. As one of the most acute examples of modern mass human cruelty, death and suffering, these horrors make us painfully aware that we are an animal capable of extraordinarily extreme cruelty, atrocity – even evil. Films like László Nemes's *Son of Saul* (2015) and Claude Lanzmann's *Shoah* (1985) bear witness to the cruel inhumanity of humanity, to minimal, bare dehumanized life. For some, it is horrendous precisely because it is a product of our time: a 'techno-bureaucratic rationality' that has brought 'the demise of an ethical consciousness' and the end of humanity.[3] The Holocaust has necessarily led to an avalanche of testaments to the experience, as well as critical commentary about all those human beings implicated in such terrors: victims, perpetrators, bystanders. The systematic, yet almost mundane, slaughtering of some 6 million Jews (but also Roma, disabled, gay people, political dissidents) by an army of ordinary operatives and technicians opens up a space for the most serious thinking about what it means to be human, inhuman and dehumanized. Just how is it possible to adequately reflect upon the masses of human lives being ghettoized, enslaved, deported, stripped bear, rendered nameless by numbering, diseased, overcrowded, starved, forced to dig their own graves, and ultimately shockingly and carelessly slaughtered? Or of children, fathers and mothers sent in the most brutalized conditions to the work and extermination camps, where they were tortured, sent for medical experiments, gassed, shot, buried alive and sent to their mass graves? This is an extreme case of the dehumanization and brutalization of life, which rightly haunts most contemporary discussions of humanity.

Even more: it is a horror that reverberates. Clearly, other groups of humans have been able to engage in such horrors, at the very deep level of dehumanization that allowed this atrocity to happen. How on earth can some people do this to other groups of people? Gradually it becomes clear that not only were there large numbers of Germans working as camp commandants, but also many in the population who were complicit as informers and bystanders. Even some Jews themselves may have been complicit. Worse still, and terrible to believe, there are now not only many people who are unaware of the Holocaust having ever taken place, but others who deny its very existence: Holocaust deniers. How can our humanity be so very, very bleak?

All this throws out many challenges. How do we find ways to think about such events, to imagine them, to know what was going on, to decipher what it all means? How do we create a human response to an inhuman act? At the outset, let's say it sharply marks out both the failure of humanity and the failure of human ethics. At the deepest level it shows the muddiest muck, the profoundest nastiness of what it can mean to be human. Call it Evil if you wish. I have little doubt that we are truly, all of us, capable of the most vile and despicable deeds. Philosopher John K. Roth claims: 'The Holocaust, genocide, and other mass atrocities confirm the singular failure of ethics, which is that ethics has not made us human beings better than we are'; he asks: 'How should it affect men and women today?' and he brings us all sharply to account:

> Defined by the intention to encourage human action that fits sound understanding about what is *right* and *wrong*, *just* and *unjust*, *good* and *evil*, *virtuous* and *corrupt*, ethics arguably is civilization's keystone. Absent the overriding of moral sensibilities, if not the collapse of collaboration of ethical traditions, the Holocaust, genocide, and other mass atrocities could not take place. Although these catastrophes do not pronounce the death of ethics, they show that ethics is vulnerable, subject to misuse and perversion, and that no simple reaffirmation of ethics, as if nothing monstrous had happened, will do.[4]

Roth makes a shocking suggestion: that every person in the world should be required to reflect on this monstrous deed every morning when they wake up; to think about these horrors of humanity before they start out into the world for the day; to reimagine them. Roth's challenge is to make us face up to value demands: being human requires us to think about and take moral and ethical stances. For now, suffice to say, the Holocaust has produced its own major humanist literature.

As one small indication, we soon find a vivid and very challenging set of vital accounts published by Auschwitz survivors, including Elie Wiesel's memoir *Night*, Viktor

Frankl's *Man's Search for Meaning*, and Primo Levi's *If This Is a Man* and *The Drowned and the Saved*. These have not just become major testimonies of Holocaust survivors; they have also edged themselves into being major testaments to humanity. Wiesel's memoir, for example, speaks to the importance of fighting to keep alive the memory of the Holocaust: 'To forget would be not only dangerous but offensive; to forget the dead would be akin to killing them a second time.'[5] Frankl's torment enabled him to pursue what he called a 'tragic optimism', whereby he could see the contrasting signs amongst those who could experience and survive the camps and those for whom life became pointless. For some, he says, 'it began with the prisoner refusing one morning to get dressed and wash or go out on the parade grounds. No entreaties, no blows, no threats had any effect. He just lay there, hardly moving ... He simply gave up. There he remained, lying in his own excreta, and nothing bothered him anymore.' In contrast, others found the will to live through the search for meaning. All people found a different meaning in life, but this meaning had to be 'very real and concrete, just as life's tasks are also very real and concrete'. Man's destiny is 'different and unique for each individual'.[6] Each person has to find their own meaning. And this is the clue to survival as well as a central feature of humanity. And finally, Italian chemist Primo Levi – sometimes called 'the austere humanist 'or 'tragic optimist'[7] – wrote much poetry and fiction after his survival from Auschwitz, most notably, in 1947, *If This Is a Man*.[8] Like Frankl, for Levi the issue concerns bearing witness to the horrors of the camp (this time in Auschwitz) and the Nazi attempt to annihilate a whole race. Even as he could embrace humanity, he could not forgive.

There are many such accounts. Together they persistently raise questions not just concerning humanity but also inhumanity; they challenge us to make sense of the rottenness of governance and the idiosyncratic meanings of life, of the importance of testimony and memory, of fragility and vulnerability, of religion and its failures, of world cruelty and justice.

The Disconnected Human World: Trauma and Atrocity at Large

The Holocaust is a prime, major modern illustration. But it is a Western concern – as sociologist Jeffrey C. Alexander says, it is a sign of 'moral universalism in the West'.[9] The Holocaust is not focused upon in the same way in other parts of the world; they have their own 'holocausts' to deal with. Indeed, some commentators puzzle over why the Holocaust attracts so much attention when we can find so many other instances in the world that are hidden or denied. Stephen Hopgood comments that 'Asia has its own legacy of mass atrocity'.[10] There was also a Spanish holocaust under Franco, which few speak of now. The Soviet famine of the Holodomor in Ukraine in 1932–3 killed some 3–12 million people. There was 'the forgotten holocaust' of the Nanjing Massacre in China in December 1937, when more than 300,000 Chinese were raped and slaughtered by the Japanese.[11] And there has been a Latin America holocaust, albeit scarcely yet conceptualized. In her brilliant study, *Cruel Modernity*, Jean Franco critically examines the widespread and deep human cruelty and dehumanization that permeates Latin America. In almost every country, from Argentina and Bolivia through Chile and Cuba to Mexico and Peru, Franco reveals deep modern inhumanities: slavery, mass killings, the raping of the dead, feminicide, torture, drug cartels, corruption.[12] Latin America is home to just 8 per cent of the world's population, but 33 per cent of its homicides. In fact, just four countries in the region (Brazil, Colombia, Mexico and Venezuela) account for a quarter of all murders worldwide. Of the twenty countries with the highest murder rates, seventeen are Latin American, as are forty-three of the top fifty cities.[13]

Librarian and scholar Matthew White has produced a devasting catalogue, a shocking book, which reveals a great chain of human atrocities running through history.[14] It is only in very recent times that we have started to develop any recognition either of how widespread and deep these events run, or of their consequences. We have here a dark flow of historical anti-humanity, of cruel governance and violent ignorance. Throughout world history, billions of people and groups have suffered, usually in silence, from the cruel dehumanizing acts of others. Their times and cultures allowed people to do this, very often in the 'name of humanity'. As late as 1800, up to three-quarters of the global population may have been living in some kind of bondage.[15]

Modern times have brought many structural atrocities, each uniquely different and horrendous. A few symbolic words will surely demonstrate this: Auschwitz, yes; also: Apartheid, Biafra, Bosnia, Cambodia, Darfur, Gulag, Hiroshima, Holocaust, Khmer Rouge, Mỹ Lai, Nanjing, Rwanda, the Thai–Burma Death Railway – not to forget 9/11. And a roll call of key names that have provoked fear in recent times include Stalin, Hitler, Franco, Mussolini, Mao, Marcos, Mugabe, Amin, Pinochet, Pol Pot, Milošević, Hussein. They can all be linked to human atrocities that have also been built into a range of social institutions: caste, colonization, genocide, inquisitions, prisons, sexual violence (including rape), slavery, torture, and wars are all vehicles for hatred and atrocity. As we have seen, the story continues with new horrors: Boko Haram, Chechnya and Russia, Darfur in Sudan, Uyghur Muslims in China, Rohingya Muslims in Myanmar.

Today there are also 'new scandals' (even as they often have long histories), involving the church and child abuse, femicide and women's abuse, refugee crises and camps, corrupt economic and political governments, the poor responses to pandemics. All could be rolled back over a history littered with examples. Similar names from a more distant past will often have been long forgotten. We are confronting a traumatized humanity, a sustained ignorance and a viscous circle of people around this process.

Regimes of Dehumanization, Disconnection and Pervasive Anti-Humanity

There is a devastating human drama unfolding here. Throughout history, large numbers of people are forced to lose their claim to being seen as human. They are disconnected from the mainstream of life, and become the objects of cruelty, torture, physical and symbolic violence, and killing. Still others become perpetrators: here are ordinary people (you and me) who have often, through the auspices of governments and economies, wreaked havoc on the lives of others, along with their land, country and world. Societies have even been structured around this: a dehumanization justified in the name of 'civilization', 'God', 'progress' or even 'humanity', often masking a deeper pursuit of wealth and power. Again, slavery, caste, colonization and genocides are key examples. All this has been marked by gender: men are more likely to be perpetrators, women the victims of sexual violence; by race and racialization: a major marker of human difference; by bodily ability and 'ableism': those who are disabled or disfigured can be discarded; by sexual difference, heterosexism and (more recently) transphobia: the differences of gender and desire become pathologies and perversions; and by nationality and nationalism: often a euphemism for racism. Taken together, we find examples of traumatized atrocity, cruelty and catastrophe that have left vast landscapes of damaged, dehumanized and dead people across the world.

Here is the large-scale destruction of lives, a widespread suffering for many people and their loved ones. Call it a traumatized humanity lodged in systemic and institutional cruelty and discrimination. The word 'trauma' here implies deep wounding. And cultural trauma becomes a term to identify the gradual collective recognition of a shared suffering.[16] And so, some key questions arise for a human future. We have to ask just how we can make narrative sense of this; how we can create memories and institutions to deal with it; and, ultimately, how we can develop a sense of justice and hope that will enable us to move on, beyond the traumas of the past world.

Confronting cultural trauma

We must look; we must remember; we must not forget. All this has deep, long-term consequences. Fuelled by a hatred of difference, an aftermath of trauma, resentment and repressed rage lingers on. A world of melancholia and sadness lives on: the world is not right. Handed down from generation to generation, this brings new problems of memory, repression, frustration, guilt and shame, anger and resentment, rage and violence. But sometimes also, maybe, reconciliations, forgiveness, justice, hope. These can all become important issues for the ways in which lives, groups and societies function, and for how humans live with a deep sense of (often concealed, denied) societal trauma or wounding. The world is full of the dead, 'ghosts', the walking wounded, and their memories. Look at almost any country or group in the world and dig a little. Scars will be found; and often a simmering rage and resentment over wounds that were never dealt with – or were dealt with very badly.

There is probably no country in the world, then, that has not been touched by some atrocity or trauma. Some more than others. They serve as a deep underbelly to humanity's malfunctioning. And they usually work in silence and a kind of violent ignorance.[17] While I surely recognize that the Holocaust is uniquely horrendous, I am also suggesting that terrible cruel deeds, putative atrocity and deep trauma can be found everywhere. I have tried to think of countries where regimes of dehumanization and disconnection have not happened. It is no easy task. There is no space here to run through every country: a few must suffice.

Australia, for example, had to face the deaths of its indigenous Aboriginal peoples (who had been living there for 40,000–60,000 years before the arrival of the British), the early days of forced migration, and the horrors of the First World War when more than 60,000 people were killed. The multiple countries on the African continent are another very apparent case: most faced colonization and the so-called 'scramble for Africa',[18] all carried out in the name of commerce, Christianity (missionization), civilization and conquest. This left a far-reaching, deep breakdown of many countries and cities with their own local cultures. Many have not recovered today. South Africa introduced the first concentration camps and the development of an unbelievably cruel system of full-scale apartheid. But each African state now bears its own trauma. Many of them are persistently identified as the most failed or damaged states in the world today. Little has gone well for them. For another example, look at Indonesia, where an estimated 0.5–1 million people were killed between October 1965 and April 1966: a mass killing field.[19]

Or take two of the major global powers: China and the USA. China, in recent times alone, undertook the Great Leap Forward (1958–62), resulting in 40 million people starving to death (the Great Famine), as well as the purge of around half a million critics of Communist Party policies. Journalist and author Yang Jisheng's *Tombstone* is the book that, as its cover pronounces, 'broke the silence on of one of history's most terrible crimes'.[20] The Cultural Revolution followed (1966–76), and in 1989 the Tiananmen Square military crackdown killed an estimated 10,000 people. China stays very silent about such events. Likewise, the USA has not been without its own horrors: dropping the atomic bomb over Hiroshima and Nagasaki in 1945; the Vietnam War (1955–75) – not to mention the invasion of Iraq and Afghanistan and even the occupation of Haiti. Earlier, there was the horror of slavery (and the Civil War) with the deep wounds of racism that have 'stamped America from the beginning'.[21] Indeed, the slavery story is one of several paradigmatic instances of the great anti-humanity (the caste system, wars, colonization and rape being other key examples). It is also the deep foundation of the modern Black Lives Matter movement. We can see some twelve or so generations of Black Americans having to deal with it.[22]

Racism and the trauma of cruel colonization

A major example, involving much of the world, arises from the modern process of European colonization from the fourteenth to the twentieth century.[23] Stretching back four centuries, key European countries (Belgium, England, France, Spain, the Netherlands, Portugal) invaded Australia, Africa, India, New Zealand, South America and much of Asia. Here was significant global subordination, subjection and, often, slaughtering of local people. The classic examples can be found in the treatment of indigenous peoples, where, if they were not killed outright, they were taken by the arrival of new diseases.[24] By 1945, nearly a third of the world's population – some 750 million people – lived in territories ruled by colonial powers. (Currently, only 2 million people live under such conditions.) Empires were built up through violence and were usually deeply interconnected with racial ideologies. And here we see early (unnamed) genocides, the spread of diseases, routine exploitation and widespread enslavement.[25]

The trauma of gender atrocity

In recent times, the extent to which war, terrorism and genocidal acts have been accompanied by large-scale atrocities towards women has become much clearer. There is a long history of such gender atrocity, as women become objects of male violence around the world.[26] Today, some 35 per cent of women worldwide have experienced either physical and/ or sexual intimate partner violence or sexual violence by a non-partner (not including sexual harassment) at some point in their lives. It is estimated that approximately 87,000 women were intentionally killed in 2017, more than half of them by partners or family members.[27] Here is a long catalogue of defilements and dehumanization: in rape, sexual harassment, sexual trafficking, honour-based crime, domestic violence, child abuse, female infanticide, online gender violence, acid throwing, obstetric violence. Violence takes place against women in a wide range of circumstances: refugees, indigenous people, lesbians, ethnic groupings, civilians in wartimes.

Owning Our Histories, Reckoning with Traumatic Pasts and Making Life Accountable

These horrors are not peculiar to the past. Take a look around the world right now. There are at least ten putative genocides going on – including the Rohingya (Myanmar), the Nuer (South Sudan), the Muslim minority in Central African Republic, the Armenian Republic of Artsakh, as well as in India, Syria, Nigeria and Iraq.[28] Modern slavery (human trafficking, forced labour, bonded labour, child marriage) affects around 40 million people (2.6 million of them in North Korea).[29] And in 2019, 243 million women and girls (aged 15–49) across the world were subjected to sexual or physical violence by an intimate partner (with the arrival of Covid-19, this is rapidly increasing).[30]

On truth and justice, peace and reconciliation

And so here we have an abiding problem for humanism, humanity and world politics. How can societies, groups and people come to recognize the atrocities and traumas of their past and deal with them? How can 'the world' frame a suitable response to the horrors it has witnessed? Indeed, is such a response possible, or even desirable? Will it be possible in the future to build world institutions that can 'make sense of the past', maybe even 'settle accounts', helping to resolve traumas of the past and ease the way into a future? How can we make sense of testimonies of atrocity, our stories, our rituals, our monuments? How can we remember this past as we handle the problems of memory, truth and justice across the changing generations? These are major, possibly intractable problems for humanity. They may never be fully resolved. But we are making a start. In less than a century, many important issues have been put on the table.[31] Table 4.1 sets out some of the basic issues here.

Institutionalized accounting

Across the world over the past century or so there have been many innovative attempts to make sense of atrocities through some kind of resolution and reconciliation. Such attempts have gradually emerged through the work of treaties, tribunals, courts, commissions and many testimonies and narratives (often linked to debates on 'transitional justice', and 'memory'). We get an early idea of the scale of the problem in the wake of the horrors around the First World War with the Treaty of Versailles in 1919 and the development of a League of Nations, when the very idea of 'crimes against humanity' first appeared. In their own time, none

Table 4.1: Making sense of atrocity and anti-humanity

Issue	Examples
Look across the world's history and identify atrocities and name the inhumanity	'Crimes against humanity', including genocide, slavery, war, caste, torture, colonization, sexual violence, etc.
Listen to all people, dialogue across voices	Who are the perpetrators, victims, deniers, bystanders, including ancestors and descendants? Who has power? Who does not?
Build institutions, create due process	Laws, courts, trials, commissions, tribunals (informal/formal; local/global)
Search memory: pursue history, truth, knowledge and wisdom	Problems of testimonies, archives, memory, truth; issues of plural pasts, post-memory, just memory, generational memory; issues of epistemological injustice
Pursue accountability, seek just and good outcomes	(a) From injustice, wounding, torture, extermination, ignorance, denial (b) Through seeking common grounds in punishment (prison, fines, etc.), retribution, vengeance, reparation, restitution, rehabilitation, forgiveness (c) Towards 'justice', 'truth' and awareness; education and symbolic morality 　(i) micro: face-to-face interactional justice 　(ii) macro: long-term and wider structural injustice
Become aware of time and generations	Short-term outcomes vs long-term outcomes: always need long-term appraisal through different generations.
Face dilemmas, looking to hope	Acts of memorialization; acts of reparation; acts of education; local and global political divides

of these ideas was really successful. For example, after the massacre of Armenians during the Turkish Revolution, the idea that this was a 'genocide' or a 'crime against humanity' was denied by Turkey – and still is to this day. But it did open the way to questions, language and debates – and even the possibility of an International Criminal Court (ICC), though this did not finally arrive until 2002. (Even then, many countries – the USA, China, India, Iraq, Libya, Yemen, Qatar and Israel – would not ratify it.) Here too, we can see that the attempt to handle the aftermath of the First World War with the Versailles Treaty was yet another failed beginning. The tasks ahead will be difficult and gradual.

Perhaps the modern zenith for making sense of all this really gets going with the Nuremberg Trials of 1945–6. Here, the Holocaust was put on trial, and three issues – crimes against peace, war crimes, and crimes against humanity – were put on the global justice agenda. Again, although something of a failure overall, it nevertheless brought into play a panoply of ideas and structures for gradually moving forward. There is a clear sense of the need for justice after an atrocity – the suffering is so great that some kind of accountability and settlement is required. Hence the idea of 'crimes against humanity' that transcended individual states and needed an international court; and an institution (in this case a court) where people would speak to truth and give witness to acts of anti-humanity.

Since these early times, many new institutions and ideas have been developed with similar concerns. It is exemplified most forcefully with the ending of Apartheid in South Africa and the Truth and Reconciliation Commission that was subsequently set up. Desmond Mpilo Tutu was a prominent figure in the commission and argued for the importance of forgiving. In *The Book of Forgiving*, co-written with his daughter Mpho A. Tutu,[32] he outlined four key stages:

1. Admitting the wrong and acknowledging the harm.
2. Telling one's story and witnessing the anguish.
3. Asking for forgiveness and granting forgiveness.
4. Renewing or releasing the relationship.

The idea of reconciliation and reparation broadens the process to include not just offenders (their accountability, their need for transformation, their desire to be reintegrated into the community), but also victims and the wider community. We are all interconnected. There is a wound in the community, and it needs correcting. And ultimately a healing will be needed. It recognizes hurt, looks at needs for reparation, and asks, whose obligations are these? It implies an underlying respect and sense of dignity. Ideas of reconciliation are centuries old, used in Africa today, for example in Acholi cultures and the *mato oput* ritual with enemies (the modern interest comes from Desmond Tutu). Other examples include the use of *shalom* in Hebrew (meaning peace, harmony, wholeness), *ubuntu* in Bantu African (meaning compassion, virtue), *hozho* in the Navajo language (meaning beauty, harmony, goodness) and *whakapapa*, a basic principle in Maori culture.[33]

There have been at least fifty truth and reconciliation commissions across the world in recent times, many in South America and Africa.[34]

Memory, pluralizing pasts and the struggle for truth

In his powerful study of memories of trauma arising from the Vietnam War, novelist Viet Thanh Nguyen remarks that 'all wars are fought twice, the first time on the battlefield, the second time in memory'.[35] A key question becomes just how these atrocities are to be recalled from the past? And how might they be linked to truth? Narrative memory raises issues of the way in which different groups can bring different memories to situations and how they can change over time. The big issues of narrative and history, truth and time, memory and justice are raised. How do our multiple stories of this past change over time with different groups, even as our sense of time, value and truth may change? Memories of the Holocaust, for example, radically changed in Germany between the 1950s and 1960s (when silence prevailed) and the 1980s and 1990s, when it became widely focused upon by later generations – as well as groups who set out to deny it had even happened. The memories of history keep changing. The challenge is to understand the ways in which narratives of atrocities change over time and throughout history: they often get silenced, denied, often justified, even normalized through differing values. What can so easily be talked away and eventually forgotten (as the dreadful acts they were) might in time come to be described as 'terrible deeds were done'.

It has, for example, taken a very long time for the US to take slavery seriously as one of the world's major atrocities. It is hard not to know about the history of slavery in the US: ever since the early slave narratives, and from the Civil War onwards, it has been part of America's story. That said, the country has not been able to face up to it in any full-scale *responsible* way, even as the long-documented 'race divide' continues. For example, unlike the 9/11 Museum (built rapidly at great cost), only one small (self-financed) museum is dedicated to slavery: the Whitney Plantation Museum in Louisiana. The first such museum in the US, it opened its doors in 2014, a full 160 years after the abolition of slavery in 1865. By contrast, after just one silent generation, the Holocaust entered full-blown public consciousness. Susan Neiman's *Learning from the Germans* provides an inciteful comparison of these two events.[36]

Conclusion

The world is struggling to frame all these issues into workable narratives and institutions. But they have brought myriad problems. They have rarely been very clear about their purpose. Their outcomes have frequently not been just. They have often outwardly failed. The United Nations has responded in very mixed ways.[37] Intense biases linked to existing power are frequently displayed. Many of the world's major atrocities – like colonization, deep racism and gender atrocity – still struggle even to be recognized, let alone seriously discussed. And there is the persistent complexity of knowing – of how we can remember differently in different times and places.

So far, much of this work has been done in a quasi-theological and therapeutic language of individuals. This is important; but it neglects the deeper and more fundamental questions of power and the macro structures of dominance, divisions and inequality that are nearly always pervasive in such encounters. In *Justice and Reconciliation in World Politics*, Catherine Lu introduces two helpful ideas of justice: interactional justice looks at the 'settling of accounts between agents', and basically looks back to the past; structural injustice looks at structures and how they reproduce 'objectionable social positions, conduct, or outcomes', and looks to the future.[38] Both are necessary: one harmonizes a past order;

one looks to a better future world. The first looks largely at reparation; the latter at wider social change. Keeping this distinction in mind just might help the arguments advance more clearly for the coming generations.

The world is full of division and damage, violence and atrocity. For the past hundred years or so, the world has just begun to take itself seriously as a planetary agent, making people and governments responsible for life on the planet. Slowly, new languages, institutions and practices are emerging to make humanity more accountable for itself. These are early days: we are just at the beginning, there is a long way to go and it will not be easy. Our future lies in doing this well.

PART III
Humanizing the World: Flourishing Humanity

Many years ago, while reading Alasdair MacIntyre's *After Virtue*, I came across a remark that has lingered with me over the years. He comments: 'I can only answer the question "What am I to do?" if I can answer the prior question "Of what story or stories do I find myself a part?"'[1] In this section of the book, I look for stories of which I want to be a part: stories that make me human. Here I look at:

- narratives of worldly care;
- narratives of human values;
- narratives of human creativity and transformation;
- narratives of acting in the world to make it a better place for all.

5
Narrating Humanity

That every individual life between birth and death can eventually be told as a story with beginning and end is the prepolitical and prehistorical condition of history, the great story without end. But the reason why each human life tells its story and why history ultimately becomes the storybook of mankind, with many actors and speakers and yet without any tangible authors is that both are the outcomes of action.
Hannah Arendt, *The Human Condition* (1998 [1958]), p. 184

The important work of the inspirational Hannah Arendt puts narrative and story at the heart of the human condition. 'Telling stories is what makes us human: we are the thinking animal and ours is a narrative humanity.'[1] We write histories of who we are, who others are, what we value, how we change, how we connect – all the time asking just what our earth, our universe, our humanity means. Narrative becomes our key vehicle for connecting to others and generating dialogues about human life and human action. We litter the earth with a multitude of such tales. In this chapter, I look a little at the *longue durée* of human stories, and chart something of its rich inheritance in helping to create our humanity. It is a big task for a little chapter.

Narrative Humanity: Capacities and Ecologies

No other life form that we know of to date has quite the conscious ability we have, given our linguistic capacity to assemble narrative, to search for the meaning of life and existence. Throughout millennia, swathes of people across many continents have explored their life worlds by telling their stories and listening to those of others. A mosaic of narratives of humanity has been created from myriad visions of life from the plurality of our pasts. And through this we cultivate our oh-so-distinctively human worlds of *empathetic hermeneutics*: worlds where we put our intelligence, our awareness of others, our compassion and meaning-making skills busily to work. These are our 'humanities': our imaginative creativities that 'investigate the expressions of the human mind'.[2]

We can look back to earlier global landscapes to find this quest for humanity and connection in the stories first found in the creativities of Palaeolithic Cave and Ice Age Art. Mainly imageries of wild animals and landscapes, here are hints of human arts and stories from our earliest days.[3] A little later we find the epic drama of family and mass war within the 200,000 verses of the Sanskrit *Mahābhārata*, compiled in the third century BCE. There is also Gilgamesh and the clash between the tyrant king of Uruk and the wild man Enkidu (along with the quest for understanding life and death as the triumph of love) on a journey in Mesopotamia that has come down to us via the twelve clay tablets of the Sumerian *Epic of Gilgamesh*, around 3,000 years ago. Here too are the ancient Egyptian *Books of the Dead* (*c.* 1991–59 BCE), written on papyrus scrolls; the I *Ching* (*Book of Changes*, written in the late ninth century BCE, whose sources and material are unknown); and Sun Tzu's *The Art of the War* (*c.* fifth century BCE) written on bamboo. It is to Herodotus and Thucydides that we look for the first major sense of our ability to be a 'history-making' animal: the need to preserve and learn from the past. And then we have the *Iliad* and the *Odyssey*. Here are tales of moral, ethical and political value helping people of their time to find some meaningful plots. Then, as now, we connect to the complexity, contingency and chanciness of life; we can find tales of our journeys, human contests, human contentment, human consummation.[4] At the heart of all this lies, simultaneously, a creative human capacity to tell stories and an environment that facilitates dialogues around the telling of tales of how we all live together.

Human capacity to tell stories

Practically, humans need stories to animate their lives, forge connections and make us pay attention to the world. Stories can lay out key plots of our existence, the characters we might come to be and central images and tropes that could guide our lives. The evolutionary significance of stories does not lie in abstraction but in making us attentive to the details of a human life and the worlds in which we live. Attending to detail, we bring into action our intelligence, cognition, memory, creativity, empathy and imagination.[5] And in more recent times the power of the story has expanded through new media into the imaginative empathetic worlds of the (increasingly transcultural) arts, drama, literature, photography, film, music and – now – the digital life world. As we will see, we now act in a deeply mediated hybrid reality.

It is through all this that we get the study of what we call the 'humanities': 'the study of how people process and document the human experience'.[6] This becomes the foundation of our cultures and education, eventually revealing the nature of our humanity through the creations of literature, drama, poetics, religion, art, music, history, dance, film, language, philosophy and more. All these 'documents of life' display the power of symbols and language alongside the creativity of human beings. They are vital in sensing who we are, where we have come from, and just where we might be heading. More than this, as the Russian literary philosopher Mikhail Epstein remarks:

> To study the human being also means to create humanness itself: every act of the description of the human is, by the same token, an event of one's self-construction. In a wholly practical sense, the humanities create the human, as human beings are transformed by the study of literature, art, history and philosophy: *the humanities humanise.*[7]

Critical humanism rightly claims that any education that fails to cultivate an awareness of this extraordinary range of classical and contemporary human stories from all around the world and in all their modes would be seriously failing in its job. Our great flow of humanity connects cave art to the Dharma of the Pillars of Ashoka; to the hieroglyphics of Egyptian pyramids; to the Bible, the Tarah and the Koran; and to *Harry Potter* and *Star Wars* of the twenty-first century. This fictive chain drapes around the world with multitudes of human documents, each bringing its own stories to tell. From their own time. And space. And each of them is potentially busy displaying some fragment of the rich multiplicity of what it is to live in a world and be a human. Every country and group has its own rich storehouse of stories to be listened to. Now, for the first time in history, there is the possibility of accessing a vast global canon of transnational literature, film, poetics and art. We neglect or forget them at our great peril.[8]

World landscapes, media and political ecologies of stories

These stories – like all wisdoms and knowledge – are not just free-floating ideas. Human narratives are rooted, grounded in specific times and places: bodies, environments, locations, spaces, ecologies, media and dialogues. As I have said elsewhere: 'Our stories do not float in from the imaginary heavens but are grounded in institutional, mediated, locational and everyday power.'[9] Here are the human worlds of cave-dwellers, pastoralists, indigenous tribes, religious movements, emerging civilizations, feudal peasants, slave plantations, subalterns, factories, city-dwellers, modernists, postmodernists, digital communicators – and the rest. All our stories 'grow' through the presence of others, and the changing modes of communication give rise to different modes of narrative culture: visual, oral, writing, reading, print, electronic, digital. We move from talk to 'text messaging'. Table 5.1 suggests a little of how this works.[10]

Table 5.1: Media landmarks of narrative humanity

Media	Society	Narrative humanity
Visual, oral, language	Indigenous peoples Ancient civilizations	*Oral and visual narratives of humanity:* a 'sentient ecology' keeps stories close to the earth, sky, waters, animals, etc.
Writing and reading	Ancient civilizations Early cave Axial Age Pre- and modern eras	*Writing narratives of humanity:* more complex manuscript writings; early religious and philosophical thinking; move towards more abstraction
Printing	China Europe Making of the modern world	*Print narratives of humanity:* print capitalism; rationality and bureaucratization
Electronic	Modern technology, science and electronics	*Mediated narratives of humanity:* mass production and reproduction; photos, recordings, radio, film
Digital media	Digital era	*Digital narratives of humanity:* algorithms and codes: platforms and big data; Facebook, Twitter, YouTube, etc.
Hybrid media	The present world	*Deeply mediated hybrid narratives of humanity* An eclectic array of media becomes embedded in everyday life

Lineages of Narrative Humanity

Where do our stories come from? Every society and group will have its own story to tell. A while back, Rachel Carson, the great pioneer of the modern environmental movement, saw a huge potential to read our earliest history by inspecting the archaeological sediments around us. As she said: 'The sediments are a sort of epic poem of the earth. When we are wise enough, perhaps we will read in them all of past history.'[11] Nowadays, these sediments have indeed become central to the new science that is building up a narrative picture of just who we once were and who we have now become. Looking back through rocks and ruins, we can catch a glimpse our story, of our 'being-in-the-world'. We can see it in the unfolding of geological forms and waves. Since Carson made this claim, there have been major developments in architecture and palaeontology. And more: our modern understanding of DNA now enables us to read the past from bones of old.

Origins stories

The human odyssey – both personally and historically – is the oldest and grandest of human narratives. It speaks to origins and journeys. And there is now a very wide array of origins stories: perpetual quests to find the origins and meaning of life and the planet. From Hopi stories of crawling out of the earth, to Norse tales of giants, to Greek myths of Gods and chaos, all 'tribes' will have their own stories. The history of narrative myths is cluttered with tales of origins. Every religion and belief system has its own tale to tell.[12]

The modern scientific origins story of the evolution of the human species, charting humanity's world time arrow, is now commonplace in schools, museums, films, documentaries and books. It can be told speedily here. Many religions and cultures will have tales that are at odds with this account; but it is one with a growing foothold in the world. Most scientists will probably agree with it in broad outline.

David Christian's *Origin Story: A Big History of Everything*, is a major well-known example, taught in schools and online.[13] It charts nine critical thresholds from the Big Bang to the creation of earth, the Holocene, and on to our Anthropocene and 'sustainability crisis'. We can see this history emerging through three spheres: (1) the cosmos (and the grand worlds of stars, moons and galaxies), (2) the biosphere and the emergence of diversities of life on Planet Earth and (3) the transformations of our human species, moving through an animal stage, a farming stage and an agricultural one before reaching our industrial Anthropocene age. Likewise, the (earth) scientists, Simon Lewis and Mark Maslin chart out their version of history through the earth's four major rock formations: from the Hadean (before life on earth), through the Archean (from earliest life about 4 billon years ago), to the Proterozoic (which begins when multicellular life can be detected in rock layers some 2.5 billion years ago) and on to the Phanerozoic (which started 541 million years ago when life became complex, visible and abundant). Lewis and Maslin finally reveal a very modern era that shows the Anthropocene emerging as the most recent stage in the development of the modern world. Ultimately, the predicted death of the sun will come in around 4.5 billion years' time. Box 5.1 suggests some of the key moments in this story.[14]

A little species with a big story

This story of our universe extends across *billions* of years. The story of humankind spans *millions* of years. The story of humanity covers the more 'thinkable' *thousands* of years. Starting to evolve around only 200,000 years ago, *Homo sapiens* truly is the new arrival – just a speck of dust – in a vast multiverse. It starts to 'think' around 70,000 years ago. Humanity, as we understand it, has existed possibly only a scant 5,000–10,000 years. So we are talking about a very short time indeed. If we think about the history of the universe as a twenty-four-hour clock, then the human species emerges somewhere between the last few minutes and the last few seconds before midnight.

Our blue planet sparkles in an extraordinarily expanding multiverse with a long and spectacular diversity of emergent life. But our human species has lived only a short while on it, evolving slowly in this deep complex world of time-space. Our vast biosphere harbours many other forms of life. There may have been 100 billion of us humans since the dawn of humanity but we are only 0.01 per cent of life on earth right now. We come and go. And life keeps evolving. There is nothing to guarantee us a place in the universe. Just as we came late, so we may go early.

Our story is one of plural human narratives: cave art, agrarian civilizations, indigenous groups, early cities, Indic, Graeco-Roman, Christian, Islamic, Sinic, African formations. As human narratives emerge, they are never pure. As they roll through history, they fragment and become entangled

Box 5.1: Stories of an emergent human species: critical moments

Universe stories: far distant
13.8 billion years ago: the universe emerges in a Big Bang.
4.5 billion years ago: our sun, solar system and earth are formed. This history has itself been divided into four aeons.

Stories of life on earth: very distant
3.8 billion years ago: a spectrum of living organisms begin to emerge on earth.
600 million years ago: first large organisms on earth.

Stories of life on earth: distant
65 million years: dinosaurs wiped out.
6–7 million years ago: hominids splits from chimpanzee lineage.

Human stories: far distant
200,000–30,000 years ago: *Homo neanderthalensis* roamed Europe – a closely linked but now extinct species.[15]
200,000–250,000 years ago: our own species, *Homo sapiens*, emerges in Ethiopia – hunter-gatherers.
50,000–70,000 years ago: first art, complex technology and religion appear – the 'cognitive revolution' brings language, fiction, history.
35,000–45,000 years ago: cave paintings and figurines.

Human stories: distant past
14,800–4,600 years ago: Neolithic age – from hunting and gathering to food production and village life.
10,000 years ago: agricultural revolution, bringing farming and permanent settlements.
8,000–12,000 years ago: first temples – e.g., Gobekli Tepe.
5,000 years ago: earliest writings in Sumer, Mesopotamia and Egyptian hieroglyphs.
2,500 years ago: the Axial Age (from 800 to 300 BCE), which brings great traditions of thinking, writing and morals/religion.

Human stories in modern times
500 years ago: scientific revolution starts; early globalization as world zones linked.
400 years ago: new world colonization to eventually impact most of the world.
250 years ago: industrial revolution, industrial capitalism, secularism, modernity – and the Anthropocene.
70 years ago: consumer capitalism; humans land on moon; creation of world institutions like the United Nations and ideas like human rights become global.
2020: the present moment – the digital, robotic and space revolutions have arrived in the last stages of capitalism, portending big changes.

with others, merging and adapting. Wide-ranging cultural hybridity is the name of the game.[16]

Only fairly recently have we started to take very seriously the global history and the underlying principles, logic and patterns of this vast universe of stories, narratives and texts. In his path-breaking book *A New History of the Humanities*, Rens Bod, who is professor of logic, language and computation at Amsterdam University, outlines the truly diverse range of the humanities from Antiquity to the present, showing its rich, cumulative, worldwide patterns and shapes.[17] Typically, a reader will focus on one discipline or one period of time and in one country. But Bod encourages us to look more holistically at the connections between different disciplines, to look across world texts in order to seek out the common patterns and principles that can be found across them. And from this we can start to find the cumulative wisdoms of humanity over time.

Narrative tensions of an axial age

Something like a narrative epiphany happened some 2,500 years ago. It was a time for humanity's great puzzlement about its own existence and the emergence of what might be seen as the great foundational narratives. It was the time for the 'great thoughts and great thinkers' about the unity of humanity. It was a time when:

> Man everywhere became aware of being as a whole, of himself and his limits. He experienced the horror of the world and his own helplessness. He raised radical questions, approached the abyss in his drive for liberation and redemption. And in consciously apprehending his limits he set himself the highest aims. He experienced the absolute in the depth of selfhood and in the clarity of transcendence.[18]

Some call this the Axial Age, identified as such in 1949 by the philosopher Karl Jaspers – though not all agree with this terminology.[19]

This was a time when bold, major contrasting claims about the meaning of human life emerged. Moral prophets, grounded in power relations, helped to shape a meta schema of assumptions to believe and live by.[20] Here are the great diverse ecologies and narratives of human thinking that will come to mark out varied political ways of thinking for large clusters of people for centuries to come. As sociologist of religion Robert Bellah remarked: 'Our cultural world and the great traditions that still in so many ways define us, all originate in the axial age.'[21] These so-called 'axial narratives' flag the emergence of the multiple political meta religions that helped shape humanity's great foundational historical civilizations and regions: minimally Confucian China, Hindu India, the Muslim Middle East, and the Christian West.

And these narratives bring deep religious power structures that order, ritualize and coerce lives – and a putative humanity – over the millennia. Each one provides sweeping stories of what it means to be human. Each one has its own regional biogeographical ecologies of life evolving over time, diversifying and spreading round the world through migratory journeys. Each one generates its own mapping of 'the human project'. And each one depicts boundless agonistic conflicts along the way. In all this, ideas of human nature in the universe are being teased out into major world narrative structures through great men and their great texts. As Darrell J. Fasching and co-authors have shown,[22] these ideas have helped shape the narratives of where we are today and given us very distinctive languages and symbolic events of what it means to be human. Many scholars see a breakthrough of major civilizations in China, Greece, Israel and India creating a tension between the mundane and the transcendental, and between the ordinary people and the elites who lead. They may also even be the pathways to what Eisenstadt calls 'multiple modernities'.[23]

And so the world's multiple, schismatic and pervasive religions become deeply woven into narratives of what it means to be human. For most of humanity's more recent history, they have provided central canopies of meaning. They have served to define who we are and what our purpose is. They have provided narrative frames for our routines and rituals, our codes and cultures, our hierarchies and symbols, our beginning, middles and ends. These are not just narratives of the past. These axial narratives of humanity live on today, shaping the lives of the vast majority of people on Planet Earth.[24]

Shaping some key early world narratives

This cannot be an exhaustive listing, but it does provide a key sense of a rough cartography, a loose world mapping that can still be found in the world today. Key narratives are created, tensions and conflicts established, and broad regions come to be shaped by such thinking.

- *Indigenous narratives* are the earliest stories (not part of the Axial Age), derived from the original 'first peoples' of a country – many now extinct, but a great many alive and trying to flourish. Such narratives suggest our deep connection to the earth and other living things.[25]
- *Sinic narratives*: Confucius 551–479 BCE. Confucianism is the earliest major narrative and remains the backdrop of one of the world's largest and most dominant regions: China. Although there might only be around 6 million followers of Confucius today, it has deeply shaped China and parts of Asia, and suggests the importance of harmony, training and education in virtues and character.
- *Hindu narratives* signpost a cluster of religions, gods and goddesses of the Indus Valley Civilization. The inspirational Vedas, Mahabharata, Upanishads and Ramayana were composed between *c.* 1500 and 60 BCE. Today, with nearly a billion followers, Hinduism is the third largest world religion, primarily found in South Asia.
- *Buddhist narratives*, founded in India by Prince Siddhartha Gautama (*c.* 563–483 BCE), spread from India to Southeast Asia and then along trade routes to Central Asia and China (*c.* 75 BCE), Japan (*c.* 594 BCE), Tibet (*c.* 645 BCE) and the West (*c.* 20 BCE). Today, there are approximately half a billion Buddhists, some 8–10 per cent of the world's population, with hundreds of small groupings worldwide. This suggests a deep compassion and connection to all life and the world.
- *Classical ancient narratives*: Homer (around eighth century BCE); Plato (*c.* 423–348 BCE), Aristotle (384–322 BCE), found in the *Odyssey,* the *Republic, The Nicomachean Ethics.*
- *Judaic narratives* are to be found in the Hebrew verses of the Tanekh, the Talmud, and the Midrash. Here are the stories of Abraham, Moses, Isiaiah and many more. There

are 13 million Jews worldwide (more than 5 million now living in Israel).

- *Christian narratives* spread widely from the first century onwards through the stories and writings of the Bible. Jesus Christ (*c.*4 BCE–AD 30/33) in Palestine. Christianity is today the world's largest religion, with more than 2.3 billion adherents and more than 33,000 denominations. It has shaped – and continues to shape – vast landscapes of life around the world.
- And many more: including African *tribal narratives*. The Persian religious leader Zoroaster (died *c.* 553 BCE) founded the dominant religion of the Persian empire, which gradually declined in importance. Sikhism was founded by Guru Nanak (b. 1539) around 1469.
- *Islam* emerges later with the Prophet Muhammad, who was born in Mecca around 622. This is outside the reach of the Axial Age, but is now the second largest world religion covering 24 per cent of the world's population (approximately 1.8 billion) and covering 25 countries.

Humanisms in the very recent past have told only the Western, predominantly Christian, narrative. Yet there are surely also Confucian humanisms, Islamic humanisms, Buddhist humanisms, Judaism humanisms and Hindu humanisms. Important as accounts of the West are, they bring a major risk of representing only Eurocentric and limited, biased standpoints. In fact, the Western narrative is only a small part of the story.

Recent Times: Modern Ecologies of Narrative Humanity

As Czech-Canadian scientist and policy analyst Vaclav Smil has pointed out, the past six generations have amounted to the most rapid and the most profound change our species has experienced in its 5,000 years of recorded history.[26] We have already noted just a few of the many significant early moments in the narrative history of humanity. I now jump to modern times. Between 1800 and today, the world population grew from 1 billion to nearly 8 billion. (There are now at least seven cities with populations larger than 20 million – Tokyo, Delhi, Shanghai, Sao Paulo, Mexico City, Cairo and Mumbai.)[27] The past 200 years have been a period of extraordinary change. The long evolution of the human species that has spanned millions of years now tapers into the most recent times. The slow changes of the long past turn into the rapid changes of the short present. And a world narrative humanity incrementally and slowly grows with it.

Stunning new narratives of change emerge. These became the big topics for sociology, which developed at this time to study the very issue of rapid social change. This is the time of the *great revolutions* (scientific, industrial, political); the *three industrial revolutions* (first steam, then electricity and assembly lines, now computers and digitalization); the *great transformation* (the rise of capitalism); the *death of God*; the *rise of individualism* – and so on. It is also the time of a major '*European colonization*' *of the world* (as Latin America, the Caribbean, Africa and India are taken over by Europe), making the narrative map of the world look quite different.[28] It is the time of *modernization* and *globalization*.

Here we find seismic changes in human narratives: the 'shock of the new' and what might be called the 'globalization of narratives'. A mosaic of narratives initially established through indigenous groups, early civilizations and the Axial Age are now joined by an array of 'modernist tales'. New nation-states appear, each gradually having to confront this global reshaping of 'multiple modernities'. There are many different pathways into this emerging 'modern world' (with many contrasting narratives accompanying them). We confront 'world history', historical geography, the history of objects in the world, a history of histories. Few can now live without a sense of being part of a large and complex narrative of global history: the big histories of dynasties in China; the making of some fifty-five different countries in Africa, forged through cruel invasion; a European Union that attempts to bring war-torn countries closer together; a Russia that becomes the Communist USSR and then returns to being a Russia; or a Latin America or an India colonized and then decolonized.[29] Vast landscapes of the world have been peopled with a wide array of cultures – all with dramatic histories. And so our world narratives now reach a peak level of complexity, change and contestation. We increasingly have to recognize the plural historical world. And this becomes a more fluid, less sure, more risky and precarious place. People and their local worlds are under serious threat. And yet: at the same time there is a sense of emerging cosmopolitanism, of convivial world narratives in the making for some, of a possible bringing together of differences.

Twenty-first-century narratives

Just when social change could not have led to any greater sense of confusion and insecurity, new changes speeded up even more. This is the era of deeply mediated hybrid narratives of humanity.[30] We entered the 'fourth industrial revolution': of intelligent machines and the internet of things.[31] New technologies start to fuse the physical, digital and biological worlds, suggesting a new and profoundly radical transformation of our humanity. Narratives arrive relating the digital revolution, the genetic revolution, AI and 'super intelligence', and body transcendence. New pervasive, deep mediated realities make more and more of us live daily with digitalism and media. All this presents us with daily routines of commercialism, celebrities and entertainment. A new narrative world of algorithms and mediated logic makes for a coded environment that defines, selects, organizes, presents and rearranges, even colonizes, the world we live in. Often this brings a lack of authenticity and a considerable simplification of the complexities of the world. Digital surveillance capitalism has arrived. According to Shoshana Zuboff, we now live in 'an information civilization shaped by surveillance [that] will thrive at the expense of human nature and will threaten to cost us our humanity'; 'surveillance capitalists know everything *about us*, whereas their operations are designed to be unknowable *to us*. They accumulate vast domains of new knowledge *from us* but not *for us*.'[32]

We are moving into another stunning new period of dramatic change, even as the narratives of the indigenous world, the Axial Age and modernity continued to unfold. The narrative is now linked to globalization, the Anthropocene, environmental destruction, space exploration, digitalism, robotics and a deeply mediated world. Each one of these distinctive processes helps to radically reshape the human story. The emerging narratives of humanity are being refashioned once again. The long historical world of the humanities has been recoded into a *digital humanities*. Stories of the past can now be digitally archived and kept alive for the present. And so many ancient documents of the past can be accessed at the click of a finger, even as we can scroll into Google Earth to cross-check the activities in every country in the world. History and geography – time and space – have compacted.

In this exuberant new period, humanity has gradually established a conflictual meta-narrative. Looking at the vast pluriverse through theories of both evolution and the cosmos, humanity can now also see its own stunning insignificance. And yet, at the same time there is a growing recognition that we just may be the only species in the universe that has been capable of moving beyond Planet Earth, both mentally and physically. It has brought the arrival of an awareness of ourselves as an interplanetary species. In this sense, we may even be a rather special little creature: A *Homo Deus*.[33]

Thinking Like a Planet: Narratives of Worldly Care

I want to suggest that a global meta-narrative of collective humanity, full of tensions, may have been struggling to make itself heard over the centuries. People dwelling in different locales find things that bring them together to act collectively 'on behalf of the world'. We start to think and act a little 'like a planet'.[34] A new transnational and cosmopolitan consciousness of connective collective care for all peoples and life on earth is gradually and slowly emerging. I call this a meta-narrative of worldly care.[35] It has many elements and its emergence can be tracked through many sources: foundational religious beliefs, trade, travel, ideas of hospitality, a sense of love, tales of moons and stars, cosmopolitanism. It will surely have been present in early migrations that created a self-consciousness about journeying across the wider world and meeting other people who lived in it. Worshiping a God, travelling the Silk Road, building elaborate cities, looking to the stars – a common togetherness has a long history. Often though, this common humanity was couched in a language of 'othering'; and humanity remained divisive. We saw something of these world journeys in Chapter 3.

The modern journey moves in various waves, starting with a long and slow period during the eighteenth and nineteenth centuries, but increasingly speeding up in the twentieth and twenty-first centuries.[36] Two critical tipping points arrive in the twentieth century in the aftermath of the world wars. Both led to a great deal of searching for solutions to problems of war, peace and international cooperation. The First World War was accompanied by major plague and led to the deaths of many millions, and a number of significant attempts were made to bring about a sense of global connection; the League of Nations was developed at this time. But it was not until after the shocking horrors of the mid-twentieth century, especially the genocides and the Holocaust, that a constellation of ideas and organizations around a 'global humanity' started to gather strength. Historian Bruce Mazlish has traced all this clearly in his *The Idea of Humanity in a Global Era*.[37] Organizations of global governance accelerate, and ideas, institutions, actions and social movements become directed towards the promotion of better worlds for all the peoples of the world.

Here is humankind on Planet Earth. We come together, develop a fragmented, hybrid world consciousness, express concern and care about humanity as a whole and stumble towards shared common values. We have a long history of trying to develop a common global humanity. Nowadays, much of this early development is seen as very flawed; but it nevertheless foregrounded some major human possibilities. Box 5.2 suggests a few key moments in history where some key elements in the creation of a meta-narrative of worldly care became more plausible.

Many events have helped shape the elements of an emerging twenty-first-century meta-narrative of connective global care. They hold some promise of connecting, of bringing things together. And they did not arrive out of the blue. This chapter has suggested, if only schematically, that there are many past signs of such universal quests. A concern with the environment, for example, is flagged with the earliest indigenous stories and earliest religions: for they usually brought an awesome sense of earth, sky, animal life and our human connection to the world.

Box 5.2: Meta-narratives of worldly care: a few symbolic moments

1648

Hugo Grotius (1583–1645) was the founder of international law, which led to the Peace of Westphalia, a common law amongst nations and 'The Free Sea'. It starts to shape narratives of the separate laws of 'sovereign nations', eventually international law, crimes of humanity and International Criminal Court (ICC).
Signs of emerging narrative of world laws and international order.

1839

The Anti-Slavery Society was formed (still in existence: https://www.antislavery.org). It was not the first such organization: the Society for the Relief of Free Negroes was formed in 1775 (with four meetings).
Signs of emerging narrative of world humanitarianism.[38]

1851

First International Sanitary Conference convened in Paris (in the wake of cholera epidemics in 1830 and 1947). A push for world public health begins, culminating in 1948 with the birth of the World Health Organization.
Signs of emerging narrative of world health and wellbeing.

1893

Parliament of the World's Religions founded, with more than 4,000 people of different faiths from around the world crowding into a hall in Chicago; a global interfaith movement was established.
Signs of emerging narrative of world interfaith.

1915–19

The Treaty of Versailles and League of Nations were established after the First World War, aiming for an *'organized*

common peace', in the words of US president, Woodrow
Wilson. Both were considered failures.[39]
Signs of emerging narrative of peace and nonviolence.

1933
The first *Humanist Manifesto* flags the creation of a global
humanist movement. Five *Humanist Manifestos* were
published in the twentieth century, which helped shape a
secular humanism (and indeed partially help to redefine it as
secular). The first three, in 1933, 1973 and 1980, built up an
argument for a secular humanism with its own morality and
without religion. In 1998, a *Declaration of Interdependence*
was published, calling for a new world community and global
ethics. As a result of the enormous changes that took place
in the twentieth century, another manifesto was published
in 2000, drafted by Paul Kurtz. All these manifestos had the
support of a wide range of signatories.[40]
*Signs of emerging narrative of a world humanism and secular
governance.*

1945
United Nations established for international peace after the
horrors of the Second World War, the Holocaust, and the
atomic bomb dropped on Hiroshima and Nagasaki on 6 and 9
August, killing between 129,000 and 226,000 people.
Signs of emerging narrative of humane world governance.

1945-9
Nuremberg Trials held for the purpose of bringing Nazi war
criminals to justice; leads to ideas of crimes against humanity,
and later, an early model for the Commissions of Truth,
Reconciliation and Justice. Ideas of transitional justice and
truth commissions spreads.
Signs of emerging narrative of world social justice.

1946
UNESCO established to bring together the global issues of
education, science, culture and communication. A world
heritage programme was created, as well as a digital
programme and a world memory programme.
Signs of emerging narrative of world heritage and culture.[41]

1946-8
Universal Declaration of Human Rights (UDHR) adopted,
enshrining and consolidating the idea of universal human
rights.

Signs of emerging narrative to consolidate a transnational world of human and collective rights.

1955
Asian–African Conference at Bandung, Indonesia. Twenty-nine Asian and African nations met to share their own traditions in search of a new world order.[42]
We begin to sense a world narrative beyond the West.

1957 / 1969 / 1972
On 4 October 1957, the first artificial Earth satellite Sputnik I was launched by Soviet Union. On 20 July 1969, Apollo 11 landed the first humans on the moon, and the first views were seen of the world, a global planet, as a whole. On 7 December 1972, a 'Blue Marble' image of the earth taken 29,000 kilometres (18,000 miles) from the earth's surface by Apollo 17.
Signs of emerging narratives of a cosmic world.

1972 / 1988 / 2000
United Nations Conference on the Human Environment (UNCHE): the 1972 Stockholm Conference raises climate change as a world issue. In 1988, the International Panel on Climate Change (IPCC) was established with 195 members and recognized the importance of the environment crisis. In 2000 the *Earth Charter* was published.
Signs of emerging narrative of earth, environment and sustainability.

1990
The first *Human Development Report* was published; an annual report has since been released.
Signs of emerging narrative of human advances across the world.

1945 / 1981 / 2018
An ancient idea is made prominent with the creation of the United Nations in 1945. International Day of Peace established in 1981. World Summit for Peace, 2018, adopted principles advanced by Nelson Mandela, whose objective was to promote global peace.

2020
Covid-19.
The first major pandemic of the digital age. A new portal opens ...

In the modern era, as vast human diversities become abundantly apparent, we can see the search for 'common grounds' through many elements: from international peace-keeping to world institutions of governance, from dialogues between different faiths to movements for world health, from a growing concern over the world's habitat and wild life to the development of charters concerned with 'crimes against humanity'.[43] Above all, the emergence of the United Nations and the human rights movements cultivated a growing sense of a common universal humanity. This was needed to transcend the self-interest of 'greedy', combative nation-states with strong ideological differences. Here, then, is a narrative that tries to look at the world from outside. It wants to tell its story with the voice of the whole planet: it wants what is best for all its living things and the planet itself. This is no easy task.

Important but difficult ways ahead

And so there is a growing movement for people to think beyond the narrow interests of their own individual needs or those of their limited states. Slowly, a global narrative has been emerging through hybrid media to help us move outwards – to 'think like a planet'. It has been in the making for millennia. In recent times, it has accelerated, becoming more organized, visible and public. The UN has to be its key contemporary institution. But in building this, many problems have become apparent.

We are dealing here with idealistic and utopian projects: trying to bring together a world of 200 nations with long conflicting histories, values and political systems is inherently fraught with difficulties. There are major inequalities between nations. We are dealing with many nation-states busily pursuing their own interests with little concern for collective connectivity. Often, blocs are constricted in their pursuit of regional interests. The intense individualism of the USA may never be reconciled with the collectivist approach of India or Japan. The East and the West may have fundamentally different modes of thinking. Past and present traumas of power exist – from tribal wars to deep atrocities – that may never allow reconciliation. The rule of authority or the rule of freedom may be in constant tension.

There are also manifest practical problems. When, for example, the United Nations organizations bring together roughly 195 nation-states all trying to put their ideas into practice and perform multiple tasks (like peacekeeping or preserving cultural heritage), we confront all the dysfunctions of large-scale bureaucratic institutions. Take a look at the UN website to get a sense of the complexity of this large organization. It employs some 40,000 people and is a top-heavy organization, even as it tries to create down-to-earth local groups. Here again are the problems of power, special interests and ideological clash. For although both the UN itself and the UDHR were assembled for world ideas, claiming a global universal narrative signed up to by numerous and growing numbers of nation-states, there has been, until recently, ample evidence of both the dominance of the West (and especially the United States) and also the formation of key voting block alliances. For a large number of participants, there is a distinct suspicion that these organizations and rights are a new disguise for a Western hegemony and require resistance. At the same time, countries form blocks to vote against other blocks: Catholic and Muslim countries unite, for example, in order to prevent rights of women and gays. Little is mandatory; all depends on good will, which is frequently not forthcoming. As a telling sign, very often nations do not pay their contributions.

Cosmopolitan connective narratives of worldly care are in the making. But they pose threats and problems for many countries. The struggles for a balanced, kind and equal world will never be easy.[44] Yet this open, shifting, contested mosaic narrative provides a key tool for 'humanizing the world' in the future. Defending and developing this narrative – its complexities, practices and institutions – becomes a key challenge.

6

Valuing Humanity

As we listened to *favela* dwellers, inhabitants of informal settlements, farmers in their fields, monks in their places of worship, we began to see that ordinary people do not generalize or systematize their thinking. *A global ethic, applicable to all mankind, is essentially unimaginable and irrelevant.* This is not because ordinary people don't reflect, and often deeply, about the injustice of the world and imagine a better one. ... The validity of a moral proposition does not turn ... on whether it can be universalized or generalized ... Its validity turns instead on whether it is true for them and their immediate community, whether it makes sense, even provisionally, of their specific context and situation.

Michael Ignatieff, *The Ordinary Virtues* (2017), p. 202
(my italics)

The very idea of humanity has been long associated with values, even if they bring much disagreement. By 'values', I simply mean the symbolic things that matter to us. Things that connect us to the world and to which we give significance and importance in our daily life. Things that become ends, goals: being in good health, having enough food, being modest, trusting others, appreciating a good film or story, having companionship, being kind, cultivating resilience, achieving success, finding love. Becoming human is largely a matter of acquiring, connecting to, narrating, habituating and living such values. Indeed, being human – the idea of 'humanity' itself – may well be something that many people treasure and value. Such values come also to be connected to broader issues like norms (the social expectations that guide us), laws (the rules that officially regulate us), ethics (the personal life we aspire to) and morals (the social good). Our values are usually embedded in stories. They are put to work in dialogues. They are often held very dearly and are not susceptible to easy change. And they take many forms.[1]

In everyday life, these values cover boundless grounds. Here is a little opening smorgasbord of some of the many things we value: *achievement, altruism, authority, beauty, bravery, care, citizenship, civility, compassion, conviviality, cooperation, cosmopolitanism, courage, craftmanship, creativity, curiosity, dignity, diligence, duty, empathy, environmentalism, equality, fairness, fortitude, freedom, friendliness, generosity, global justice, hard work, harmony, honesty, hope, human rights, humane governance, humility, humour, integrity, intelligence, justice, kindness, liberty, love, loyalty, nonviolence, objectivity, piety, politeness, rationality, resilience, respect, responsibility, security, selflessness, skilfulness, solidarity, spirituality, sustainability, tolerance, transcendence, trust, truth – and much more.*

Which of these values might you favour? Are there any common grounds across world cultures that might share some of these values? In this chapter I give a central focus to the importance of values in making sense of humanity.

On Values, Narrative and Humanity

Values are closely bound up with the language and narratives of humanism. To speak of 'human nature' or 'the human condition' is to immediately open up a Pandora's box of value dialogues over whether we are good or evil, free or determined, responsible or not. To speak of 'humanity' usually suggests some value we should aspire to. And to speak of humanism itself raises issues of what it means to be human, and ultimately how this might help create a better for world for all. Humanity is organized through values in ways that other animal and plant life is not. For sure, there is plenty of evidence that some animal life may well have a kind of evaluative world;[2] but it does seem that only humans can develop complex systems that can be coded, written down, developed, even cherished. Our cultures are then deeply 'moral', even 'sacred', as we become the 'moral, believing animals'.[3]

The complexity of values

Values come in many forms. Sometimes they fly into worlds of *abstraction*. They float to us from the high heavens coded in key texts as world religions. Or they can arrive as complex, Kantian-style analytic arguments lodged in Western philosophical political and ethical discourses. (In Western thought, for example, deliberative and rational argument around values is often focused on 'virtues', or 'justice'.) Values can also become *institutionalized* – found at work, for instance, in economies (as market values, for example), in governance (as democratic values, for example), in health (as health ethics and care ethics) or as educational values, family values or even digital values when they instruct us in daily life. And many values become *ritualized*: in daily prayers, frequent church going, court rituals, medical procedures, etc.

Critical humanists are most interested in what might be called *grounded pragmatic values*: how we live our values practically with the challenges involved in negotiating everyday experiences. How do people assemble and 'live' values? In the introductory quote to this chapter, Canadian political thinker Michael Ignatieff speaks of ordinary lives lived far away from the abstract values talked about by priests, intellectuals, global rights theorists or lawmakers. In his research on human values, spanning six countries, he finds just how little people are concerned with the grander abstractions of ethics and values.[4] Academics may talk about care theory, or dignity, or human rights. Ordinary folk rarely do. Yet they do regularly put values into practice. A growing number of studies (often identified with anthropological ethics) have moved away from abstraction to field work engagement with gang behaviour, coping with illness, facing the death of children, family struggles for the good life, etc. They ask how moral dilemmas are lived, felt and practised in everyday life. For example, anthropologist Nancy Scheper-Hughes looks at how impoverished women on a mountainside *favela* in Brazil confront the poverty and imperilled longevity of their children, demonstrating values of love and care.[5]

In such studies, what matters is not religious or philosophical abstraction (important as these may also be), but the down-to-earth ways in which humans make muddled and messy subjective practical decisions about the problems in their lives. As people get on with facing their myriad daily problems, values are lived as practical things: they emerge chaotically out of interaction, conversation, stories and dialogues. They arise as daily practical and problem-solving activities are confronted. As American philosopher John Dewey put it: 'Moral conceptions and processes grow naturally out of the very conditions of social life.'[6] We face them as we confront suffering and precarious moments. So, as we are busy talking, living and dying with one another, we develop our values. Ignatieff's study did not find abstractions; but he did find that people everywhere now have a grounded sense of a right to their voice. They lived by uncomplicated 'ordinary virtues – trust, honesty, politeness, forbearance, respect'.[7] And, maybe, dignity.

The language of academic folk, though, usually focuses on values in highly abstract and rational arguments. Here, languages of justice, virtue, responsibility, human rights, democracy, dignity and care will often very likely lie at the core of their thinking. And these can often become the more cognitive and rational arguments for our everyday acts (often as 'justifications'). Yet such abstractions can have a way of taking us away from the human, the lived life and the experienced. In truth, our values are also always connected to our *emotions, feelings and brute bodies*, made from what Kant famously called the 'crooked timber of humanity'.[8] The psychologist Jonathan Haidt speaks about the irrationality of our values, while the philosopher Martha C. Nussbaum grounds many of our values in emotions.[9] Our bodies can become *angry* about unfairness; lives can be emotionally *engaged* with beauty; we *feel* compassion. Throughout history, these feelings and rationalities will get translated socially into norms and laws, ethics and morals, religion and politics. They are also often values put into rituals, notably with systems of religion and governmentality. A challenge for critical humanism is how to better understand these associated values of everyday life around the world.

Another vital feature of human values is that they tend to be ambiguous and plural, bringing the potential to clash, confuse, contradict and change. Tensions have to be confronted and choices have to be made. Indeed, many values lead to antimonies and dilemmas that make them wide open to debate and contestation, argument and dialogues.[10] And these discursive potentials are also distinctive features of what it is to be human. Our values will also evolve; which means they have histories and genealogies as they flow through lives and the backgrounds of whole groups and societies. And they can therefore change. But much of this value debate is tacit and unshaped – we do not follow textbook manuals of ethics but instead live life as best we can.

The pragmatic account of values

How do we find our values? We are not short of research on this. Some link to biology, some to evolution, others to political economy; many are developmental and psychological, while others span cultural historical and anthropological work. Still others remain more philosophical or metaphysical. All have much to offer. Here I take an inclusive pragmatic humanist account.

The pragmatic account of values claims that they arise out of embodied experiences through a complex bundle of activities in the vast sweep of the everyday grounded historical world. They then become habits and stories from which we can learn to live an ethical life. Character may be built. In order to understand this, philosopher Philip Kitcher suggests we need to look back historically to capture this ongoing creation of a human ethical project. Throughout history we can see the gradual emergence of values – like altruism and cooperation – through the activities of people. He argues: 'Ethics emerges as a human phenomenon, permanently unfinished. We, collectively, made it up, and have developed, refined, and distorted it, generation by generation. Ethics should be understood as a *project* – the ethical project – in which we have been engaged for most of our history as a species.'[11]

There is a very long tradition of speaking about 'the evolution of morals' or, more recently, the 'natural history of morality'. Within these wide-ranging abstract ideas, particularities of local cultures and people are always present. So a useful stance is to examine just how human values arise practically out of our everyday problems of living. Values become tools for connecting us to life's problems. The classic example would be the value of 'cooperation' that would enable early tribes to work together. 'Care' would always be a practical value – for example, raising children, looking after the sick, caring for the dying. Or 'nonviolence', which could become a tool to prevent constant conflict and war. And 'human rights' itself becomes a value(able) tool for handling the problems of treating one another with equal respect. In the end, human beings are grounded, creatively engaged creatures who struggle in their various ways to make sense of the world and give meanings (and languages) to their life and world; part of this sense-making will raise questions of what it is to live a good or bad life. Putting this in the widest context, we get a little toolbox of ways through which to create and connect to our values. We do this pragmatically as a result of our experiences in the world, using:

- our brainy, active, cognitive and emotional intelligence developed through our evolutionary past – a brain, with emergent reasoning and reflective abilities;
- our intuitive consciousness of practical problems needing resolution in the world;
- our ability to regularize conduct through habits, and ultimately the development of what might be called character;
- our empathetic capacity towards others and their suffering;
- our social capacity to live with others, cultivate some kind of relational skills and adapt to the values of 'our groups';
- our language skill for telling stories of life (valued and devalued);
- our capacity for dialogues and conversation through language;

- our generations of ancestors who have gone before and become exemplars and moral leaders and who left us with 'generational wisdoms';
- our continuous and contentious historical and cultural development through conflicts with others.[12]

We move from body and brain to history and power. Critical humanism works with a pragmatic and pluralistic account of human values. Values are always grounded in the rich plurality of real embodied experiences and practical world problem solving. And multiple problems lead to multiple values, just as common problems might lead to common values.

In this process, we return to our problem of differences. And their contexts. Right at the heart of this lies the idea that different contexts will bring different problems and different values. Values become embedded in time and space. And much of our long past can be characterized as the promulgation of ethnocentric values, where the value of one group comes to see its own values as the values for the whole world. 'Our tribe is better than yours'; 'our religion is better than yours'; 'our science is the correct truth'; and 'our civilization or nation is quite simply better than any another': our story is best. We start to see the paradox of humanity at work again here, creating differing sets of inclusive and exclusive values. Just who exactly our 'other' will be has been a recurrent historical and sociological problem. Religious and tribal wars become a prominent feature of social life.

We now have a rich *geography of morals* that shows how all across the world and its human groupings, people come to value different things in different ways at different times. Sometimes these differences may be quite profound, as suggested in the divide between Asian and Western values, beliefs, ways of seeing.[13] We can see a long historical flow of societies and human life as vast conflicting webs of 'experiments in values'. Organized in deeply different ways by a multitude of various historical cultures, values arise through shared problems in living, becoming embedded in collective social routines and habits and organized into social institutions, even as they may change as time moves on. As our lives twist and turn, so we confront different kinds of problems that in turn bring different kinds of value epiphanies.

The human world can be seen as orchestrated through a splendid cacophony of historically evolving mosaics of multiple values lodged in religious, ethical, moral and legal stories. Values materialize in key different institutions as we create and tell stories: from those very earliest cave drawings to the latest digital design. Again, we can see a grand narrative march moving from Gilgamesh and the *Odyssey*, through the Bible and the Koran, and on to large Kumbh Mela gatherings and the latest soap operas and social networking. Human lives become inescapably drenched with normativity, meaning and morality that speak to what we can or should value, or even who we should be. Human societies are storytelling flows about human values, always in perpetual process as humans engage with the multiple everyday troubles and joys as they work and play, live and love. And such stories and values are always embedded in political processes – our values are bound up with states, religions, economies, communications: the key sources of power.

In the previous chapter, we have seen the emergence of stories from the cave age to postmodernity. Embedded in all this are the stories of value, often in the forms of good and evil. There have been many attempts to trace this genealogy of human values from the earliest of indigenous peoples. Here we look for evidence of the value of cooperation between small groupings, as well as early presence of values and enemies in these small populations. All this would have been grounded in the small-scale daily struggles for survival. Strategies of cooperation and competition and modes of handling conflict and aggression would have taken elementary forms.[14] What we also saw in Chapter 5 was a phenomenal explosion of values taking place in the Axial Age about 3,000 or so years ago. Here is the initial orchestration of meta value systems. Some highlighted many gods (the polytheisms of Hindu belief and the monotheisms of Judaic, Christian and Muslim beliefs); others had no core god (Confucianism, Buddhism). All provided central narratives of states, word religions and philosophies creating (or discovering) major accounts of how to live a good life. And all were embedded in struggles for and about power.[15]

Older narratives suggest a necessary taming of some of our aggressive instincts (to prevent a war of all against all) as we became more and more cooperative (even civilized) with each other. More recent research draws out sophisticated comparisons with our nearest evolutionary animals, telling the story of just how our values and moral lives are intertwined with both animals[16] and the evolving complexities of the cultures we create. This has also involved the search to narrate the evolution of the human mind itself – the 'making of the prehistory of the human mind'.[17] This might be the time when the Big Bang of culture happened: the emergence of Palaeolithic art and religion, and with this the rise of more complex and imaginative reasonings. Gradually we also see the rise of moral leaders and exemplars. Throughout history there have been individuals who have denounced the ways of dominant groups and who have seen the need for a change of values. The list of such moral figures is long: starting perhaps with Confucius, Moses and Buddha and moving on to Mahatma Gandhi, Martin Luther King and Nelson Mandela.[18]

Martin Luther King is an important modern example. He brought together a number of key issues, he was an outspoken humanist, a wide-open passionate Christian, a protagonist against race hatred, a nonviolent civil rights activist – and a charismatic speaker. He inspired a movement and a politics that still flourishes in the USA today, representing a plea for the centrality of grounded values, ultimately looking for values that might be shared across the world:

> A true revolution of values will soon cause us to question the fairness and justice of many of our present policies. ... A true revolution of values will soon look uneasily on the glaring contrast of poverty and wealth with righteous indignation. It will look across the seas and see individual capitalists of the West investing huge sums of money in Asia, Africa, and South America, only to take the profits out with no concern for the social betterment of the countries, and say, 'This is not just.' It will look at our alliance with the landed gentry of Latin America and say, 'This is not just.' The Western arrogance of feeling that it has everything to teach others and nothing to learn from them is not just.[19]

Modern Narratives of Humanity: Transforming Values

We jump on to current times. Capitalist modernity in all its varied forms inevitably brought profound social change and with it 'the shock of the new' and a proliferation of complex values. Many traditional values of the past were called into question. The new power of the capitalist market, the politics of rationality and science, the rise of the city along with the decline of the traditional community, the growth of individualism, the threat to religion and rise of secularism, the imposition of colonial values, and the spread of new political ideologies of democratic liberalism and socialism: all this and more led to a radical shifting and challenging of older values.

Documenting this widespread shift in human values is bread and butter to social thinkers. Some, like German sociologist Norbert Elias, have linked it to the rise of civilizing values; others, like French philosopher Michel Foucault, as regulative and controlling.[20] It has been centrally linked to an 'elective affinity' with Christianity (the rise of the Protestant ethic), the growth of rationality, the demise of the godly values and the rise of a certain disenchantment with the world. Many have shown the decline of community values and the rise of more impersonal ones. And all have had to deal with the emergence of new kinds of markets that give prior value to money, wealth and economic development above all – and which are happy enough to live with the degradation of much human labour. Above all, the shift has been associated with the rise of individualistic values rather than collective ones. And it has been a predominantly Western change.

All of this has complicated the plurality of world values. We now live in a world of traditional religious values living side by side with the rise of new modernist ones. This has been one of the key findings in the research of the World Values Survey (WVS) led by political scientist Ronald Inglehart. Running since 1981, a comparative survey is conducted every five years that provides a global overview of human values (WVS Wave 7 covers the years 2017–21). Currently, about eighty countries are involved, many with their own local research centres. Asking fairly basic questions, the surveys have come to be depicted on two major world axes of values. The first tracks the well-established values of the past, which are usually religious (traditional), alongside emerging secular, rational and capitalist values (modern). The second tracks two other dimensions, which the authors call survival values and self-expression values. The world can be mapped across these dimensions (see Figure 6.1).

- societies that have high scores in traditional and survival values include Zimbabwe, Morocco, Jordan, Bangladesh;
- societies with high scores in traditional and self-expression values include the US, most of Latin America, Ireland;
- societies with high scores in secular-rational and survival values include Russia, Bulgaria, Ukraine, Estonia;
- societies with high scores in secular-rational and self-expression values include Sweden, Norway, Japan, Benelux, Germany, France, Switzerland, Czech Republic, Slovenia, and some English-speaking countries.

Connecting and disconnecting: value narratives in the twenty-first century

Human values have been transforming over a long time. Moving from locally based, ethnocentric and relatively simple situations to multiple globally connected, polyvocal and complex systems, human values have become less absolute, less clear, less secure. In the past, we have often mistakenly taken our own little local stories to be the values of the whole world, discrediting or dehumanizing those in other parts of the world with different values as barbarians, heathens, primitives, savages. Many big wars have been fought over who holds the One True Story. Colonialism embodied this very spirit and took it to an extraordinarily cruel extreme, proclaiming, is it did, that our world and our values were the best. On the basis of this simple yet seriously misguided view, vast tribes of indigenous peoples were wiped out, slavery legitimated, and races exterminated.

This process continued as globalization gathered pace. We now see a world capitalist system, a rise in global mediated realities, and core commercial values colonizing

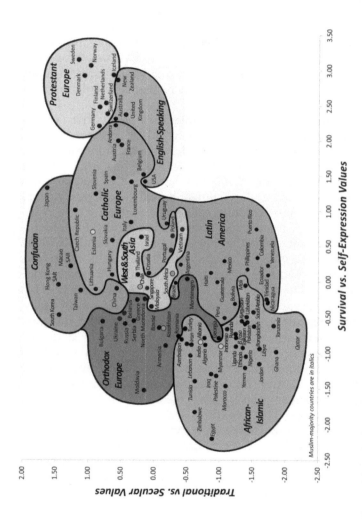

Figure 6.1: The Inglehart–Welzel World Cultural Map

Source: World Values Survey 7 (2000; provisional version). (http://www.worldvaluessurvey.org)

the entire planet – even as the old tribal world of Axial Age religions continues. We find a human world where the market and money, competitiveness, greed, celebrity, entertainment, commercialism and a desire for unrelenting growth have become key values for our time. So-called neoliberalism has arrived. The mutilation and disconnection of the world continues (see Chapter 2). Yet globalization has never just been about economic matters alone. It has also brought a shift in awareness of differences around the world in many spheres: religion, science, governance, media, popular culture, decolonization and ethics.

For growing numbers of people, the twenty-first century world has become a speeded-up world of mediated, digital and robotic values. While there have been numerous value narratives throughout history, the scale has now become widely unmanageable. What has happened is that not just different countries and religions, but also different groups are taking a stand, claiming their own values. For at least half the world's population now, human reality has already become a mediated and digitalized reality; people are living in a *deep mediatization of human values*. More and more lives exist through media of all kinds and our values are embedded within them. The values here may be quite wide-ranging but there is a pervasive concentration on entertainment, play, celebrity, consumption. Documentaries often take the form of 'info-entertainment'. As one author famously said: 'We are amusing ourselves to death.'[21] We live with simplified messages, muddled values and persistent speed, complexity and bafflement. And 'becoming human' (socialization) now requires a deep immersion into media of all kinds from a very young age. The self, now a data self, comes to exist through digital life. Increasingly, we apparently fail to exist if we are not online. And this creates another core emergent value system: of performing a self – agency becomes a matter of self-presentation and self-promotion. And we come to develop a quantified self as we finely monitor this valued self. Behind all of this is an emerging and enveloping extreme atomization and even narcissism.

For many, contemporary global human values seem to be in a muddle. And it is too soon to see quite where this all might be headed. But certain themes are becoming quite clear. These can signify powerful messages of the rich diversity of the values of human life: we are world humanity and we are plural. A stream of global events (like Covid-19, the environment, migration, racism, authoritarian states, religious conflicts or gender troubles), alongside a multiplicity of human rights issues and a global media, have all helped shape an awareness of global diversity and value polarizations. All this leads to a plural consciousness: a potential to move us away from just one set of values to an awareness of the many. We have to confront openness, diversity and tolerance in the pluriverse. Being ethnocentric makes it harder to live in the world or be part of a global humanity. And it can lead to dire consequences.

Consider the key example of religion. The diversity of different world religions means they are often seriously in tension with each other. Most of the major conflicts in the world in 2020 can be linked back to religions. Bloody battles are regularly fought. They are often at odds with themselves, as they degenerate into a multitude of schisms. Religious war has been a regular feature of history. But globalization has brought a growing awareness of this diversity and conflict of religions. How can this now be lived with? Violent sectarian and religious conflicts have become central features of the mutilated world. These range from Islamic extremists waging global Jihad and power struggles between Sunni and Shia Muslims in the Middle East to the persecution of Islamic Rohingya in Buddhist Myanmar and outbreaks of violence between Christians and Muslims across Africa. According to the World Economic Forum, in 2018 more than a quarter of the world's countries experienced a high incidence of hostilities motivated by religious hatred, mob violence related to religion, terrorism, and harassment of women for violating religious codes.[22]

And yet, on a more positive front, different world religions are now coming together to help form multifaith and interfaith gatherings. His Holiness the Dalai Lama, for example, speaks of moving 'beyond religion', bringing mindfulness to our thinking.[23] Nowadays, there are numerous religions, many of which are becoming more and more flexible and open to other faiths (and even to no faith). It is not just that we have reached a partially secular age; religions are (sometimes) being transformed, using language such as 'after Buddhism', 'Buddhist atheists', 'secular Buddhism', 'beyond Islam'.[24]

Searching for Signs of Fallible Shared World Values

Most of the world's perpetually unbearable conflicts are over values – and there may never be agreements. Critical humanism recognizes that conflict and contestation are the name of this game of mind, body and emotion. But that said, it can also claim that some values have featured so regularly throughout history, across so many cultures, and are so widely held today, that they are worth noting as being potentially vital, human, worldly – yet fallible. I use 'vital' deliberately to stress that they are life-giving.[25] And I stress 'fallible' because of the complexity of values and knowledge in the world.[26]

So these are not absolute universals: there can hardly be values that will cover all societies for all time. For the critical humanist, values are always messy: potentially diverse, historically contingent, and always contested, fallible and negotiable. There is no absolute necessity about any of them. They grow from actual experiences and can function to order the personal, social and political life *in situ*, in their time and place. Traditionally, religions have provided major guidance as to how to deal with values. But modern and postmodern world values have become far more precarious.[27]

And yet. Even as it is easy to find multiple differences between values around the world, it is also not really that hard to find great commonalities that keep recurring. There are many of them, including the Golden Rule, the flourishing life and its goods, and virtues; and, more recently, human rights and global ethics. Cosmopolitanism may be another.[28] While sometimes discussed abstractly, such values are more commonly found operating in very local, specific grounded experiences.

The *Golden Rule* is one of the earliest and most widely held candidates for being some kind of vital universal value.

Bluntly, this says: treat others as you would like to be treated. The *Analects of Confucius* sums it up: do not do to others what you don't want them to do to you (15:23). But it can be found in all religions, from the Jewish 'Love your neighbour as yourself' (Leviticus 19:18) through to Christianity. It can be seen as the norm of natural law and is most surely one of the most common of all moral and ethical dictates. Oddly, it is usually ignored by 'serious' Western philosophers and intellectuals (except perhaps Kant), but it can be found widely everywhere in rough-and-ready practice. In his study of the Golden Rule, philosopher Harry J. Gensler devotes more than thirty pages charting the very long history of its multiple use, beginning with the hunter-gatherers (where he suggests that tribes that worked cooperatively and acted with each other had a better chance to survive).[29]

Like all general guides, the Golden Rule is riddled with problems; but the grounds for its wide appeal is surely that it brings together a vocabulary of many other, often dimly sensed, linked concerns: empathy, sympathy, compassion, care, fairness, reciprocity and mutuality, the sense of other people, alterity, connection. These ideas are often seen as part of a Western style of valuing; but they can surely be found across many cultures (even if not organized in the same way). Here most clearly we sense a prime feature of humanity: the significance of the awareness of others, of what has come in the West to be called 'the second person standpoint', of being able to see the world from someone else's point of view, and ultimately the ideas of cooperation, reciprocity, altruism and a recognition of other people. Many ethical stances arise to distance themselves from crude self-interest towards concern, even a care, for the other.[30] Even as it may go out of intellectual fashion, it remains as one of the key bases of everyday thinking about values.

Another perennial moral value found in most cultures through much of history is that of the realization of human potential and the living of a good life: *the quest for their world to flourish and to find the good (virtues)*.[31] Flourishing and the virtues present in diverse ways across many world religions and philosophies, in the foundational arguments of Confucius, Aristotle, Christ, Buddha and much of African ethics.[32] Confucians, for example, highlight the five constants of *ren* (benevolence, humaneness), *yi* (honesty, righteousness, justice), *li* (proper rites, cultivating nature), *zhi* (knowledge, practical wisdom) and *xin* (integrity); Hindus highlight *ahimsa*, nonviolence; while Buddhists stress *karma*, compassion and alleviating ill-being. In most religions, the realization of flourishing lives ultimately depends on strict adherence to their faith: their life is realized through service to their God and not to live such a life signals failure. In classical Greek culture, ideas of flourishing were also widely developed, most prominently in the writings of Socrates, Aristotle, Plato and Epicurus. And such ideas have been modernized for today. Sociologist Christian Smith has reviewed around twenty recent accounts of human flourishing, all of which come up with lists of the various goals and attributes of a life.[33] A couple of influential examples will help get the idea clear.

A very popular idea half a century ago was developed by the humanistic psychologist Abraham Maslow in a succinct listing which placed our human needs in hierarchic order. Very much out of fashion these days, but widely used in the mid-twentieth century, he suggested five classic pyramidical levels. Humans have basic physiological needs, security needs, social needs, esteem needs and, ultimately, actualizing needs. With this self-actualizing, people come 'to have for human beings in general a deep feeling of identification, sympathy, and affection ... they have a genuine desire to help the human race. It is as if they were all members of a single family.'[34] An ideal life would spiral through all these needs.

The most prominent recent example, and probably the most widely used modern Western version of this 'virtue' theory, is found in the influential work of the economist Amartya Sen and the philosopher Martha C. Nussbaum. Their ideas were used as a foundation for the creation of the United Nations Human Development Index (UNHDI); their aim was to investigate ways of understanding human development that were not rigidly linked to economics and GDP. The purpose, instead, was to examine underlying structural or social opportunities that could lead to a fulfilling life. This moved the emphasis away from the centrality given to economic understanding that had long dominated discussions of human development, and instead asked questions about human rights, justice, capabilities and the social conditions under which these can flourish. The UNHDI highlighted both longevity and education alongside GDP, gender differences and, latterly, also includes dimensions of social inequality and sustainability. Nussbaum refined her ideas as 'capability theory', where the question posed is: 'What is each person able to do and to be?'[35] From this, she built an account of human capabilities grounded in ideas of freedom, polarity, justice and dignity. Here is an idea whose time has certainly come: it is now widely used and is constantly evolving and changing, especially through the work of the Human Development and Capability Association (HDCA) and its *Journal of Human Development and Capabilities*. Nussbaum outlined ten global human capabilities: (1) life itself – to live a life of at least normal length; (2) bodily health – including nourishment, shelter and reproductive health; (3) bodily integrity – the ability to move freely and be secure against assault, including sexual assault; (4) senses, imagination and thought – creativity, education, an ability to seek the meaning of life; (5) emotions – and especially to be able to love, grieve and be angry; (6) practical reason – 'to form a conception of the good and critically reflect on it'; (7) affiliation – to empathize, connect, dignify others; (8) other species – to show concern for and to live with other animals, plants and the environment at large; (9) play – to be able to laugh, play and enjoy recreational activities; and (10) control over one's environment.

This strikes me as a very appealing listing, though Nussbaum has always been quick to point out that it is a work in progress which she invites readers to add to and modify (though in the thirty years since she first proposed it, it has not changed much). The ten capabilities are all equally important.[36]

In a way this is a modern virtue theory. Virtues suggest an excellence, the good and the better ways of cultivating a life. Standards of excellence are suggested, modes of education and character training are given, and lives are then lived in an attempt to enhance and improve them. A good character comes to embody these virtues. As a major world tradition, virtue theory went out of fashion in the West, seen as conservative and moralistic; but it is now showing signs of making a comeback.[37] But it has always been deeply rooted in the rest of the world.

Thinking about virtues and flourishing can bring a vast listing of possibilities. Confucius, for example, highlighted benevolence, righteousness, wisdom, propriety and trustworthiness. Aristotle listed eighteen virtues. In current times, psychologists such as Christopher Peterson and Martin Seligman have produced very long lists; Judith Andre suggests honesty, compassion, generosity and humility; and Michael Brady distinguishes four classes of virtue: strength (fortitude and courage), vulnerability (adaptability and humility), morality (compassion) and the practical and epistemic excellences that make up wisdom.[38] Brady argues that virtues flow from suffering, which is also a common theme in Buddhist, Hindu and Confucian thought. The puzzle for me with this thinking is that so many virtues and ways of flourishing are highlighted. Which ones should we choose?

Another possible candidate for being a vital human value is more recent: the idea of *human rights*. We have encountered this before. While nowhere near as prevalent as the ideas of the Golden Rule or human flourishing, there are certainly traces to be found in the past. There is a latent history of human rights.[39] As we have previously seen, it comes into its own as a universal standard through the creation of the United Nations Universal Declaration of Human Rights (UDHR), which elevated it in a major way to a feature to be raised for all societies. Despite very severe critics (see Chapter 1), many have claimed that the current human rights paradigm is the world's first universal, indigenous, moral system. In a short space of time it has brought about many significant changes for many groups.[40]

Finally, modern times have brought a distinctive quest for something like *global values*. Canadian economist Rodrique Tremblay has laid out 'Ten Commandments for a Global Humanism', opening with: 'First humanist rule: Proclaim the natural dignity and inherent worth of all human beings, in all places and in all circumstances.'[41] There are now many courses, research programmes, centres and textbooks that detail this quest for a global ethics and global justice. Usually, they involve courses that are global and interdisciplinary and they try to link theory and practice. The focus of their debates is often on specific world issues, like migration, war, technology, space. Often present in much of this writing is a continuation of the dominant modes of ethical thinking, either from traditional religious values or from a Western viewpoint. For example, two texts, both called *Global Ethics: An Introduction*, one by Heather Widdows and another by Kimberly Hutchings, provide important statements but also draw heavily from Western ideas.[42] Hutchings sets up a debate between rationalist and nonrationalist ethical foundations, while Widdows examines classical (Western) moral and political theory and applies it to world issues.

A search for fragile values in a twenty-first-century pluriverse

On inspection, then, it is possible to find signs of multiple 'world values' at work in the past. Today, as the world's nations and media increasingly intertwine, the time has come to take this gradual yet perpetual quest for shared narrative values very seriously. There have clearly already been many attempts to do this. But conditions today now make it all the more urgent. We are necessarily more reflective about the plural world as a whole as it faces major world crises: from global plague to environmental crisis and digital surveillance. Chapter 5 has already suggested that we may be nudging towards some kind of world consciousness, a need to 'think like a planet'. A provisional kind of cosmopolitan narrative of living together is in the making. Seeking some putative 'common grounds' over values must be one of the tasks ahead. Such values would have to be suggested tentatively, without making grand or authoritarian claims. They would have a prime goal of bringing us all together. The above discussion shows both a little of the possibility of this debate even as it hints at its complexity, maybe impossibility.

Here I return to the spiral of humanity that was outlined in Chapter 1 and sketch out a simple, provisional tour of some of the puzzles we face. Each puzzle suggests some pragmatic values that might be able to help us. This is not meant as any kind of fixed, finished or final code. Rather, it is open, porous, flexible – always open to perpetual debate and modification. The starting point is to be attentive, to think, even to meditate a little. The challenge is to engage in dialogue about the problems people face while living in this world and to act a little to make it a better, more connected human place. Finding human problems, we try to resolve them. We make connections to life's domains through a long lineage of human values, some of which seem to be pretty, if fallibly, universal.

Environmental, earthly values

How can we live well on this earth and the commons along with other living life? This raises issues of living alongside other biological life cooperatively (animal ethics), while caring for the resources of the planet on which we live (earth ethics). Out of this arises the basic values and virtues of our environment: of living well and in life's ecologies, with other animals, and things. Above all it leads to sustainability. *These are the values of the commons, the environment, animal ethics and a sustainable world.*

Existential values

How are we to confront birth, life and death, human vulner- ability and human suffering? These are the big human problems of our existence. Out of this arises the need to be recognized as a creative valued person in the world, given respect and dignity and, in return, the need to act with an awareness of others, with a certain responsibility to others and future generations. *These are the values of dignity, respect and responsibility.*

Interpersonal values

How do we face the challenge (and joys) of meeting other people, of raising and looking after children, of encountering 'strangers'? These are issues of relating and connecting. The roles of empathy and compassion – maybe even love – are present in many animals, but they also need cultivating. Care, which takes different forms in different parts of the world, becomes a key general value. We ask how we can best connect, relate and live well with self, others and the world. *These are the values of care and compassion, love and kindness.*

Community and identity values

How do we come to belong with some groups and identify with them: from family to team to neighbourhood? We confront the problem of 'belonging' to social communities and worlds and the ways in which can find and live well with 'our' groups, sensing who we are. But how can we, at the same time, avoid the narrowness and parochial limits that come with this? We need to expand our circles of belonging and reduce the need for enemy others. *These are the values of belonging and identity, sharing and cooperation.*

Society's values

How are we to face the problems of living in a society, including its systems of education, economy and governance? How can we best help to form a society that is fit for all human beings to live in? At its core, this usually means confronting the classic values of social justice and their linked components of freedom and equality. We seek the freedom of peoples as we also seek their fair treatment. This raises a perpetual tension. If freedom pushes too far, it may well lead to marked inequalities. Likewise, greater equality may require serious restrictions on freedom. This is revealed in the longstanding historical question of governance veering between authoritarian states and democratic states. All this has raised voluminous debates about the meanings of justice, freedom and equality – along with some component dimensions of human rights (to both freedom and equality), the nature of inequality, of intersectionality and justice, of human capabilities and, of course, the nature of democracy. Multiple forms of freedom and justice are identified (for example, economic, social, gender, intersectional, world), along with a range of contrasting theories (utilitarian, social contract, conflicts). A very elaborate language or discourse now exists to evaluate all these critical values.[43] *These are the values of justice, freedom, equality, rights – and maybe democracy.*

Cultural / pluriversal values

How do we face the problems of making a good life and flourishing in our cultures? To do this, we need a sense of human flourishing and of 'the good'. These 'virtues' help us to live well in the world and to appreciate the cultivation of good habits and character. But what might these virtues be? How do we flourish? To tackle the problem of how to be secure in the world, how to feel confident and safe, we need the values of trust. *These are the virtues and the flourishing of life – a good life in a good world.*

World values

How do we face the problems of living in the wider world, an international order, a pluriverse of differences? We try to live with our differences, not to quarrel, fight or be aggressive towards one another; we try to seek peace and nonviolence. We face issues of living together well, being hospitable towards one another, and developing tolerance and conviviality. *These are the values of cosmopolitanism, nonviolence, dialogue and peace.*

Cosmic issues

How are we to face the problem of living a planetary existence in a wider cosmos? As Brian Cox has asked: Who are we? Where are we? Are we alone? Why are we here? What is our future?[44] No bigger questions exist. How can we recognize our smallness yet also the value of our own life, the vastness of the multiverse and its long expansive future? And how do we face the need to live and die as best as we can within it? *These questions lead us to planetary values of hope, sustainability (again) and transcendence.*

Humanity is bound up with the search for meaning in the world and a core feature of this is the values that human beings make. This chapter has roamed over the complexity of such values, even opened a Pandora's jar. Looking for key vital values for the world will be an ongoing challenge for the future.

7
Transforming Humanity

The fact is we all live within the Earth as pluriverse; we weave
the pluriverse together with every existing being through our
daily practices. We are all summoned to the task of repairing
the Earth and the pluriverse, one stitch at a time, one design
at a time, one loop at a time … Some of our stitches and loops
will likely contribute to the web of relations that sustain life,
others less so or not at all.
                    Arturo Escobar, *Pluriversal Politics* (2020), p. xvii

What kind of future will we make for the world and
for humanity? According to Arturo Escobar, as he puzzles
over the question of how we might move forward, we are
confronting a world of 'pluriversal politics'.[1] We have to
engage with multiplicities of life worlds and societies. We
ask how can we connect well to the planet on which we live?
How might flourishing human lives be revitalized across
generations? What is to be done? These are big political
questions that animate humanism in the twenty-first century.
Here I look to humanity's creativity and its future: cultivating
a politics – and pedagogy – of humanity.

Narratives of Future Humanity

Of one thing we can be sure: lives and societies will change. As
Yuval Noah Harari says in his bestselling book *Homo Deus*,

'The single greatest constant of history is that everything changes'.[2] In this chapter I look at change and start with just a few stories of where humanity might be heading; towards a world of the future with unpredictable possibilities.[3] As I write, we are facing a global pandemic, Covid-19, that looks as if it is likely to change everything: work, economies, housing, intimacy, travel, education, health, families, communication, rituals, time and space. It may even change the meaning of life and humanity itself. The point to remember though is that when the virus struck, we were already witnessing momentous changes in capitalism, the environment, governance, religions, communications, technologies. The world was already facing crisis – even regression.[4]

One thing is clear: we cannot know what the future will be like, but we can be sure it is going to change. Here are just four of many possible future narratives.[5]

An apocalyptic world

I start with the narratives that takes us to the precipice.[6] We are stumbling towards 'Apocalypse Now', a condition documented in films and books galore.[7] Earlier writings include works by Shelley, Wells, Forster, Huxley, Orwell. A new generation of films then emerged: *Blade Runner* (1982) and *The Terminator* (1984); we got lost in *The Matrix* (1999), confronted the fearsome *Aliens* (1986) and *Prometheus* (2012) from other planets; and came to live with *Annihilation* (2018). More concretely, we arrived in an era of catastrophic ecological change conducted in slow motion,[8] a world on the precipice of catastrophe and existential risk. There is now a pandemic, of course. But we also face a world of deep human division and incompetent and inhumane governance alongside a risky nightmare of an emerging surveillance, digital and robotic order. Sociologist John Urry spends two pages of his book *What Is the Future?* simply cataloguing works on this theme.[9] He lists more than 100 books with titles ranging from *Our Final Century* and *The Next Catastrophe*, to *Requiem for a Species* and *Catastrophic Times*. One odd title is *The Collapse of Western Civilization: A View from the Future*. None of this makes for a pretty picture.

We may well ask, as people have so often done in the past: can we survive? Perhaps no humans will ultimately survive. It may signify the end of our grand but short human story. We will join the already told stories of the great mammalian extinction. There have been five major species extinctions since the dawn of the earth; and now we are facing the sixth. More likely, perhaps, a few people and groups will survive. But these few may yet again be divided between the poor with nothing and the rich, the privileged, who can escape to other planets or find special enclaves on earth. There are signs that some of this elite group are already preparing to do just this.

The catastrophes that humanity faces have been called existential risks. Swedish philosopher Nick Bostrom has come up with more than twenty-one possible catastrophes that could wipe us out – ranging from nuclear destruction and asteroids and comets colliding, to major world epidemics and some kind of digital collapse. At present, the most significant problems are the eco-crisis of climate warming and biodiversity decline. We can see this happening before our very eyes as weather patterns change and we find ourselves facing heatwaves, floods and other dramatic events. The subtitle of David Wallace-Wells's book *The Uninhabitable Earth* is *A Story of the Future*. He documents the dying oceans, the freshwater drain, the unbreathable air, the wildfires and the plagues of warming.[10]

Others have carefully evaluated the full range of disasters awaiting us. We have arrived at the age of the Anthropocene and the Precipice. The Anthropocene is that newly designated and controversial ecologic era where human beings have altered the very shape and structure of the nature of the planet, bringing great potential risk. It indicates a 'Great Acceleration' of mobilizing 'energy and resources on ... an unprecedented scale'.[11] It highlights the ways in which humans are destroying the planet. Starting in the mid-nineteenth century with the wide extraction and use of fossil fuels, it marks not just damage to the earth, but also an intensive polarization of wealthy and poor. The Precipice is the time in human history when 'humanity is at high risk of destroying itself'.[12]

The themes of destruction and collapse are clear. But this is most likely to be gradual: making impacts on some groups and some parts of the world before others. Many past societies have regularly collapsed.[13] It is not so much that humanity will be instantly obliterated, but how some might survive to live falteringly, unequally and painfully in new rotting and declining social conditions.

Techno-futures and transhumanism

A less harrowing tale is told by the Swedish-American physicist and cosmologist Max Tegmark, who claims we are about to move into *Life 3.0* (the title of his bestseller), where AI and technological evolution will become central from now on. Earliest life was biological evolution (Life 1.0) which moved into cultural evolution (Life 2). But now, under Life 3.0, 'Technology is giving life the potential to flourish like never before – or to self-destruct'. Tegmark charts some twelve directions life could travel over the next 10,000 years, showing a wide range of possible directions, from self-destruction through reversion to libertarian utopias.[14]

Many 'transhumanists' suggest we are potentially heading for a marvellous future. Look at some of the technological changes we are already becoming familiar with in the early decades of the twenty-first century – and multiply them. We can already see the enormous potential (but also the problems) of new technologies that aim to:

- prolong life and improve health so that we may live for 500 years, 1,000 years – or even forever (but then we are surely also forced to ask: how long do we really all want to live? what would be the consequences?)
- transform life by creating new forms of being in the world that we can hardly imagine in the present (but what might these forms be? are they likely to bring huge risks? do we really want this?)
- extend intelligence into machines and robots so they can think more speedily, with greater variety and complexity: a superintelligence; brains may well be able to function outside the human body (but do we want to be just brains, or just regulated by brains?)
- extend digital surveillance so there is no private world of being human anymore: no inner world, no 'personal',

no secret life (do we really want our lives to become a complete machine-based algorithm?)

- put men on the moon and start to colonize other planets; to make interstellar travel a commonplace and hence to make a new human world in the wider cosmos (but can we ever actually do this? at what cost? and even if we could, surely it would be for just for a few?)

Welcome to the 'hyperlands' of the transhumanist: the scientists who want to extend, enhance and enlarge humanity into a super hyper-functioning humanity plus. This pathway will lead to a deep metamorphosis of our being. Humanity as we have known it becomes something very different. In a near future, we will not be able to recognize who we once were.

What, then, happens as nanotechnology, gene therapy, digital expansion and robotic development expand, accelerate and take over more and more lives over the next few generations, in the next 50, 100 or 200 years? Here is a human future where we give power to the machine makers. Blessed be the machine makers, for they will indeed have inherited the earth! Some, like inventor Ray Kurzweil, argue that we can expect an acceleration of machine intelligence that will overtake human intelligence. Once this happens, machines and humans will merge. Our humanity becomes *a singularity*. How humans act in all spheres of life will radically change: our current world will become unrecognizable.[15] Meanwhile, other scientists, like Michio Kaku, take us in a different direction. He leads us into the world of space exploration that has only recently appeared in these last few moments of humanity's history.[16] Such discoveries have changed the way human beings can understand and live in the vast universe. We are only at the earliest of days, but already there are plans by some to colonize the universe. Our future is becoming an *interplanetary humanity*.

A progressive world

A third narrative claims that the world will continue to progress. This is the hallmark of Steven Pinker's bestselling book *Enlightenment Now*. Drawing largely from a review of major world indicator statistics, the case for human progress is made in some 550 readable pages.[17]

So here is the good news. Science and rationality have helped human beings to live much longer. Life expectancy hovered at around 30 years for much of history (some people lived longer than this, but there was heavy toll in the first year of life). By 2020, life expectancy in Spain, France, Italy and Australia was over 82 years. In Japan it was the highest, at 86 years. And even in the countries with the worst health, life expectancy was between 50 and 60 years. The population of the Central African Republic and Namibia had the lowest life expectancy, hovering at around 50 years.[18] Or we could take the rise of literacy, something unknown even as an issue for most of human history. While 88 per cent of the world could not read or write at all in 1820, today it is more like 17 per cent, and falling. Since the mid-twentieth century, the global literacy rate increased by 4 per cent every five years – from 42 per cent in 1960 to 86 per cent in 2015, with the global literacy rate for all people aged 15 and above being 86.3 per cent. The global literacy rate for all males is 90 per cent and the rate for all females is 82.7 per cent. There are differences across countries, but overall we can also see better global health, expanding education, declining poverty, reduced violence, the growth of knowledge, the development of human rights, growing women's equality, enhanced political participation and the rise of claims for LGBTQT equality. I could go on. Over the past 300 years, the struggle and gaining of freedoms and justice for the ordinary person have been placed firmly on the agenda in ways that simply wasn't imaginable in the distant and longer past. And the last 200 years have brought both more scientific knowledge and greater artistic creativity than all the previous centuries combined. The past half-century or so has made all this more accessible to more people than ever before in history.[19]

A case in point: The Human Development Project

Some of these changes will happen by chance. Some will flow from radicalism. Some have been by human design. Consider the now well-known example of the Millennium Development Goals (MDGs), signed into being by the United Nations in 2000. This brought eight rather grand aims of action to improve the world: such things as reducing global poverty and infant mortality, enhancing global literacy, and improving the situation of women. This is the first time 'global humanity' had set itself such a broad goal for the entire world. (We might say, again, that humanity was starting to think like a planet.) Although the MDGs were far from being wholly successful and certainly had their many critics, by 2015, at the end of this project, a lot of success could be claimed. Global poverty had significantly fallen. Across the world, the number of people living in extreme poverty had declined by more than half, from 1.9 billion in 1990 to 836 million in 2015. Likewise, the numbers of starving and chronically undernourished people in low-income societies had declined from around 40 per cent in 1990 to 12.9 percent in 2013. There was also greater access to drinking water in 2015 (by more than 90 per cent), and there were more reasonable sanitary conditions (open defecation had fallen by half since 1990). In low-income societies there had been a clear improvement in child mortality: from 165 deaths per 1,000 live births in 1990 to about 43 in 2015. Literacy had increased from around 16 per cent in 1990 to about 91 per cent by 2015, and education at all levels was recognized and significantly on the increase, especially for girls. There had been a striking growing global concern about the situation of women; by 2015, there was greater gender equality in employment and in political institutions.

This has to be big news. We see very large groups of human beings working hard to make the world a better place for a significant number of people, even if not as much as had been hoped for in the original goals was actually achieved. What is striking here too is the very way in which the world was becoming organized to battle these problems. It is no longer always a matter of each country on its own. This was a global project for the betterment of humankind.

And this project has gone further. As it came to an end, a new one emerged, reshaped at the UN General Assembly in 2015 as the Sustainable Development Goals (SDGs). Again, reactions brim with critics and naysayers, but after a long and complex debate,[20] the SDGs were adopted as a universal set of seventeen goals, with 169 targets and accompanying indicators, which were agreed by UN member states to frame

Table 7.1: The Sustainable Development Goals for a world in 2030

1	No Poverty
2	Zero hunger
3	Good health and well being
4	Quality education
5	Gender equality
6	Clean water and sanitation for all
7	Affordable and clean energy
8	Decent work and sustainable economic growth
9	Industry, infrastructure, and innovation
10	Reduced inequalities
11	Sustainable and resilient communities
12	Responsible consumption and production
13	Climate action
14	Conserve and sustain life below water
15	Conserve life on land
16	Peace, justice and strong institutions
17	Partnerships for the goals

their policy agendas for the fifteen-year period from 2015 to 2030. Table 7.1 lays out the goals in their shortened and rather striking form. This is quite a list. Before Covid-19 hit, fair progress was being made; it is now very unlikely that the goals will be met by 2030. For instance, some seventy global vaccination programmes were stopped within a few months.[21]

Creative cosmopolitan communities

The dominant narratives of our putative futures highlight the ways that technology and rationality, or both, will change our lives, for better or for worse. But a critical humanism starts with different possibilities: with value-inspired, feeling human beings who look for imaginative connections to act to build better worlds. The question must never simply be what technological change will do to us; but always what we are to do with technological change. The issue of future possibilities can never be one that will ignore the technological, nor can it be unprepared for the catastrophic. But it has to be one that foregrounds the creative, contingent, political human actions that we do. Humans make human worlds. Critical humanism lives in practical action, in pragmatic narrative and value making. We create imaginaries of futures where our creative human actions can make multiple better worlds happen. It is to this that I now turn.

A Politics of Humanity: Creativity, Connection, Challenge

Critical journalist Rebecca Solnit wrote: 'What we dream of is already present in the world.'[22] Solnit has witnessed how human beings bring hope to dark times. She sees that we are active creative people, who can transform our futures. It is up to us, our visions and our actions. And already, across the world in a multitude of ways, millions of people are busy acting together to try to make the world a better place for all. We have to take this to heart. When it is set to play, we can see an effervescent cascade of people, small groups and communities working to make the world better. At least six features underpin this slowly emerging politics of humanity.

Connective consciousness: thinking like a planetary person

At the centre is the development of a *connective consciousness*, balancing and connecting many very different ideas simultaneously. It thinks both like a planet and like a person. Thinking like a planet, it starts with the widest mappings of Planet Earth and our fragile world and its nations. Like Google Earth, it starts 'above' the world, mapping its contours, zooming in on detailed parts of the planet. It is only very recently that anybody (with access to a computer) has been able do this. We can start to see the world as an interactive and connective whole. Here we see a pluriversal world. Look at documentaries like *Earth from Space* to get a sense of how this big picture is created.[23] But we can also zoom in from the holism of Google Earth to the uniquely vulnerable individual and their local groups. This creates a connective double consciousness of local and global, person and planet. Google Earth maps out a Planet Earth in a cosmos – an emergent planet of worldly wisdom. From this we can gradually create a cosmopolitan geopolitical awareness. But zooming in on a country or community, town or building, we can soon find a local world abuzz with human creativity and action. Here is a 'politics of small things' at work in everyday life.[24] And so we also think like unique *creative human persons*: we bring a microscope to our unique vulnerable human being, living in local creative worlds, engaged in practical value and political worlds of everyday life. Let's be very clear: both humanity and politics are about active, creative people who are busy making larger human worlds.

Cultivating this connective awareness – a globalization of a multiple consciousness – means that across the world we learn to think both big and small, global and local, general and particular, macro and micro: world and life.[25] From this, we develop a way of politics that will make connections and bridges. One concern is with how, on a day-to-day level, human creativity can flow upwards to change the more conventional broader structures of power. At the same time, broad general narratives of worldly care can flow downwards. An emerging 'world care project' looks beyond nations to think like a planet, to think holistically of the complexity of the world as a whole and not get caught up too much with narrow parochial sectional interests – important as they must be.

With these two different ways of thinking, we try to bring together human actions, human imaginations and human connectivity to make bridges into wider global political processes. Here is a fusion of micro projects of life with macro projects of a wider worldly care – all with the common aim of making life better for all people in our rapidly changing, troubled and insecure times.

A mosaic of participatory worlds of pluriversal politics

In the miasma of global social life, there exist multitudes of active people building grounded little communities and groups steeped in dreams for a better world (see Box 7.1). Here is a worldwide participatory mosaic of creative human life unmistakably and irredeemably grounded in the local multiple cultures of the world. One step at a

Box 7:1: A cascade of effervescent politics of humanity

'You just have to look. People are telling stories everywhere to change the world': so say Rickie Solinger et al. in *Telling Stories to Change the World*.[27] In this book alone, we hear voices showing the power of stories in creating political change in twenty-three communities around the world, from Darfur and Jaghori to New Orleans and Kampala.

Or look at Peter Weibel's powerful collection of essays by activists and scholars on a very wide range of movements, countries and modes of action.[28]

Look also at *Pluriverse: A Post-Development Dictionary*, which brings together an extraordinary range of dynamics for change from all around the world, creating a people's pluriverse of transformative issues: from agroecology, body politic and deep ecology to permaculture and queer love. All work within a 'Global Tapestry of Alternatives' (GTA), which shows how the recent world has witnessed the emergence of 'an immense variety of radical alternatives to this dominant regime'.[29]

Or look at Nicholas Kristof and Sheryl Wudunn's *Half the Sky: How to Change the World*,[30] which documents the ways in which many women are changing the world. Or Joe Willis's work, which looks at how the 'food sovereignty movement', the 'access to medicine movement' and the 'water justice movement' developed to question and challenge neoliberal regimes where profit, self-interest and often corruption are predominant. Here is a 'transformative politics', which seeks to 'fundamentally transform and transcend those structures'.[31]

There are many people all round the world working to make it a better place in so many ways. Go to the website of the Union of International Associations (UIA): https://uia.org. Or look at Wikipedia's list of social movements: https://en.wikipedia.org/wiki/List_of_social_movements. Thomas Davies has traced the history of several hundred years of an emerging transnational civil society where NGOs have grown.[32]

time, we find people all around the planet getting into groups to make the world a better place: activist groups, community groups, caring groups, church groups, counselling groups, digital networks, humanitarian groups, militant groups, mutual aid, nongovernment organizations (NGOs), transnational NGOs, utopian colonies, participatory groups, radical movements, religious groups, self-help groups, social movements, support groups, volunteer groups. And day-to-day care. On a narrower and more formal level, the 2020 Yearbook of International Organizations profiles some 67,000 organizations across 300 countries and territories.[26] All these groupings have histories, often well documented. Usually they work in distinctive spheres, for example, abuse, animal protection, antiracism, civil strife, communications, disability, drug issues, economic change, environmental, gender, health, human rights, homelessness, honour-violence, housing, mental health, refugees, religion, sexuality, slavery, social justice, torture, water, wildlife – and much more. Some well-known examples include Amnesty International, the Red Cross, Médecins Sans Frontières, the women's movement, the environment movement, the international lesbian, gay and queer movement, Wikipedia, the international forum on femicides, the Popular University of Social Movements, Buen Vivir. In their most well-known forms, these groups often bring manifestos for change, the growth of international social movements, and major civic or global organizations that seek to do good for all in the world. And they pursue many different kinds of change: to maintain the status quo, to reform the world, to assist people, to revolutionize.

The emancipatory ideas of a caring world humanity

A key to the politics of humanity is an emancipatory thinking for a flourishing world, one that moves critically beyond some of the dominant modes of thinking and listens to a wider range of 'voices' and narratives. This has to build out from both the global South and global North, as well as the East and the West, recognizing the failures and successes of both.[33]

Some ideas will come from religiously inspired foundations: ideas that grow from *agaciro* in Rwanda, Buddhist wisdom-based compassion, *buen vivir* in South America, earth spirituality and ethics, Kawsak Sacha in the Amazonian Rainforests, *kyosei* in Japan, liberation theology, *ubuntu* in South Africa, Zapatista autonomy in Mexico. Links can be made to a Confucian politics, to Taoist politics, to Islamic ethics and politics. Other ideas will come from grounded thinking all over the world where new non-Western ideas are being developed, representing a new vocabulary and consciousness from the global South. Box 7.2 suggests some of these themes.

Box 7.2: Thinking beyond the West: an emerging consciousness

Portuguese sociologist Boaventura de Sousa Santos has commented: 'The understanding of the world by far exceeds the Western understanding of the world; the cognitive experience of the world is extremely diverse, and the absolute priority given to modern science has entailed a massive epistemicide.' How can we move beyond the limits of the current Western moment? Here are some ideas:

Connective humanity: linking human existence and values to earth, living things, society, world and the cosmos.

Pluriversal politics: the cultivation of thinking and action across many different worlds, ideas and groupings.

Planetary social thinking: thinking inclusively to include wider planetary and cosmic existence.

Transnationalism: thinking beyond nations.

Decolonization: thinking beyond colonization – the critique of colonization and the rethinking of past modes of thinking in colonized countries.

De-Westernization: thinking beyond the West, reducing the hegemony of Western thought.

Subaltern politics: thinking beyond dominant voices, listening to the oppressed, marginalized and subordinated (includes indigenous polities: Third World feminism, the inequalities of the land).

Cultural translation: understanding the diversities of languages and texts across the world: an awareness of different great traditions (the non-Western canon).

Emancipatory thinking: thinking beyond dominant ways of thinking – 'conscientization', 'radical pedagogy' – developing world emancipatory ideas.

Dialogues across civlizations, faiths, cultures: talking with the vast differences of the world.

Local knowledge: thinking beyond Western and modern forms of knowledge.[34]

Ideas also come from recent generations of critical thinkers over the past half century, often working in and around universities across the world, cultivating a wider canvas for discussing the political than the one provided by standard Western Enlightenment thinking. A new language is arriving that speaks of the transformative: a politics of agonistics, belonging, care, compassion, cosmopolitanism, decolonization, dialogue, difference, disability, environment, ethnicity, feminism/gender, global justice, hope, ignorance, intersectionality, love, posthumanism, queer, race, rights, vulnerability. These are all key ideas that seek to move the world on. It is a listing that is rich with ideas on how to move ahead, how to transform the world into a better place. All have their followers; all have their critics. We get glimpses of new and better worlds slowly arriving.[35]

Grounded real utopianism

I am sensing a grounded utopianism in the making. Utopianism has a long and troubled history. These days it is usually considered a failed idea on three major counts. Theoretically, it is too idealistic. Practically, no utopia has ever been achieved. And politically, attempts to build some kinds of utopia have often floundered in authoritarianism and totalitarian systems. Utopianism is widely held not to be a good idea.

And yet: recent (largely sociological) research has argued for a modified utopianism. Sociologist Erik Olin Wright developed the idea of *real utopias* (built out of emancipatory projects found already existing in the world). Ruth Levitas, another sociologist, has argued for *utopia as method*, to be a tool – a way of thinking, researching and suggesting a 'prefigurative' way to change the world. They both suggest pathways to what I call a *grounded real utopianism*.[36] This is a pragmatic refined version of utopianism through which the focus is on an existing world practice, or institution, so that its best features can be evaluated, developed and taken forwards. Here we look especially for the multiple practices of creative politics, worldly care and their narratives; from this, we can examine the ways they are being put into practice; we can probe their weaknesses and failures; and we can aim to rebuild and enhance them. We engage in a politics of recreating the world.

These practices will *not* be utopian, but they will have utopian narratives – or at least the possibilities for positive future imaginaries. While recognizing the impossibility of utopia in itself (by definition almost), the idea can be used as a method, a strategy for change. Put simply, it suggests that procedures might start by looking at groups and institutions striving for better worlds. It takes these as a starting point, and then looks for the ways in which they are failing and how they may be enhanced. In a sense, the idea applies something like a scientific method to projects of life: checking and counterbalancing and looking for better solutions.

Start to look for solutions and you can see them in many places. For example, although they all come with associated problems, there are now many global institutions that have already been established for environmental sustainability, peace, knowledge and cultural heritage, human rights and harm reduction: they harbour magnificent dreams and ideas of how a harmonious world might work. And yet these institutions have as yet been constantly thwarted by bureaucratic, political and financial pressure, and deeply tainted by geopolitical conflicts and tensions. As with all politics, key lobbies and ideologies become entrenched – in this case, on a global scale.

A caring, compassionate and critical digital citizenship

More and more, the digital has become the creative space of political action. Politics increasingly works with the 'algorithm' – the 'online', the 'bubble', the 'selfie', the 'celebrity', the 'demotic'. A critical humanist politics looks for humane governance that works ultimately for the flourishing of all its peoples (citizens). Part of this now has to include the flourishing of human beings who are interconnected across digital worlds and planetary life. It looks for what some have called a digital republic, others a digital citizenship.

All this suggests a politics of humanity whereby how people act in the world shapes the world we live in: for good or bad. Ultimately, this asks us to see the big picture (a little like a planet) and work towards a pluriverse of worldly care and wisdom. But it also grounds understanding in the practical activities of human beings, including the digital. It detects a multiplicity of creative groupings all around the world who are busy right now working actively to build a more human, compassionate, cooperative, value-aware, connected and worldly future for all across the planet. It sees a world where our human actions can try to tame the damaging potential of technology, reduce corrupt abusive power, prevent an environmental crisis, weaken immiserating inequalities – and more.

Cultivating humanity's hope: movements and education for change

A politics of humanity must also be a politics of education and a politics of hope. It is grounded in passion for the creativity of human actions to bring about new and better things in the world. Sadly, for many people, humanity is lodged in suffering: they face a damaged, divisive, disconnected life. With that, a kind of pessimism can take hold. The world has failed; little can be changed.

Here there is a pessimism of old-style politics of both the right and the left. For the political right, there is the desire to return to an imagined idealized past, to conserve traditions and to reject the idiocies of radicalism that are thought to have wreaked havoc on the world.[37] For the political left, optimism can provide a false palliative for humankind.[38] Lauren Berlant, for example, links it to 'cruel optimism'.[39] Encouraged to want unachievable futures, those very things we desire become the obstacles of life. Either they are unattainable, or they are worthless in themselves. For both right and left, the very idea of hope often seems a false hope. The very idea cheats us. Likewise, the idea of grand utopias – so beloved of thinkers of the past – have generally been shown to be failures, with unforeseen consequences and relationships.[40]

And yet. For both religion and humanism, hope becomes a key value and a vital feature. The two are intertwined.

Religion's hope has a long history and suggests that the future for humanity depends upon faith and the sacred. For Buddhism, this faith lies in an ultimate and eternal recurrence: we will return to the earth in different forms. For monotheists, hope is usually linked to some kind of salvation, forgiveness and an afterlife. The Christian view brings together love, faith and hope. Faith is certainty about salvation and love is the key. For Thomas Aquinas, hope is for a future glory, called out as a communion with God.

Humanity's hope is different. It lies in a perpetual search for creative building and critical engagement with vital, common, human values: as a cosmopolitan world, as a community, as a generation, as a good person. It has to think pragmatically, concretely and holistically across the world. Humanity's hope sees the future of humanity through the lenses of what people do on this earth to make it a better place for all, for its own sake and for its place in the pluriverse. It is another key to what is meant by humanity, as well as a guide for humanist action.

Hope knows about the darkness (the gloomy), yet looks to the light (the positive). Hope is aware of a dark past, but looks to a possible future that just might be better. Hope is built on memories that help make new ways of knowing life. Hope is necessary, because it sees a value that provides us with both an ultimate challenge and a directive to 'move on'. Hope is willing to, indeed must, dream a little.[41]

Humanity's hope takes many forms. There is a kind of habitual pragmatic hope that looks for the little acts of kindness in everyday life and in the everyday: in positive sightings of life in the stories people tell. Cosmopolitan hope looks at the rich diversities of life as a planet and at the big picture, and celebrates the luxuriant complexity in the world, signs for a positive experience living here. Grounded utopian hope dreams of better worlds, but finds the grounds for such dreaming in real, existing local worlds. And there is ultimately a generational hope which makes us think about the complexity of time, of the here and now in a world of pasts and futures, forcing us to ask whether we are leaving humanity in a better place for subsequent generations.

Ancestors, activism, futures and generational hope

After the darkness of the Second World War, Marxist philosopher Ernst Bloch wrote his magisterial three-volume world history of hope.[42] He documented the history of our little daydreams and wishful images through to our full-blown outlines for a better world and dreams of utopias in myriad future forms of life. People are on the lookout for a better future, developing an anticipatory consciousness, dreaming ahead. It may perhaps be yet another universal of humanity. Another philosopher, Hans Jonas, highlighted the need to think about future generations and to consider an ethics of collective responsibility in the political sphere.[43]

The future of generations and the importance of responsibility

We all live in a time we call the here and now. But our here and now moves within labyrinths covering at least five generations: from our grandparents to our (putative) grandchildren, the world rolls on. In the vastness of universal time, a more limited generational time – for us, around 200 years of life – provides a manageable time space to think within. We can look at 'ghosts' of the past and assemble fictions of the future that are linear, life stories composed like straight lines. Or we can construct lives of past and future as omnipresent in the current moment; we can see the dead in the living time as memories, and future children and people as wishes and dreams ahead. A key challenge for temporal thinking like this is how to address the puzzle of human advance: how to live with ancestors and yet move the world on for a new generation. How to make the world a little better for each generation to come.

In recent times, at least in the West, we have not always made a good job of this. For the continuation of humanity, each generation has to have a belief in a future for their children, hoping that their children will have good lives, at least as good as theirs and probably better. Each generation will act in the world in which they dwell so as to make it better for their children. In distant times, change was not really significant: every generation would face a similar world. But in current times, the problems of generations become more acute given the speed and rapidity of potential future change. For much of history, progress was not an issue: life was just lived; generational hope was unstated. But now, the speed, scale and critical nature of changes that create a perpetually damaged humanity have made the problem of generational hope a necessary and urgent one.

Hope can grow from our day-to-day creativities of change. A vital micro politics is being developed that focuses on grounded local change. In recent times we have witnessed a fast acceleration in worldwide global activisms. They develop repertoires of action and make 'contentious claims', looking to wider issues of inequality, division, colonization, world suffering. They raise new 'voices of difference' across the world. A feature of the last several hundred years has been the gradual advance of a new kind of grounded politics based on social movements and a new politics of identity.[44]

Extinction Rebellion is one major recent example of generational hope. In 2019, this new movement appeared, pushing forward an agenda for significant immediate change to avoid environmental catastrophe. It was spearheaded by (mostly) young people concerned about their future. A young Swedish activist, Greta Thunberg, led the youth movement that quickly developed to challenge governments' environmental practices, and to bring home the issue of generational hope. And it was clear: the connection was being broken. As Thunberg declared at the UN Climate Action Summit on 23 September 2019:

> This is all wrong. I shouldn't be up here. I should be back in school on the other side of the ocean. Yet you all come to us young people for hope. How dare you! You have stolen my dreams and my childhood with your empty words. And yet I'm one of the lucky ones. People are suffering. People are dying. Entire ecosystems are collapsing. We are in the beginning of a mass extinction, and all you can talk about is money and fairy tales of eternal economic growth. How dare you!
>
> For more than thirty years, the science has been crystal clear. How dare you continue to look away and come here

saying that you are doing enough, when the politics and solutions needed are still nowhere in sight.

You say you hear us and that you understand the urgency. But no matter how sad and angry I am, I do not want to believe that. Because if you really understood the situation and still kept on failing to act, then you would be evil. And that I refuse to believe that. ...

With today's emissions levels, our remaining CO_2 budget will be gone in less than eight and a half years. ...

You are failing us. But the young people are starting to understand your betrayal. The eyes of all future generations are upon you. And if you choose to fail us, I say: we will never forgive you.

We will not let you get away with this. Right here, right now is where we draw the line. The world is waking up. And change is coming, whether you like it or not.[45]

Extinction Rebellion is one instance of a worldwide flourishing in the animation of human struggle: of being and working together to make a better world. A multitude of projects for change, large and small, are being developed. This becomes a rich fertile ground for a politics of connective humanity and generational hope as they work to reduce harm, cultivate flourishing and connect well with life and world. They echo the Filipino José Rizal, who claims that 'the youth is the hope of our future'.

Acting to Transform the World

Throughout this book, I have been signposting much that needs to be done: a damaged world that needs repairing, a divided world that needs bringing together, a trauma-tized world that needs healing, a narrative of worldly care that needs developing, and a cultivation of worldwide connective values of care, justice and flourishing. Powerful groups exist that seek to impede a creative and diverse humanity for all.

My closing argument is straightforward: each generation has the challenge of finding where such emancipatory projects are under way and helping to develop them to a higher level. In doing this, they help foster a worldwide politics of humanity alongside a growing pedagogy and literacy of hope. Drawing on ideas in the book, the final section summarizes these ideas into a more direct manifesto for this kind of humane world politics.

PART IV

Transforming the World: A Politics and Literacy for Humanity

- *create a connective planetary imagination*: a politics of humanity;
- *heal the mutilated world*: a politics of harm reduction;
- *live well with difference*: a politics of inclusion, dialogue and compassion;
- *reconcile with the troubled past*: a politics of memory and truth, justice and reconciliation;
- *understand the history of the narrative world*: a politics of narrative worldly care;
- *pursue common shared values*: a politics of world values;
- *create a connective world*: a politics of generational hope and movements grounded in utopian realism;
- *transformative futures*: a politics and literacy for a better world;
- *ultimately connect*: thinking like a planetary person, build a politics and literacy of connection.

8

A Critical Humanist Manifesto for the Twenty-First Century

Critical humanism brings a wide-open politics and literacy of humanity. It encourages multiple critical projects that work for a more connected, transformative and better planetary human world future – projects that are political, cultural and educational. Each generation looks to others and tries to:

- *reduce the harm and hazards of the planet, especially for the vulnerable, exploited and marginal;*
- *connect lives to the continuity and richness of the earth and cosmos we live in;*
- *build creative and flourishing human worlds for all life.*

Many words are walked in the world. Many worlds are made. Many worlds make us. There are words and worlds that are lies and injustices. There are words and worlds that are truthful and true. In the world of the powerful there is room only for the big and their helpers. In the world we want, everybody fits. The world we want is a world in which many worlds fit.

'Fourth declaration of the Lacandón Jungle', trans. in Marisol de la Cadena and Mario Blaser, eds, *A World of Many Worlds*,

p. 1

Preface: A Crisis for Humanity – Beyond Covid-19

It is 2020. Covid-19 stalks the world, changing everything. Indeed, pandemics provide 'tipping points' for such change: moments where everything is open for reconsideration since everything is provisionally under threat. As Albert Camus noted in his 1947 novel *The Plague*: 'The Pestilence is at once blight and revelation.' Radical moments like this bring the question: is this a time to reassert the (failing) old order; or is this a time of possibility, for a rethink and a change?

And yet. When the pandemic entered the world in January 2020, humanity was already in crisis, facing a major stage of upheaval. Covid-19 might be seen as advance warning, a threatening virus arriving in a world already under siege from many fronts. For several decades before, there had been warnings: a concern over environmental degradation, digital dehumanization, a robotic end to humanity, polarizing inequalities, political breakdown, migratory exclusion, growing culture wars and widespread existential risks. As well as being the age of Covid-19, this is also the age of the Anthropocene, a decolonizing world, a digital lifeworld, a global mediated reality, a fourth revolution – even a potential sixth extinction. The catastrophes and damage of ever-expanding growth make an environmental crisis plainly visible to all who would see. Here is also the time of Brexit in Europe, Trump in the United States, Bolsonaro in Brazil. Key players and powerful states are undergoing change. Global strategist Parag Khanna reminded us in 2019 that 'for most of recorded history, Asia has been the most important region of the globe'.[1] And now China once again has become a major dominant hub in the new interconnected, multipolar world order. Although China's history carries a latent humanist Confucianism, it also includes an unmistakable authoritarian stance. Today it incorporates a strong moral credit surveillance system run by the state, is no celebrator of human rights, and does not focus on the individual in the way democratic systems do. A political map of the world in 2020 shows many other states moving towards authoritarianism, even totalitarianism.

Very old debates between left and right, capitalism and socialism, democracy and authoritarianism often make little sense as new possibilities are glimpsed. Part of this coming future must continue to be the ceaseless coming to terms with the settlements of the past. After three generations, there remain many unresolved tensions left over from the cataclysmic horrors of the twentieth century. The gradual emergence of a world system of humane states that started after the Second World War is now seriously at risk. Along with this, we see the fragility of democracy in a world now marked by the rise of authoritarian populism. Autocratic leaders are on the march. Reviewing the crisis of the neoliberal modern world, journalist Edward Luce comments: 'Many of the great questions facing humanity will be answered largely in India, China and Africa – not in the West. For the first time in centuries, the West must get used to that.'[2]

Another factor of great significance for the future is digital politics. As always, those who own the technology (Big Tech) exert great power over people and the wider political and educational process. The rise of media and digitalism is changing the face of politics at all levels. The core feature of politics is rapidly becoming the algorithm. The new surveillance capitalism is colonizing the world. We have to consider that we may be entering a new world where not all the political participants will be human.

Politics and education perpetually transform life. There is now a strong need for a digital pedagogy. The world is being politically rewired, and new forms of politics, literacy and education are starting to emerge. Education can never remain what it used to be. It has to move on to adapt to changing times. This is more apparent than ever. At such a time, we can surely suggest that a new world of humanity – with its political, social and economic reconstruction – should also be in the making.

The need for a politics of humanity and a pedagogy of hope

Bluntly put, one likely imminent future will be authoritarian, cruel, divisive and chaotic. Values are being claimed that are far, far away from those usually claimed for any kind of worldly humanism. What may now be at stake is the very existence of the 'human being' and a belief in some kind of 'humanity'. Critical humanism suggests a transforming political narrative: a politics of connected humanity, a quest for common values and narratives, a revitalized education, and a literacy for humanity's hope. It is a time for change from the dominant worlds of neoliberalism that have brought us to a tawdry state of market, material and commercial values pervading all in sight, including education – a time when politics has taken a profoundly nasty authoritarian turn. We need a vision of something better. Putting the earth, people and planet together in the age of a pandemic is surely the time to hear the call of a planetary humanity. What follows is a call for a new politics and a new education.

A MANIFESTO: NINE THESES

I   Creating a Connective Planetary Imagination

We have to reimagine: to hear the call of humanity across the world and universe, making connections with earth, being, others, life and the cosmos. We need to create a connective politics and education for a better world.

> Today perhaps it is wise to try to transfigure the old humanisms that have played important roles in Euro-American states into multiple affirmations of entangled humanism in a fragile world.
> William E. Connolly, *Facing the Planetary: Entangled Humanism and the Politics of Swarming* (2017), p. 168

Political philosopher William Connolly joins a wide range of thinkers and activists who think the time has come to think like a planet – to develop a planetary imagination. And this is part of a critical humanism that seeks an energetic revitalized imagination towards humanity and humanism in the cosmos in a twenty-first-century world. Humanism has always been concerned with the ways human beings look for the meanings of life. Critical humanism claims humanity has to be a plural and constantly debated idea. It brings an aspirational and ethical imagination, a transformative politics, an educational practice and an aesthetic for living in the cosmos. It suggests an open-ended creative project in the universe.

Critical humanism encompasses a global and planetary humanism, not simply a Western one. It arises from the fragility of the universe, the plurality of the world and the vulnerability of life. It suggests a human consciousness that is very aware of its own insignificance in the universe. Yet one that is also aware of the powerful creativity of humanity. Its actions in the world can change the world, and the planet. It becomes aware of the suffering of the world, the muddle of world thinking, the power imbalances and cruelties enacted by the human world. Never fixed nor settled, it is perpetually contested, drawing on insights from a wide range of earlier world thought, directing us to our deep interconnections with earth, existence, relationships, others, community, culture, society, world and cosmos. All weave together across the planet in a vast and puzzling entanglement. Sensitizing us to what it means to be a connected acting human-being-in-the-world, it provides us with the core elements for building a cosmopolitan narrative of a worldly care, a flourishing humanity and a sustainable planet. It can give us a hope for meaning and sense in the world, an open wish to make pluriversal, planetary life a better place for all. But it has to do this with modesty and scepticism – there are many different pathways to do this.

We start by putting the classical idea of 'humanity' under question, as something worthy of investigation in itself. Critical humanism is just that: a critical stance. It appreciates that meanings of humanity shift over time and space. It moves beyond a focus on the rationality of Enlightenment thought, to incorporate affect, feelings and bodies. It moves beyond secularism and limiting religions. And it moves beyond the ideas and structures of the dominant, colonizing and totalizing 'male' West to incorporate the multiplicities of other world cultures and the plural planet. The whole world, even the universe, now needs to be our canvas. The humanities of our past have become damaged, divided and disconnected from the world. Now we look for the globalization of an – albeit fragile – cosmopolitan human narrative, consciousness and politics. An agenda is being shaped.

1. *Humanity is damaged.* We need to heal the mutilated world. We try to make sense of the sufferings of the world

and act positively towards them. We build a politics of harm reduction.

2. *Humanity is divided.* We need to live well with human differences across the world. We try to resist the cruelty of division, enlarge the human circle, cultivate compassion and dialogue. We build a politics of dialogue, compassion and inclusion.

3. *Humanity has been traumatized.* We need to confront our troubled past and their atrocities. We try to build institutions and develop practices that enable us to cope with the trauma of the past. We build a politics of memory and truth, justice and reconciliation.

4. *Humanity is shaped by narrative.* We need to understand the long history of our narrative world. We try to develop a narrative that 'thinks like a planet' while bringing a multiplicity of responsible world narratives that enable flourishing and bind us all together on one planet. We create a politics of narrative worldly care.

5. *Humanity is shaped by values.* We need to pursue the globalization of common shared human values. We try to appreciate the world's historical struggle to find a good world and to negotiate this into the present. We create a politics of global values.

6. *Humanity is transformative.* We create a politics and education to create a connective and flourishing world for all. We try to make each generation aware of human flourishing, cultivating a human creativity directed towards a better world and a future with hope. We cultivate a politics of humanity and literacy: of generational hope and social movements grounded in utopian realism for this better world.

Ultimately, then, we are building a politics and literacy of humanity, an imagination for better worlds, a new world politics for the present world. We try to help bring about social changes to help make a better world for all. We create *a politics of connective humanity*. Right now, creative life is going on all over the world to face such issues. We can find them in a multitude of projects through the work of millions of people. This manifesto is dedicated to them.

II Healing the Mutilated World: A Politics of Harm Reduction

We have to understand just how badly we have damaged our world and work to repair it (even as we also attend to its joys). We need to pay attention to human suffering and ask what we can do about it.

> We are threatened with suffering from three directions: from our own body, which is doomed to decay and dissolution and which cannot even do without pain and anxiety as warning signals; from the external world, which may rage against us with overwhelming and merciless forces of destruction; and finally from our relations to other men. The suffering which comes from this last source is perhaps more painful to us than any other.
> Sigmund Freud, *Civilization and Its Discontents* (1930), p. 14

Sigmund Freud taught us much about the inevitability of human suffering. That said, we might ask ourselves what good a politics of humanity will be if it does not work to eliminate, reduce, repair or reform the sufferings of the world. This has been a central concern of many of the world's religions and past humanisms; it becomes a core concern for critical humanism. For many, our current world remains a world of damaged, degraded, dehumanized life. So this is one of humanity's core challenges: to repair the mutilated world.

With full irony, the world for some may seem never to have been better as they march gloriously into the new scientific age of space travel, robotic technology, gene editing and superintelligence. But for large numbers of others, the end stage of humanity may be approaching: a world of inequality, neglect, precariousness, cruelty, unkindness – even atrocity. The benign view of this is that we are becoming posthuman; the dark view is that we have reached the end of the human. For many, it is still a world where many do not get the most basic food, health, safety or security. They live a bare humanity.

Our twenty-first century is a world of *disconnected, damaged, divided humanity*. And since the arrival of Covid-19, the damage has accelerated. Critical humanism takes a strong

Table 8.1: Social imaginaries for a post Covid-19 world: from damaged humanity to a humanized world

Damaged humanity: a society unfit for people *Imagining troubled humanity* Dehumanization and despair	Humanized world: a society fit for people *Imagining better human worlds* Humanization and hope
Breakdowns and deficits in health, food, housing and income	*A secure society* Basic levels of service for health, food, housing and income for all
Environmental collapse	*A caring and sustainable society* Caring for the planet, the environment and all living things: creating a sustainable common and a low carbon society
Technological dehumanization (digital, genetic and surveillance)	*Creating a plurality of compassionate technologies* Digital citizenship, ethics for human technology
Perpetual capitalist crisis (greed, inequality, competition)	*Creating a plurality of economies 'fit for all people'* Rethinking economics and building a new economic order based on human values
Widening and growing inequalities within and between countries	*A just and fair society* Narrowing inequalities by creating a plurality of fair and just mechanisms with the rights to dignity for all
Dividing others/excluding others: expulsion and othering of others	*An inclusive and sympathetic society* Expanding the circles of sympathetic others, resisting 'otherness', reducing discrimination and exclusion
Growth of social ignorance: failing education, media and rise of fake news and prejudices	*A society with epistemic justice and responsibility for knowledge* A literacy and pedagogy of hope: expanding a plurality of cultural knowledge, creating critical informed ways of thinking across transnational boundaries
Violence, terrorism, war	*A nonviolent world* The pursuit of perpetual peace, reduction of violence; support of antiviolence across spheres of life
Failure of governance; reassertion of authoritarian states; breakdown of democracies	*Humane world governance* Creating a plurality of open participatory governance with both local and global societies of civility, citizenship and compassion

Corruption	*The trusting society* Building a foundation of honesty, respect and truth
The malaise of the world	*The flourishing mind* Establishing secure contexts for creativity, critical thinking, hope and 'mindfulness'
Historically traumatized societies: shame, anger, lack of trust	*The reparatory society* Creating institutions that deal with their damaging pasts and seek justice

stand against this mutilated world, and becomes a project for harm reduction; it aims to:

- challenge bare humanity by establishing world institutions that help sustain, maintain and repair human life;
- challenge the degradation of the environment and the perpetual pursuit of growth by seeking a sustainable and nourishing world;
- challenge destructive technology by seeking to make technology and digitalism compassionate;
- challenge dehumanized economics by setting up economies fit for all people, based on human values;
- challenge dangerous violence by establishing worldly institutions that promote world peace and nonviolence;
- challenge divisive exclusion in search for a harmonious and inclusive world for all;
- challenge damaging governance by seeking humane and caring governance for all peoples across the world;
- challenge cruel ignorance by expanding worldly cultural awareness of knowledge and creating a transnational, critically informed way of thinking about truth and wisdom;
- challenge the corrupt world by aiming for honesty, truth and trust in relations;
- challenge the mishandling of the traumas of the past world and aim to make the world responsible for its past.

Critical humanism lays out many challenges but it also lays out many possibilities.

1. *Transform degraded environments.* We are destroying our planet: its air, its water, its earth, its life. We have created catastrophic, collapsing environments. *Cultivate environmental care and justice.*

2. *Transform destructive technologies.* We have invented destructive digital and robotic life, which puts humanity at risk. This certainly brings advances, but we do not give enough attention to the dangers and risks. The world is being colonized by surveillance capitalism and humanity is being lost. We are facing the coming deep digitalization and mediatization of humanity. We have created depersonalized, risky, often soul-destroying, digitalized data-based life. *Cultivate compassionate digitalism and digital citizenship.*

3. *Transform dehumanized economies.* We have created a runaway economy based on money, markets and profits that brings dehumanized and exploitative economies with alienated, degraded work. We need a plural world economics: an environmental economics, a majority economics, a feminist economics, an economics of wellbeing, a participatory economics, a human economics. *Rebuild a human economy organized with people and human values in mind* – see Table 8.2.

4. *Transform immiserating inequalities.* We have divided the world into a small haven of 1 per cent elite rich and a 99 per cent remainder of lesser mortals. Many of the world lives in slums and *favelas*. Over the past few decades, we have created increasing and immiserating inequalities that make life precarious and bitter. *Minimize inequalities and work for global social justice.*

5. *Transform excluded peoples.* We have segregated vast swathes of people from the mainstream of planetary life. A disposable humanity snakes the earth – *a human flow* of displaced people, environmental refugees, political refugees, asylum seekers, the mass incarcerated. We have created divided and excluded peoples. Migration processes have long produced large groups of marginals, even outcasts. We see people without any rights at all – 'denizens', as they have been called. The rise of a specific group that had been called the precariat. *Facilitate the harmonizing inclusion of all people.*

Table 8.2: Humanizing economies: from market values to human values

Market values	Human values
e.g., Hayek, neoliberalism	e.g., Green economics
Importance of freedom	Importance of care and justice
Growth and GDP	Wellbeing
Competition	Cooperation
Money, cash nexus	Circle of others, care, empathy and compassion
Egoism, self-interest	Altruism, otherness
Consumption and commodification	Creativity, skill, action
Self-promotional, advertising, marketing	Mutuality, sharing
Trickle down: from top to bottom	Bottom up: from the people
Wealth of capital and money	Wealth of people/wellbeing/ humanity
Economy progressively incorporates all previous autonomous form of life (e.g., universities become academic capitalism)	Economies coexist with other flourishing and relatively autonomous institutions (e.g., education, media and governance)

6. *Transform troubled truth and ethnocentric ignorance.* We have created an era where knowledge and truth have become increasingly complicated. We live in worlds of irresponsible realities of ethnocentric ignorance. Knowledge and truth are in crisis: from diverse religious dogmatisms, from postcolonial awareness, from digital bubbles, from marketed, metric education and from trivialized media and news. *Work for truth and trust.*

7. *Transform perpetual dangerous and cruel violence.* We continue to be a violent species. For many, violence pervades and invades everyday life – not only in the realities of new wars and civil strife, homicide, rape and abuse, but also in our very mediated imageries of a prevalent extreme violence. We have created (and normalized) ubiquitous cruelty and violence – rape, terrorism, war. And there is an enormous gender skew to this: men are more prone to be violent, women to being the victims/survivors. *Cultivate nonviolence and peace.*

8. *Transform weakened governance.* We create governments that are often weak, dominating, self-seeking, corrupt, insecure. Often siding with the wealthy, they simply do not manage to look after the mass of their people. Often, they neglect or abuse their citizens. Governance fails when leaders are driven ultimately by economic (and status) self-interest, often connected to major (frequently concealed) corrupt actions. It fails when they perpetuate and generate inequalities and have little concern for the suffering of many of their people. And it fails when they refuse to take seriously the claim that all the world's people are equally human. Today, democracy is in decline and authoritarianism and populism are on the rise. Many states are fragile. And digital power is shifting the way we do politics. *Build a world of humane governance.*

9. *Transform corrupted life.* We create organizations, groups and ways of life that generate corruption, crime, drug abuse, sexual terrorism – developing cruelty and inhumanity, and in the process destroying the lives of many. *Fight corruption in all its forms.*

10. *Transform damaged minds.* We find a breakdown in mental health. Humans find themselves unable to function in the world, often at odds with it. *Pursue healthy, positive, good habits of thinking.*

III   Living Well with Difference: A Politics of Inclusion, Dialogue and Compassion

How can we come to live cooperatively with our diverse yet common humanity, rendering it neither divisive nor dehumanizing? How can we best live together with our differences? The task is to examine how we can live well with others, how we can expand our circles of humanity, communicate through dialogue and cultural exchange and resist cruel division. We look to harmonize human division.

> Three possibilities ... have always stood before man whenever he has encountered an Other: he could choose war, he could fence himself in behind a wall, or he could start up a dialogue.
> Ryszard Kapuściński, *The Other* (2008), p. 82

Polish thinker Ryszard Kapuściński introduces us to the puzzle of the 'Other'. We face a paradox of humanity. Of difference versus commonality; of inclusion versus exclusion; of uniqueness versus universalism. Humanity can be seen as a way of all peoples coming together. It becomes an inclusive ideal. But this common humanity, a universality, also highlights the extraordinary heterogeneity of life. Unable to handle this, it leads rapidly to the exclusion of others who are not like us. It brings the possibility of a cruel humanity: one based on fear, hate, polarization and violence. Seeking some kind of common humanity with others who are unlike us, we become estranged from them through their differences. And with this, we start to use the very idea of humanity as a weapon to divide people and exclude some. *People who are not like us come to be seen as less then human.* They become what the Polish thinker Kapuściński called the 'Other'. And this provides a warrant for us to abuse them in all kinds of ways. This is anti-humanity. It has a long history: of inhumanity, dehumanization and atrocity, all growing out of a seemingly positive word.

The paradox of humanity leads us to a series of resistances. It becomes a politics of the dehumanized other. Critical humanism resists this 'making of the other' by suggesting that we must:

- resist sexism and patriarchy: living well across gender borders;
- resist inequalities, rankism, classism and minimize socioeconomic differences: living well across class distinctions;
- resist racism: living well with the fullest range of ethnic diversities;
- resist ageism: living well across age and generational boundaries;
- resist (dis)ablism: living well with a wide variety of health issues, (dis)abilities and bodies;
- resist heterosexism: living with the rich flourishing of diverse sexualities;
- resist fundamentalism: living well with the exuberance of diverse worlds of the spiritual and the sacred;
- resist nationalism: living well with different cultures across borders;

- resist speciesism: living well with other animals and life forms in harmony;
- resist anti-environmentalism: living well with a flourishing earth and cosmos;
- resist anti-humanism: living well with a celebrated common humanity.

There are many ways to move through the paradox of humanity and live well with differences. We aspire to reduce human division and appreciate the universal – what holds us together. We seek to build a *toolbox of skills* for human connection.

1. We can live attentively to the presence of others – their faces, bodies, words, being.
2. We can recognize the human ability for listening to multiple voices and the cultivation of empathy, compassion and translation – we can understand difference and engage with cultural exchange; the growth of literature, film and the arts, especially when transnational, can only enhance this.
3. We can develop dialogues across different voices – we interpret and make sense of difference; the growth of locations where different cultures meet – on vacation, in business, in art and culture – amplifies this.
4. We can resist norms of discrimination and hostility found in institutions (like institutional racism, sexism, ableism or homophobia).
5. We can create norms of hospitality and conviviality – we can build rituals, norms and common ways to bring friendliness and kindness to strangers.
6. We can expand our circles of humanity to ever widening circles – we extend our sense of who we are by meeting, mixing with and appreciating more and more varied 'others'.
7. We can facilitate an awareness of the power of language (the politics of labelling) and a care about words used: words matter – they can wound and damage – and degrade and generate shame and guilt.
8. We can cultivate a cosmopolitan ideal – even if flawed, it helps us envision a world consciousness and world activity where we can come together.

9. We can build institutions that harmonize relations between people (transnational organizations).
10. We can resist the cruelty of human divisions, and the fears, hostility and hatred that underpin them.
11. We can seek a common humanity.
12. We can be kind, be kind, be kind.

Our human world can be understood as a relational network of people struggling to make sense of each other and live well together. It is framed in stories and dialogues that can move us into a widening of the circle of human understanding and a more inclusive humanity. We can think of a *circle of connective humanity* that bridges human commonalities. It starts with differences, which can then become divisions (and indeed result in social inequalities, exclusion, dehumanization). Finally, we can return back to commonalties and universalism through human encounters with others and our dialogues across differences.

IV Reconciling with the Troubled Past: A Politics of Memory and Truth, Justice and Reconciliation

How can societies, groups and people come to face the atrocities and traumas of their past, and deal with them? How can the world frame a suitable response to the horrors it has enacted? The task is to make sense of traumatized life, to face history and come to terms with our tragic pasts and to help make the world accountable for itself.

> The Evil that men do lives after them, the good is oft interred with their bones.
> William Shakespeare, *Julius Caesar*, Act 3, sc. 2

We live in a global history of anti-humanity. Past generations have debased billions of people through slavery, torture, the caste system, wars, massive colonization that slaughtered large numbers of people, genocides, the killing of indigenous peoples, and the perpetration of cruel systems of class, race, gender and sexual terrorism on large numbers of people. 'Less we forget', there have relatively recently been two world wars, the Holocaust, the atomic bombings of Hiroshima and Nagasaki, the Gulag, the great Chinese famine, Khmer Rouge in Cambodia, the Mỹ Lai massacre, genocide in Rwanda, Apartheid in South Africa, the Thai–Burma Death Railway, 9/11, wars in Bosnia, Cambodia, Darfur. Ongoing today, we have a brutal war in Syria, the displacement of the Rohingya in Myanmar, global 'terrorism', refugee camps, the Uyghur genocide in China. People and societies all over the world have been deeply affected. How do we make this past matter and become accountable? What should be done?

All this brings a world full of suffering and anger that cannot easily be overcome by subsequent generations. Out of this has gradually arisen the need for a world politics of accountability, reconciliation and justice. How are we to face the past and deal with this anti-humanity? The challenges include:

1. How to build institutions of responsible reconciliation, social justice and dignified world accountability. We have already started this process through the International Criminal Court, commissions for truth and justice, amnesties, and organizations of transitional justice, etc. But they are very imperfect and need critical enhancement.
2. The need to develop strong narratives of the purposes of this accountability: of truth seeking, reconciliatory justice and future peace in the world. Again, early elements of these narratives can be found in such ideas as crimes against humanity, epistemological injustice, reparation, nonviolence, and the peace process.
3. How to cultivate multiple generational memories of traumas past, how to build a sense of the complexity of the truths of the past and the changing values that shape these. We are building new ways of thinking about 'generational memory', 'post-memory' and 'just memory' alongside a new awareness of acts of memorialization and commemoration.

V   Understanding the History of the Narrative World: A Politics of Narrative Worldly Care

We ask: how can our stories humanize the world? Of which wider narratives are we a part? The task is to understand the complexity of our emerging plural stories; to see how they connect both with unique and local tales alongside an emergent narrative of worldly care, wisdom and flourishing.

> Stories animate human life: that is their work. Stories work with people, for people, and always stories work *on* people, affecting what people are able to see as real, as possible, and as worth doing or best avoided … A good life requires living well with stories. When life goes badly, a story is often behind that too … Narrative makes this earth habitable for human beings.
> Arthur W. Frank, *Letting Stories Breathe: A Socio-Narratology*
> (2010), pp. 3, 46

Narratologist Arthur Frank tells us to take care of our stories: they are what make us human. We are little planetary creatures with a unique ability for narrative. And we can reflect on our own existence; our connection to others, the world and the cosmos; the very nature of being human. We have long lived in a world awash with stories that suggest how to live as humans: how to suffer, go on journeys, meet others, fall in love, engage in conflict, find harmony.

As we create a vast pluriversal landscape in time and space, our narratives become the vehicles through which our stories can be told to bring us together. We started with cave art, small tribes, indigenous groupings. We built great civilizations – many now long dead. And we were inspired by the multiple narratives from the Axial Age – Hinduism, Buddhism, Judaism, Christianity, Zoroastrianism and thousands more. We have built a mosaic of world narratives about the great odyssey, war and peace, crime and punishment, love and hope. We tell stories to one another in order to live, make connections and to sense the meaning of the world around us.

Over long periods of time, we have slowly developed fragments for a globalized narrative connectedness. They bring us dialogues, hope and a sense of a common human flourishing. Call them *narratives of worldly care.* We can find elements of them in vital ideas like environmental justice, human rights, sustainability, humanitarian compassion and aid, world peace, world cultural heritage, global literacy and, most recently, sustainable development goals. As we start to familiarize ourselves with these narratives, we act with them and recraft them for future generations. We bring together a sense of our past ('lest we forget'), our futures ('making the world a better place') and our present (our actions today).

Here are a few of the world narratives we are starting to imagine we are part of:

1. *World narratives of sustainable earth and environment flourishing* tell stories of how we care for the natural world: all living things, the commons, the earth and the universe. It speaks to our connectedness with all things. Look for such stories in the work of the World Wildlife Fund, Greenpeace, the World Resources Institute, UN-Habitat (the Human Settlements Programme), the UN Sustainable Development Goals, the UN Conference on the Human Environment.
2. *World narratives of health and wellbeing* tell stories of promoting good world health and wellbeing for all. These have developed out of a long-term global concern over earlier pandemics; all aspects of human wellbeing, physical and mental, are now covered. These narratives tell the story of human suffering, of knowledge being developed to cure troubled bodies, of people caring for other people, of resilience and compassion. Look for such stories in the work of the World Health Organization, the People's Health Movement and its report *Global Health Watch*, the International Disability Alliance and the thousands of organizations dedicated to looking after different kinds of illness groups across the world.
3. *World narratives of social justice* tell stories of the fight against the inequalities of the world that resists the exclusion, discrimination and oppression of other peoples. They tell stories of people trying to live together well, fairly and inclusively. They tell tales of human rights, social justice and international law for all. Look for such stories in the work of, e.g., the UN Human Rights Council,

the UN Development Programme, the International Court of Justice (in the Hague), Amnesty International, Human Rights Watch, Anti-Slavery International and World Vision International.

4. *World narratives of world heritage, wisdom and culture* tell stories of the value of all different cultures and aim to cultivate a world knowledge, culture, literacy and education for all. They aim for cross-cultural literacy, translation, pedagogy and tell stories of seeking world truths and wisdoms. Look for such stories in the work of, e.g., UNESCO and the World Literacy Foundation and in Wikipedia.

5. *World narratives of care and humanitarianism* tell stories of people in distress being looked after. Here are stories of suffering and of those who nurse and attend to it. From a sick friend to disaster relief, human care is needed. Look for such stories in the work of the UN Office for the Coordination of Humanitarian Affairs, UN Disaster Assessment and Coordination, Médecins Sans Frontières (Doctors without Borders), the International Red Cross, Oxfam, Save the Children, the Bill and Melinda Gates Foundation.

6. *World narratives of humane governance* tell stories of making governments accountable for the care and security of their populations. Here are stories of care and justice, of human rights, dignity and social justice for all. Stories are told of governments looking after people well and ensuring the most marginal come to have flourishing lives. Look for such stories in the work of the UN Democracy Fund, the World Movement for Democracy, the Human Rights and Democracy Network (Europe).

7. *World narratives of peace and nonviolence* tell stories of the failures of war and the long history of pursuing nonviolence and perpetual peace. Look for such stories in the work of, e.g., UN Peacekeeping, the International Peace Bureau, Search for Common Ground, Nonviolent Peaceforce, Peace Brigades International.

8. *World narratives of cosmic existence* tell stories of our wider interplanetary existence.

9. *World narratives of common humanity* tell stories of how we live together, work together, come together. We find connective narratives, ones not based on an individual

religion, country or charismatic leader, but ones that generate a conversation about the world as a whole, about a common good for all its peoples. They ultimately breathe life into some kind of common humanity.

VI   Pursuing Common Shared Values: A Politics of World Values

The task is to understand how values emerge through our grounded problems in living, to cultivate a conversation about the very value of humanity itself and to see if we can find ways that some of our values might be shared over the world collectively. We look to share our diverse human values across a plural world.

> If we are to get on the right side of the world revolution, we as a nation must undergo a radical revolution of values. We must rapidly begin the shift from a thing-oriented society to a person-oriented society ... A true revolution of values will soon cause us to question the fairness and justice of many of our past and present policies ... The Western arrogance of feeling that it has everything to teach others and nothing to learn from them is not just ... A genuine revolution of values means in the final analysis that our loyalties must become ecumenical rather than sectional. Every nation must now develop an overriding loyalty to mankind as a whole in order to preserve the best in their individual societies. This call for a worldwide fellowship that lifts neighbourly concern beyond one's tribe, race, class, and nation is in reality a call for an all-embracing and uncondi- tional love for all mankind.
>
> Martin Luther King, 'Beyond Vietnam: A Time to
> Break Silence'

On 4 April 1967, one year before his assassination, Martin Luther King gave a powerful speech at New York's Riverside Church.[3] It called for a major world revolution in values. His message, from over half a century ago, still rings loud and clear today. Values are vital to human life – but they are failing us. We need a transformation of our values. We need an 'all-embracing and unconditional love for all mankind'.

Values and humanity are deeply entangled, interconnected. Such values, the things we treasure, are always multiple, changing, contested. Above all, they are grounded and practical. All human groups face their problems, and it is out of these diverse problems that values arise. Values are the toolbox for solving our problems. We face problems when raising children and when looking after other people: we need values of care, compassion, love. We face problems of living a good life and flourishing: we need 'the virtues' and the cultivation of good habits. We face the problem of being recognized as a valuable person in the world: we need a sense of a right to dignity, respect and equality – along with a sense of the responsibilities and obligations this will also bring. We face the problem of being treated fairly in the world – how to resolve 'the thought problem' of 'the original position':[4] we need the major ideas of justice, freedom and equality. We face the problem of being secure in the world, of feeling confident and safe: we need the values of trust and truth. We face the problem of living together well, of being acceptingly hospitable to each other: we need the values of cosmopolitanism, tolerance and conviviality. We do not need to quarrel, fight or be aggressive to each other: we need the values of nonviolence and peace. In doing all this, we find a form of resistance to anti-humanity as well as some guidelines for living.

Life is a combination of a wide array of problems and a long history of diverse religions bringing strong multiple values into the world. Confucianism looks for harmony in relations. Buddhism tells how to live with suffering. Christianity brings love and redemption. Many values have made their mark on the past and present world.

Today, we live in a world of multiple changing values and a major challenge is to negotiate pathways between them. We can find some values like the Golden Mean, the virtues, justice and rights that provide emerging pathways towards some kind of global ethics and a broad sense of a 'common ground'.

Life becomes embedded in human-made values: laws, norms, rules, tacit understandings, ethics. From the grandest of public moral laws laid down by world religions to the hidden but taken-for-granted rules of street gangs, humanity lives through values. To think about values, we need to look at the problems involved in living in this world and the acts needed to make it a better, more connected human world. What values would emerge from this? Are we already living with them?

There will never be one sure, fixed or final common ground. That is neither the way of the world nor the way of values. Within the domains of life, we can find human problems, try to resolve them and in this discover a lineage of human values that we can draw upon. In doing this, we may start to find some provisional working vital values. We think about a future world and its values as we engage in dialogues and negotiations about:

1. *Our earth*: cultivate a respect for the environment and the interconnection with all living things on earth in which we find ourselves: an animal ethics, a commons ethics, an earth ethics, a sustainable ethics.
2. *Our being*: develop a respect for all life and treat all people – humans – with dignity; recognize responsibilities through this respecting of all life: give dignity and equality to all life; and encourage the creativity of all people.
3. *Our relationships*: live well with others; be kind, compassionate, caring and loving for self, other and world.
4. *Our community*: connect to others and build community, belonging and solidarity with an expansive world of 'others'; resist exclusion and foster 'dialogues of difference'.
5. *Our society*: Work for social justice, human freedom, equality and rights embedding them in social institutions; take care of downgraded people especially.
6. *Our culture*: look for the good (the virtues) across the generations, and facilitate the flourishing and potentials of life and lives, developing core values like truth, love, humility, peace and the Golden Rule; try to build truth, trust and transparency in the world.
7. *Our world*: cultivate worldly wisdom and care, harmony, peace, nonviolence and a cosmopolitan hope; resist violence, encourage dialogue and engage in peacebuilding processes.
8. *Our cosmos*: recognize our smallness in a vast universe; but

cultivate human creativity to bring about peace and hope, even transcendence, in the planet we inhabit.

A note on humanizing the digital world and connecting to human values

Shoshana Zuboff has declared: 'Let there be a digital future, but let it be a human future first.'[5] The digital life is clearly here to stay and there are undeniably enormous benefits flowing from it. But it is seriously changing what we know to be the human. Many foresee a coming nightmare: multiple digital and robotic risks are already bringing disenchantments and dangers. In its most extreme form, this will mark 'the end of humanity'. And so one of the key value problems of the twenty-first century becomes how to prevent the dehumanization of life by digitalism and create a valued, compassionate digital world.

For technological experts who believe that the success of machines is enough to justify their power over people, the value problem has not always figured on their list of concerns. We have been here before throughout human history (and recently, notably, with the industrial revolution). Technology has often been a cruel story for many people. We have let the technologists race ahead, while the humanists, the ethical thinkers, the sensitive politicians, the caring employees have all been left behind. And so we start to answer our basic question. We need to shape the digital life by bringing to it human values: of *care, dignity, justice, rights, cosmopolitanism, truth, beauty, love – and compassion.*

Humanism and digitalism can work together. Humanism may help reduce the harms and hazards of digitalism, while digitalism may assist in the flourishing of human beings. Critical humanism starts with creative human actions – with us resisting the overwhelming rise and dominance of the machine in our lives. But a critical digitalism examines ways to enhance ways of being human. Table 8.3 gives some indications of these; the task is to infuse the digital world with the values, narratives and creativity of humanity.[6]

Table 8.3: Humanizing the digital world

Value domain	Negative values: how do we prevent this happening	Positive values: tasks ahead
Environmental	Catastrophic risk	Making digital safe so that it does not harm humans, animals or earth
Existential	Degradation and dehumanization of relations, even death of humanity	Human beings use digital as an aid for living: Creativity, dignity, responsibility
Interpersonal	Machine as others	People as others: digital empathy, compassion and networks of care, connectivity of kindness and love
Community	Breakdown of human community: communities made mechanical and exclusionary	The human network and human web: the digital as a means to inclusive human communities
Society	Digital inequality Digital injustice Digital cruelty Digital surveillance	Online social care, justice and equality: digital citizenship, resisting surveillance
Culture	Digital pollution Damaged culture Fake news Breakdown of trust	Enhancing the good and flourishing life: building digital institutions of truth, trust and transparency
World	Polarized divides Parochialism, populism, sectionalism and 'bubbles' Violence	Enhancing cosmopolitanism via the web: digital conviviality, regulating digital abuse and violence
Cosmos, planetary	Trashing world and universe	Sustaining worldly care in the universe

VII   Creating a Connective World: A Politics of Generational Hope and Movements Grounded in Utopian Realism

Our task is to think where we might be heading and what our role in this is. Human narratives, human values and human creativity will help us shape this future. A politics of humanity brings a generational hope that looks to past, present and futures – to worlds that reduce harm, connect life and make creative life flourish.

> The earth, the womb of all life, is in trouble. Humanity, ridden with its own crises of inequality and exploitation, has mistreated its only home to the extent that life as we know it is itself imperilled. Do we have the wisdom and foresight to save ourselves and the planet? Can we take the urgent, widespread and deep-rooted actions that are needed for this? A world which is built on respect, compassion, love, responsibility, freedom, diversity and humility – not only in the relations amongst humans but also between humans and the rest of nature – surely we can not only dream this but also forge paths towards it?
>
> Vikalp Sangam Process, *The Search for Alternatives: Key Aspects and Principles*

Here we have an extract from an early position paper for world discussion of an alternative future politics (Vikalp Sangam Process) organized initially in India. It is now part of the Global Tapestry of Alternatives (GTA).[7] It flags the fact that the world we live in today may soon be transformed out of all recognition. We might just meet an apocalypse through catastrophe. A pandemic plague, a climatic change, a nuclear explosion might (almost) wipe us out. The growth of authoritarian regimes may mean all our hard-won past 'freedoms' are lost. We may become a digitalized, robotic, post-humanity.

But different futures are possible. And millions across the world are trying to make this happen. Through our own creative acts of planetary care, we might just be able to make the world a kindlier, fairer and more connected place. We cannot predict futures. *But we can act now for the sort of world we wish to see.* We can create the plural global paths to a politics of worldwide human care and connectivity. It would aim to reduce harm in the world, connect lives to the continuity and richness of the earth and cosmos we dwell in and build creative and flourishing human worlds.

We need to cultivate thinking like a *planetary person* by developing:

1 *World connective consciousness* that bridges local and global, personal and public, earth and planet: a fusion of micro projects of life fusing with macro projects of worldly care. It appreciates simultaneously the diversity of world cultures and the uniqueness of persons.

2 *World emancipatory thinking* that connects the world's wide range of cultural understandings of human flourishing and works to put them to good use. Western ideas now need to be bridged with ideas from the wider pluriversal world.

3 *World grounded utopianism* that looks for projects and actions already succeeding to make the world a better place, learns from them, and aims to enhance them.

4 *World generational hope* that enables us to think of time long past, time future to come, and time as we live in the here and now. Our here and now is hedged in by at least five generations. From our grandparents to our grand-children, the pluriverse rolls on. How we have changed over the past sixty generations of human life! Five generations, the 200 years or so around our life, is a manageable time frame to think within. We can construct pasts and futures in the present that are linear, life stories that move in straight lines. Or we can construct lives of past and future as omnipresent in the current moment: we can see the dead and ghosts in living time as memories. The challenge in all temporal thinking is how to move the world on for a new generation. How to make the world a little better for each future generation. In recent times, we have not been doing this very well.

A note on the importance of hope: the idea of hope is necessary for future and humanity. It has a long (his)storical narrative. Little lights shine in the darkness. Hope enables us to keep going. It gives us some comfort and makes us look to a better future. It is another key to unlock what is meant by humanity, as well as a guide for humanism. It takes many forms:

- a *radical hope* will help us to imagine a life 'beyond', even when life is at its darkest;
- a *pragmatic hope* will help us get through the day – we

all have our ups and downs; we look for the little acts of kindness to be done in everyday life.

- a *narrative hope* will attend to the stories we tell and looks for the ones that can bring us to a better place;
- a *cosmopolitan hope* will look at the exuberance and delight of human differences and encourage better ways of living and learning from this – there can be harmony in difference;
- a *grounded utopian* hope will enable us to look for those actually existing local worlds that generate human flourishing; they need encouraging, to bring forth more and better creative things to be done;
- a *generational hope* will bring the dream that each generation lives, works and creates to make a better world for each generation to come.

VIII Transformative Futures: A Politics and Literacy for a Better World

Our task is to connect to the world and change it. We move between the local, the pluriversal and world politics, engaging in a connected, emancipatory life of revaluing, reconciling, resisting, repairing, rebuilding, recreating and reimagining.

> Care for the future of mankind is the overruling duty of collective human action in the age of technological civilization … This care must obviously include care for the future of all nature on this planet as a necessary condition of man's own.
> Hans Jonas, *The Imperative of Responsibility: In Search of an Ethics for the Technological Age* (1984 [1979]), p. 136

Hans Jonas was concerned with confronting the change of our times by building a strong 'imperative of responsibility' to pass from generation to generation. A new politics had to be built to care for the world and humanity. Many have coalesced on views like this. A new politics and literacy of world humanity is called for.

This can work in many ways, through millions of little, local actions from groups with visions of a fairer, kinder, more connected planetary life; and through wider shared narrative imaginaries of worldly care and responsibility. It can be local and grounded but also transnational and abstract. Ultimately, there is a responsibility for each generation to pass on to the next generation a world that is better than the previous one. This is a big task; and it has to work in a multiplicity of ways – building a 'global tapestry of alternatives'. There is no one way of doing this. The challenge is to build an open, flexible, multiple awareness and politics.

Here will be a planetary politics that will reduce harm, cultivate flourishing life for all, and connect to life and the cosmos. It will think and act in both big and small ways (as planetary persons) and with the long term in mind, not just the short term – at least several generations, not just several years. It will bridge the gap between local and personal life (micro politics) and a worldwide concern with global human values (macro politics). It will gradually trace the connectivity of life from cosmos to earth, from world to person, from human to all of life. Here is a politics of connectivity and generational hope: each generation continues our connection with the earth, existence, relations, communities, societies, cultures, the planet and the cosmos. In doing this, it brings together ten deep practices, all already introduced:

1. *Repair*: heal the world.
2. *Resist*: stand against the divided world.
3. *Reharmonize*: live well with differences.
4. *Reconcile*: understand the failed past world.
5. *Re-story*: search for narratives of worldly care.
6. *Revalue*: share connecting values.
7. *Recreate*: make life flourish across generations.
8. *Remake the world*: build a politics of humanity.
9. *Reimagine*: cultivate future human imaginations and imaginaries.
10. *Re-educate*: develop a literacy of hope with each generation.

IX Ultimately Connect: Think Like a Planetary Person

In practice, the politics of humanity engages with the (gradual) creation of and connection to a multiplicity of new progressive human worlds for all. It starts by connecting to imagination: to imagine a distinctive planet in a cosmos with the worlds and lives and values we want. It connects to care for the building of an interconnected planetary life and humanity and assembles a social imaginary for a future cosmic world humanity. It requires a thinking politics that draws from its damaged past and looks towards a better future for all. It thinks holistically and pluralistically, not focusing on just the one cause, the one interest, the one idea, the one country, or the one concern. With great difficulty, it aims to be persistently wide-ranging, open-ended, plural in its aims, tolerant of ambiguity and aware of the impossibility of many of its tasks.

And this politics of humanity brings with it a concern not just for the creativity of politics but also for a vision for education – a pedagogy of hope and a literate humanity. To guide us in all this, we need both a future world *imaginary* (see Table 8.1, above), a collective sense of a better world ahead, and an *imagination*, a personal vision of the creative world. Both are concerned with reducing harm, enhancing connectivity across the world and enabling a flourishing world. They will always be under discussion, but both suggest ways of flourishing in the world, values to be shared together, new ways of seeing, some kind of provisional map for a future. It will be a perpetually negotiated world struggle for a worldly care: our shared human values with goals like care and kindness; earth sustainability and human flourishing; dignity, rights and responsibility; world social justice; truth and trust; living with difference and cosmopolitanism; as well as non-violence and love.

These have been the dreams of dreamers for a long while. They provide both generational hope and a pedagogy for hope: a basis for a better world for all and for the perpetuation of humanity's hope.

Epilogue: On Being Well in the World – The Joys of Everyday Living

> One of life's quiet excitements is to stand somewhat apart from yourself and watch yourself softly becoming the author of something beautiful, even if it is only a floating ash.
> Norman Maclean, *A River Runs Through It* (1976), p. 68

Norman Maclean's novel (and the film derived from it) is a wonderful exploration of the passion some people have for nature and the act of fly-fishing. Here is a sense of being well in the world. And so, from this Manifesto's dizzy heights of hope and future creativities, I return to ordinary everyday life and its little joys.

Some while back, confronted by a daily deluge from an all-invasive media about the real horrors of the world we inhabit, and on the edge of getting depressed from this daily onslaught, I started to assemble a daily log of joys. I set my task: to simply name as many joys as I could find. The sources of human contentment are many and varied. We might even call them the 'joys of living'. Joy suggests a feeling of great pleasure and happiness. I drew randomly from my own experiences, from people I have known in my life and also from what I have read. It did not take any time at all to come up with quite a long listing. The world, it seems, is full of wonderful things. Put into alphabetical order, here is a far from exhaustive list. Many people enjoy life – even find a calm joy – while engaging with:

acting, adventuring, angling, animal loving, antiques, architecture, art, astrology, astronomy ... babies, badminton,
baking, ballet, bees, birds, boating, bodies, books, bowling,
boxing, boyfriends, Buddhism, butterflies ... campaigning,
carnivals, children, choirs, Christianity, climbing, clubbing,
collecting, collective joy, computing, concerts, conversation,
cooking, crafts, cricket, croquet, cycling ... daffodils, dancing,
darts, debating, deep-sea diving, discussing, drawing, dreaming,
dress, drinking ... eating, entertaining, environment, exercise,
extreme sports ... Facebooking, faith, family, farming,
fashion, festivals, films, fishing, fitness, flowers, flying, folk
music, food, football, forests, friendship ... gambling, gaming,
gardening, gardens, girlfriends, god, golf, groups, guitar ...
hair, health, heritage, Hinduism, hobbies, 'home', hospitality
... ideas, idling, intellectual work, Islam ... jazz, jogging ...
karaoke, knowledge, kung fu ... laughing, leisure, literature,
looking, love ... magic, make-up, making things, martial arts,
maths, meditation, moon, mountain climbing, music, musicals
... nature, nothingness – doing nothing ... oceans, opera ...
painting, parties, performing, piano playing, plants, play,
playing pool, poetry, politics, pornography, practical things,
prayer, programming, protesting ... queer politics, questioning
... radicalism, radio, reading, relationships, religions, repairing
things, ritual, rock climbing, rugby, running ... sex, science,
shopping, singing, the sky, sky-diving, sleep, smells, social
media, speaking, sports, spirituality, stamp collecting, stars,
storytelling, swimming ... tai-chi, television, tennis, theatre,
thinking, touching, travel, truth seeking ... walking, watching,
water-colouring, wilderness, woodlands, working, world
affairs, wrestling, writing ... YouTubeing

This is quite a list. It is far from exhaustive. It suggests a lot
of possibilities. Some of my own joys are there. I hope some
of your joys are too. These little joys of life can be infinite.

There are many diverse things that these little worlds
display, but is there anything they have in common? Perhaps
they all bring:

- *creativity* – we do things, make new things, have new
experiences, bring new things and meanings into the world;
- *connectivity* – we connect with others, with life, with
things on the planet;
- *care* – we show engagement with something or someone
that matters to us, beyond our own world;

- *contemplation* – we attend to what we are doing, take an interest, think about it or use it as a space to think, and we become attentive to the fragile meanings of life;
- *calm and contentment* – we become at ease with the smallness of our world, 'at home'; however tenuously, some kind of calm or peace or inner joy may arrive.

Here then, are little social worlds of everyday contentment, goodness, maybe even wisdom. They have long roots back to Buddhism and Epicurus. We may need to be planetary persons in a cosmos of multiple galaxies; but we are also tiny little animals living minuscule unique lives in microscopic social worlds that are ours alone. Today, perhaps more than ever before, there is more human creativity in writing, the arts, music; more sporting talent; more 'education'; more enthusiasts for leisure and the little arts – nature, cooking, gardening. The potential for more delights of life and joys in living has probably never been so available. And yet the challenge is such that many people are not able to find this small contentment in the world. It surely suggests the need to see their importance for a future. It may well be that, ultimately, the human project is a uniquely tiny but diverse one. It creates minuscule local worlds that enable the little interests, loves and hopes of an everyday life to develop the small joys of being a tiny but vital human.[1]

Short Guide to Further Reading

Here is a short tour of selected readings. Detailed references can be found in the notes. A detailed annotated guide to reading, websites – and more – can be found on the website accompanying this book: **kenplummer.com/criticalhumanism**.

Introducing Humanism

Yuval Noah Harari, *Sapiens: A Brief History of Humankind* (Vintage, 2011): https://www.ynharari.com. See also the comic book version: *Sapiens: A Graphic History* (Harvill Secker, 2020).

Yann Arthus-Bertrand, *Human: A Portrait of Our World* (Thames and Hudson, 2015). http://www.yannarthusbertrand.org.

Steven Pinker, *Enlightenment Now: The Case for Reason, Science, Humanism and Progress* (Allen Lane, 2018).

Recent Humanist Writings

Hannah Arendt, *The Human Condition*, 2nd edn (University of Chicago Press, 1998 [1958]).

Martha C. Nussbaum, *Creating Capabilities: The Human Development Approach* (Harvard University Press, 2011).

Christian Smith, *What Is a Person? Rethinking Humanity, Social Life, and the Moral Good from the Person Up* (University of Chicago Press, 2011).

Marcus Morgan, *Pragmatic Humanism: On the Nature and Value of Sociological Knowledge* (Routledge, 2016).

Daniel Chemillo, *Debating Humanity: Towards a Philosophical Sociology* (Cambridge University Press, 2017).

Andrew Copson and A. C. Grayling, eds, *The Wiley Blackwell Handbook of Humanism* (Wiley-Blackwell, 2015).

Critical Problems

Anne Phillips, *The Politics of the Human* (Cambridge University Press, 2015).

Rosi Braidotti, *The Posthuman* (Polity, 2013).

Raewyn Connell, *Southern Theory: The Global Dynamics of Knowledge in Social Science* (Polity, 2007).

Boaventura de Sousa Santos, *The End of the Cognitive Empire: The Coming of Age of Epistemologies of the South* (Duke University Press, 2018).

Ali Meghji, *Decolonizing Sociology: An Introduction* (Polity, 2021).

Gurminder K. Bhambra, *Connected Sociologies* (Bloomsbury, 2014).

Jairus Victor Grove, *Savage Ecology: War and Geopolitics at the End of the World* (Duke University Press, 2019).

The World: A Background *circa* 2020

Manuel Castells, *Rupture: The Crisis of Liberal Democracy*, trans. Rosie Marteau (Polity, 2018).

Peter N. Stearns, *World History: The Basics* (Routledge, 2010).

Fareed Zakaria, *Ten Lessons for a Post-Pandemic World* (Allen Lane, 2020).

Nick Couldry and Ulises A. Mejias, *The Costs of Connection: How Data is Colonizing Human Life and Appropriating It for Capitalism* (Stanford University Press, 2019).

Heinrich Geiselberger, ed., *The Great Regression* (Polity, 2017).

Roy Scranton, *Learning to Die in the Anthropocene: Reflections on the End of a Civilization* (City Lights Publishers, 2015).

Covid-19: A Time of Pandemic

Gerard Delanty, ed., *Pandemics, Politics and Society: Critical Perspectives on the Covid-19 Crisis* (De Gruyter, 2021).

Klaus Schwab and Thierry Mallert, *Covid-19: The Great Reset* (World Economic Forum Publishing, 2020).

Martin Parker, ed., *Life after Covid-19: The Other Side of Crisis* (Bristol University Press, 2020).

Damaged Humanity

Iain Wilkinson and Arthur Kleinman, *A Passion for Society: How We Think about human Suffering* (University of California Press, 2016).

David Wallace-Wells, *The Uninhabitable Earth: A Story of the Future* (Allen Lane, 2019).

Jonathan Porritt, *Hope in Hell: A Decade to Confront the Climate Emergency* (Simon & Schuster, 2020).

Derek Wall, *Economics After Capitalism: A Guide to the Ruins and a Road to the Future* (Pluto Press, 2015 [2005]).

Kate Raworth, *Doughnut Economics: Seven Ways to Think Like a 21st-Century Economist* (Random House, 2017).

Thomas Piketty, *Capital and Ideology* (Harvard University Press, 2020).

Shoshana Zuboff, *The Age of Surveillance Capitalism: The Fight for a New Future at the New Frontier of Power* (Profile Books, 2019).

Saksia Sassen, *Expulsions: Brutality and Complexity in the Global Economy* (Harvard University Press, 2014).
Michiko Kakutani, *The Death of Truth* (William Collins, 2018).
John D. Caputo, *Truth: The Search for Wisdom in the Postmodern Age* (Penguin, 2013).
Lothar Brock, Hans-Henrik Holm, Georg Sorensen and Michael Stohl, *Fragile States: Violence and the Failure of Intervention* (Polity, 2012).

Divided Humanity

Ryszard Kapuściński, *The Other* (Verso, 2008) is a readable and short introduction to thinkers and issues.
David Livingstone Smith, *On Inhumanity: Dehumanization and How to Resist It* (Oxford University Press, 2020).
Patricia Hill Collins and Sirma Bilge, *Intersectionality*, 2nd edn (Polity, 2020).
Kwame Anthony Appiah, *The Lies that Bind: Rethinking Identity* (Liveright, 2018).

Traumatized Humanity

Tzvetan Todorov, *Hope and Memory: Reflections on the Twentieth Century* (Atlantic Books, 2005).
John K. Roth, *The Failures of Ethics: Confronting the Holocaust, Genocide and Other Mass Atrocities* (Oxford University Press, 2015).
Jean Franco, *Cruel Modernity* (Duke University Press, 2013).
Robert Gildea, *Empires of the Mind: The Colonial Past and the Politics of the Present* (Cambridge University Press, 2019).
Jeffrey C. Alexander, *Trauma: A Social Theory* (Polity, 2012).
Pankaj Mishra, *Age of Anger: A History of the Present* (Macmillan, 2017).
Martha Minow, *Between Vengeance and Forgiveness: Facing History after Genocide and Mass Violence* (Beacon Press, 1998).

Catherine Lu, *Justice and Reconciliation in World Politics* (Cambridge University Press, 2017).
Susan Neiman, *Learning from the Germans: Confronting Race and the Memory of Evil* (Allen Lane, 2019)

Narrative Humanity

Ken Plummer, *Narrative Power: The Struggle for Human Value* (Polity, 2019).
Kay Schaffer and Sidonie Smith, *Human Rights and Narrated Lives: The Ethics of Recognition* (Palgrave Macmillan, 2004).
Arthur W. Frank, *Letting Stories Breathe: A Socio-Narratology* (University of Chicago Press, 2010).

Emerging ideas of Global Humanity

David Christian, *Origin Story: A Big History of Everything* (Penguin, 2018). See also the Big History Project website: https://www.bighistoryproject.com/home.
Bruce Mazlish, *The Idea of Humanity in a Global Era* (Palgrave Macmillan, 2009).
Siep Stuurman, *The Invention of Humanity: Equality and Cultural Difference in World History* (Harvard University Press, 2017).
Jeremy Rifkin, *The Empathic Civilization: The Race to Global Consciousness in a World in Crisis* (Polity, 2010).
Nigel Clark and Bronislaw Szerszynski, *Planetary Social Thought: The Anthropocene Challenge to the Social Sciences* (Polity, 2020).

Valuing Humanity

Kenan Milk, *The Quest for a Moral Compass: A Global History of Ethics* (Atlantic Books, 2014).

Michael Ignatieff, *The Ordinary Virtues: Moral Order in a Divided World* (Harvard University Press, 2017).

Michael Sandel and Paul J. d'Ambrosio, eds, *Encountering China: Michael Sandel and Chinese Philosophy* (Harvard University Press, 2018).

Philip Kitcher, *The Ethical Project* (Harvard University Press, 2012).

Nira Yuval-Davis, *The Politics of Belonging: Intersectional Contestations* (Sage, 2011).

Owen Flanagan, *The Geography of Morals: Varieties of Moral Possibility* (Oxford University Press, 2016).

Transformative Humanities

John Urry, *What is the Future?* (Polity, 2016).

Toby Ord, *The Precipice: Existential Risk and the Future of Humanity* (Bloomsbury, 2020).

Amitav Ghosh, *The Great Derangement: Climate Change and the Unthinkable* (University of Chicago Press, 2016).

Rickie Solinger, Madeline Fox and Kayhan Irani, eds, *Telling Stories to Change the World: Global Voices on the Power of Narrative to Build Community and Make Social Justice Claims* (Routledge, 2008).

Rebecca Solnit, *Hope in the Dark: Untold Histories, Wild Possibilities* (Haymarket Books, 2016).

The Politics of Humanity

Arturo Escobar, *Pluriversal Politics: The Real and the Possible* (Duke University Press, 2020).

The Care Collective, *The Care Manifesto: The Politics of Interdependence* (Verso, 2020).

Steve Crenshaw and John Jackson, eds, *Small Acts of Resistance: How Courage, Tenacity, and Ingenuity Can Change the World* (Union Square Press, 2010).

Peter Weibel, ed., *Global Activism: Art and Conflict in the 21st Century* (MIT Press, 2014).

Paul Mason, *Clear Bright Future: A Radical Defence of the Human Being* (Allen Lane, 2019).

Rutger Bregman, *Utopia for Realists – and How We Can Get There* (Bloomsbury, 2017).

Hilary Cottam, *Radical Help: How We Can Remake the Relationships between Us and Revolutionise the Welfare State* (Virago, 2018).

William Martin, *The Activist's Tao Te Ching: Ancient Advice for a Modern Revolution* (New World Library, 2016).

On a practical level, see Mike Berners-Lee, *There Is No Planet B: A Handbook for the Make or Break Years*, 2nd edn (Cambridge University Press, 2021), which is very down to earth.

Christiana Figueres and Tom Rivett-Carnac, *The Future We Choose: Surviving the Climate Crisis* (Manilla Press, 2020).

Closing Thoughts

David Attenborough, *A Life on Our Planet: My Witness Statement and a Vision for the Future* (Ebury Press, 2020).

Notes

Introduction

1   I have provided a short account of my illness in 'My Multiple Sick Bodies: Symbolic Interactionism, Autoethnography and Embodiment', in Bryan S. Turner, ed., *Routledge Handbook of Body Studies* (Routledge, 2012), pp. 75–93.

2   In a short space of time there has already been a mad rush of publications about Covid-19. Everything is in flux, but one early useful book is Fareed Zakaria, *Ten Lessons for a Post-Pandemic World* (Allen Lane, 2020).

3   See Zygmunt Bauman, *Liquid Modernity* (Polity, 2000). Bauman has written many works on this theme, including *Liquid Love: On the Frailty of Human Bonds* (Polity, 2003), *Liquid Fear* (Polity, 2006) and, with David Lyon, *Liquid Surveillance: A Conversation* (Polity, 2013).

4   I use the word 'pluriverse' a lot in this book and it may not be familiar. It has three genealogies. First, William James wrote of the plural experience and 'the pluralistic universe' (see *A Pluralistic Universe*, CreateSpace Publishing, 2015 [1909]). He suggested a world of human multiplicities. Second, the term 'multiverse' is used by physicists to claim that the universe is not one but multiple. And third, it has been used recently to capture diversity in world politics, developed in the works of Arturo Escobar in *Pluriversal Politics: The Real and the Possible* (Duke University Press, 2020). These are not incompatible. The challenge is to think in the local and specific diversity, to see worlds in the plural.

5 It is present in my *Documents of Life: Introduction to the Problems and Literature of a Humanist Method* (Allen & Unwin, 1983); but I make it much more apparent in the major revised second edition: *Documents of Life-2: An Invitation to a Critical Humanism* (Sage, 2001). I expand on it in several other works: for example, *Cosmopolitan Sexualities: Hope and the Humanist Imagination* (Polity, 2015), *Narrative Power: The Struggle for Human Value* (Polity, 2019) and 'A Manifesto for a Critical Humanism in Sociology', in Daniel Nehring, *Sociology: An Introductory Textbook and Reader* (Pearson Education, 2013), pp. 489–516.

6 Anne Phillips, *The Politics of the Human* (Cambridge University Press, 2015), pp. 14–15.

7 As well as the discussion in Phillips's *Politics of the Human*, see discussions in Yuval Noah Harari, *Sapiens: A Brief History of Humankind* (Vintage, 2011) and *Homo Deus: A Brief History of Tomorrow* (Vintage Books, 2015); Siep Stuurman, *The Invention of Humanity: Equality and Cultural Difference in World History* (Harvard University Press, 2017); Alexander Harcourt, *Humankind: How Biology and Geography Shape Human Diversity* (Pegasus, 2015); John Hands, *Cosmo Sapiens: Human Evolution from the Origin of the Universe* (Duckworth, 2015); and Bruce Mazlish, *The Idea of Humanity in a Global Era* (Palgrave Macmillan, 2009).

8 Trees account for some 82 per cent of biomass; tiny bacteria some 13 per cent; we humans account for a mere 0.01 per cent. For a summary of these ideas, see https://www.theguardian.com/environment/2018/may/21/human-race-just-001-of-all-life-but-has-destroyed-over-80-of-wild-mammals-study. The original study can be found at: Yinon M. Bar-On, Rob Phillips and Ron Milo, 'The Biomass Distribution on Earth', *Proceedings of the National Academy of Sciences*, 115/25 (19 June 2018): 6506–11: https://www.pnas.org/content/115/25/6506/tab-article-info.

9 Discussions of the 'person' raise many issues – especially concerning dignity and agency. It corresponds roughly to what I will refer to as existential being, but I do not discuss it here. An important clarification is to be found in Christian Smith, *What Is a Person? Rethinking Humanity, Social Life, and the Moral Good from the Person Up* (University of Chicago Press, 2011). See also Margaret Archer, *Being Human: The Problem of Agency* (Cambridge University Press, 2000).

Chapter 1: Critical Humanism

1 Anne Phillips, *The Politics of the Human* (Cambridge University Press, 2015). For a recent analysis, see Daniel Chernilo, *Debating Humanity: Towards a Philosophical Sociology* (Cambridge University Press, 2017).

2 Marcus Morgan, *Pragmatic Humanism: On the Nature and Value of Sociological Knowledge* (Routledge, 2016), ch. 2. Morgan also enumerates some seven responses to this recurrent death of man/humanity/humanism.

3 See John Dewey, 'What Humanism Means to Me', in Jo Ann Boydston (ed.), *John Dewey: The Later Works, 1925–1953, Volume 5: 1929–1939* (Southern Illinois University Press, 2008), p. xxxi.

4 See Lawrence Grossberg, *Cultural Studies in the Future Tense* (Duke University Press, 2010), p. 20ff.

5 William Du Bois and R. Dean Wright provide an overview of the development in the USA in 'What is Humanistic Sociology?', *The American Sociologist*, 33/4 (Winter 2002): 5–36. In its earliest days it was associated especially with Florian Znaniecki, Charles Cooley, Margaret Mead, Jane Addams and Charles Wright Mills.

6 Identified mainly with some of the Frankfurt School intellectuals, such as Erich Fromm, Erik Erikson and even Theodor Adorno in some of his work. See for example, Kieran Durkin, *The Radical Humanism of Erich Fromm* (Palgrave Macmillan, 2014).

7 See Introduction, note 4.

8 Louis Menand provides an outstanding history of early pragmatism in *The Metaphysical Club: A Story of Ideas in America* (HarperCollins, 2001). He discusses, among others, Charles Sanders Peirce, William James, Jane Addams and John Dewey. Of the later pragmatists, see Sidney Hook, *Pragmatism and the Tragic Sense of Life* (Basic Books, 1975).

9 Alfred McClung Lee, *Sociology for Whom?* (Oxford University Press, 1978), pp. 44–5.

10 See Edward W. Said, *Orientalism* (Penguin, 2003 [1978]), p. xx; see also Said, *Humanism and Democratic Criticism* (Palgrave, 2004).

11 More recently, sociologist Daniel Chernilo, in *Debating Humanity: Towards a Philosophical Sociology* (Cambridge University Press, 2017), has approached the problem another way. With a careful scrutiny of major theorists from just one particular discipline (sociology), he shows how humanist ideas – like responsibility (Hans Jonas), reflexivity (Margaret Archer) and language (Jürgen Habermas) – develop in their work. Here,

a multiplicity of key words for humanity could be traced back to such discussions.

12 Steven Pinker, *Enlightenment Now: The Case for Reason, Science, Humanism and Progress* (Allen Lane, 2018).

13 See Pankaj Mishra, 'Grand Illusion', *New York Review of Books*, 19 November 2020, pp. 31–2.

14 A small sampling of this work, which I draw on here, includes: Raewyn Connell, *Southern Theory: The Global Dynamics of Knowledge in Social Science* (Polity, 2007); Boaventura de Sousa Santos, *Epistemologies of the South: Justice against Epistemicide* (Paradigm, 2014) and *The End of the Cognitive Empire: The Coming of Age of Epistemologies of the South* (Duke University Press, 2018); Bernd Reiter, *Constructing the Pluriverse: The Geopolitics of Knowledge* (Duke University Press, 2018); Marisol de la Cadena and Mario Blaser, *A World of Many Worlds* (Duke University Press, 2018); Arturo Escobar, *Pluriversal Politics: The Real and the Possible* (Duke University Press, 2020).

15 See de Sousa Santos, *Epistemologies of the South*, p. 164.

16 Bertolt Brecht, *Life of Galileo*, trans. John Willett (Methuen, 1986), p. 108.

17 For some of this debate, see Hans Joas and Klaus Wiegandt, eds, *Secularization and the World Religions* (Liverpool University Press, 2009); Peter L. Berger, ed., *The Desecularization of the World: Resurgent Religions and World Politics* (Eeerdmans, 1999).

18 Richard Dawkins, *The God Delusion* (Black Swan, 2006); Sam Harris, *The Moral Landscape* (Free Press, 2010); Christopher Hitchens, *God Is Not Great: How Religion Poisons Everything* (Atlantic Books, 2007).

19 *The Wiley Blackwell Handbook of Humanism*, ed. Andrew Copson and A. C. Grayling (2015), brings together more than twenty contributors. There is a wonderful opening essay, which outlines many main features of humanism today. It is also made very clear that the anti-religious definition is the real definition of humanism. Stephen Law's *Humanism: A Very Short Introduction* (Oxford University Press, 2010) also takes this view. See also Philip Kitcher, *Life After Faith: The Case for Secular Humanism* (Yale University Press, 2014).

20 Yuval Noah Harari, *Sapiens: A Brief History of Humankind* (Vintage, 2011), p. 465.

21 See Brian Cox and Andrew Cohen, *Wonders of the Universe* (HarperCollins, 2011), p. 241.

22 See John Gray's *Seven Types of Atheism* (Allen Lane, 2018). With a long history he suggests that secular humanism is only one version of atheism and the least substantial.

23 See Phil Zuckerman, *Society Without God: What the Least Religious Nations Can Tell Us about Contentment* (New York University Press, 2008).

24 See Pew Research Center, 'The Changing Global Religious Landscape', 5 April 2017: https://www.pewforum.org/2017/04/05/the-changing-global-religious-landscape/

25 Ulrich Beck, *A God of One's Own: Religion's Capacity for Peace and Potential for Violence* (Polity, 2010).

26 See Mark Juergensmeyer, Dinah Griego and John Soboslai, *God in the Tumult of the Global Square: Religion in Global Civil Society* (University of California Press, 2015). See also Michael Jordan, *In the Name of God: Violence and Destruction in the World's Religions* (Sutton Publishing, 2006); Oliver Roy, *Holy Ignorance: When Religion and Culture Part Ways*, trans. Ros Schwartz (Hurst, 2010).

27 Hans Küng and Karl-Josef Kuschel, eds, *Global Ethic: The Declaration of the Parliament of the World's Religions* (Continuum, 1993).

28 See Sandy and Jael Bharat, *A Global Guide to Interfaith: Reflections from Around the World* (O Books, 2007). An illustration of this at work can be found in Kwok Pui-Lan, *Globalization, Gender and Peacebuilding: The Future of Interfaith Dialogue* (Paulist Press, 2012).

29 Dalai Lama, *Beyond Religion: Ethics for a Whole World* (Houghton Mifflin Harcourt, 2011); Daisaku Ikeda, *A New Humanism* (Tauris, 2010); Felix Unger and Daisaku Ikeda, *The Humanist Principle: On Compassion and Tolerance* (Tauris, 2016).

30 Beck, *A God of One's Own*, p. 197.

31 See 'For Darwin Day, 6 Facts About the Evolution Debate': https://www.pewresearch.org/fact-tank/2019/02/11/darwin-day/; 18 per cent of Americans reject evolution entirely, saying humans have always existed in their present form.

32 See Elizabeth Kolbert, *The Sixth Extinction: An Unnatural History* (Bloomsbury, 2014).

33 David Reich, *Who We Are and How We Got Here: Ancient DNA and the New Science of the Human Past* (Oxford University Press, 2018); Steven Rose, *Lifelines: Life Beyond the Gene* (Vintage, 2005); Adam Rutherford, *A Brief History of Everyone Who Ever Lived: The Stories in Our Genes* (Weidenfeld & Nicolson, 2017).

34 Cox and Cohen, *Wonders of the Universe*, p. 3.

35 Compare the rather sober Martin Rees, *On the Future: Prospects for Humanity* (Princeton University Press, 2018) with the rather extravagant Michio Kaku, *The Future of Humanity:*

Terraforming Mars, Interstellar Travel, Immortality, and Our Destiny Beyond Earth, 2nd edn (Penguin, 2019).

36 This is a key argument in both Cox and Cohen, *Wonders of the Universe*, and Harari, *Sapiens*.

37 This is life during the age of AI and more. See sociologist Steve Fuller's *Humanity 2.0: What It Means to be Human, Past, Present and Future* (Palgrave Macmillan, 2011) and physicist Max Tegmark's *Life 3.0: Being Human in the Age of Artificial Intelligence* (Allen Lane, 2017).

38 See, for example, Angela Saini, *Superior: The Return of Race Science* (Fourth Estate, 2020); Jonathan Marks, *Is Science Racist?* (Polity, 2017).

39 Nikolas Rose, *The Politics of Life Itself: Biomedicine, Power and Subjectivity in the Twenty-First Century* (Princeton University Press, 2001), p. 105; see also Raymond Tallis, *Aping Mankind: Neuromania, Darwinitis and the Misrepresentation of Humanity* (Routledge, 2011).

40 Iain Wilkinson and Arthur Kleinman, *A Passion for Society: How We Think about Human Suffering* (University of California Press, 2016), p. 196.

41 See the history by Michael Barnett, *Empire of Humanity: A History of Humanitarianism* (Cornell University Press, 2013). More widely, it is captured well in Jeremy Rifkin's *The Empathic Civilization: The Race to Global Consciousness in a World in Crisis* (Polity, 2010), and Natan Sznaider's *The Compassionate Temperament: Care and Cruelty in Modern Society* (Rowman & Littlefield, 2000). For a much more critical appraisal, see Didier Fassin, *Humanitarian Reason: A Moral History of the Present* (University of California Press, 2011).

42 Lionel Trilling, *The Liberal Imagination* (New York Review of Books, 1950), cited in David J. Rothman, 'The State as Parent', in Willard Gaylin, ed., *Doing Good: The Limits of Benevolence* (Random House, 1978), p. 72.

43 Tony Vaux, *The Selfish Altruist* (Earthscan, 2001), p. 203.

44 Philip Cunliffe, *Cosmopolitan Dystopia: International Intervention and the Fall of the West* (Manchester University Press, 2020).

45 Fassin, *Humanitarian Reason*, p. 3. A useful lecture given by Fassin, 'Critique of Humanitarian Reason', can be found at https://video.ias.edu/critique-of-humanitarian-reason.

46 It can be found at https://www.un.org/en/universal-declaration-human-rights/.

47 See two very positive evaluations of human rights by Kathryn Sikkink, *The Justice Cascade: How Human Rights Prosecutions Are Changing World Politics* (Norton, 2013), and *Evidence*

for Hope: Making Human Rights Work in the 21st Century (Princeton University Press, 2017).

48 See Lawrence M. Friedman, *The Human Rights Culture: A Study in History and Context* (Quid Pro, 2011).

49 See William F. Felice, *Taking Suffering Seriously: The Importance of Collective Human Rights* (State University of New York Press, 1996).

50 For example: although indigenous rights may be officially recognized, in practice many problems remain. See Colin Samson, *The Colonialism of Human Rights: Ongoing Hypocrisies of Western Liberalism* (Polity, 2020). Similar problems remain for each category listed in this Box.

51 Stephen Hopgood, *The Endtimes of Human Rights* (Cornell University Press, 2013), p. ix; see also Cunliffe, *Cosmopolitan Dystopia*; Samuel Moyn, *Not Enough: Human Rights in an Unequal World* (Belknap, 2019). Hopgood distinguishes between human rights (lower case) as grounded activism, which is important and will always be with us, and a Human Rights (upper case) – a large global structure more like a worldwide church, of which he is very critical. By contrast, Alison Brysk provides the positive case for rights in *The Future of Human Rights* (Polity, 2018).

52 See Chandra Talpade Mohanty, *Feminism without Borders: Decolonizing Theory, Practicing Solidarity* (Duke University Press, 2003); Jasbir K. Puar, *Terrorist Assemblages: Homonationalism in Queer Times* (Duke University Press, 2007).

53 See Robert W. Fuller and Pamela A. Gerloff, *Dignity for All: How to Create a World Without Rankism* (Berrett-Koehler, 2008).

54 Christian Smith, *What Is a Person? Rethinking Humanity, Social Life, and the Moral Good from the Person Up* (University of Chicago Press, 2011), p. 435. Smith argues that it is impossible not to be an essentialist. There is always an essential core hanging around somewhere or we could not even talk about such things. He builds his personalist account (a theory held by a distinctive group of largely Catholic theorists) with dignity and agentic human purpose at the core. See also Chapter 4 of Phillips, *The Politics of the Human* for a critical commentary of essentialist ideas of dignity. Maria Kronfeldner's *What's Left of Human Nature? A Post-Essentialist, Pluralist and Interactive Account of a Contested Concept* (MIT Press, 2018) is a rigorous and systematic philosophical development of modern non-essentialist ideas around human nature.

55 Martha C. Nussbaum's ideas can be found in, especially, *Cultivating Humanity: A Classical Defense of Reform in*

Liberal Education (Harvard University Press, 1998); *Creating Capabilities: The Human Development Approach* (Harvard University Press, 2011). Much of her recent work is concerned with taking seriously the importance of emotions in social, ethical and political life. For examples, see, *Upheavals of Thought: The Intelligence of Emotions* (Cambridge University Press, 2001); *Hiding from Humanity: Disgust, Shame, and the Law* (Princeton University Press, 2004); *Frontiers of Justice: Disability, Nationality, Species Membership* (Harvard University Press, 2006); and *Political Emotions: Why Love Matters for Justice* (Harvard University Press, 2013).

56 Cary Wolfe, *What Is Posthumanism?* (University of Minnesota Press, 2010), p. xv.
57 This idea is well detailed and discussed in the writings of Deborah Lupton; see her *The Quantified Self* (Polity, 2016); and *Data Selves* (Polity, 2020).
58 See David Roden's *Posthuman Life: Philosophy at the Edge of the Human* (Routledge, 2015), esp ch. 1. I have drawn mainly on Rosi Braidotti's three key works: *The Posthuman* (Polity, 2013); *Posthuman Knowledge* (Polity, 2019); and, with Maria Hlavajova, *Posthuman Glossary* (Bloomsbury, 2018).
59 Braidotti, *The Posthuman*, p. 65.
60 See Cunliffe, *Cosmopolitan Dystopia*.
61 Braidotti and Hlavajova, *Posthuman Glossary*.
62 E. M. Forster, *Howards End* (1910), ch. 22.
63 José van Dijck, *The Culture of Connectivity: A Critical History of Social Media* (Oxford University Press, 2013).
64 There are many precedents for thinking about connectedness. The early work of Carol Gilligan was very influential – e.g., 'Hearing the Difference: Theorizing Connection', *Hypatia*, 10/2 (1995): 120–7; but see also Gurminder K. Bhambra, *Connected Sociologies* (Bloomsbury, 2014), and, on relationality, Nick Crossley, *Toward Relational Sociology* (Routledge, 2011).
65 C. Wright Mills, *The Sociological Imagination* (Oxford University Press, 1959).
66 A wonderful book for children used in primary schools asks us to '*imagine if the world were a village*' – children often learn the shape of the world through tales of comparative size. See David J. Smith and Shelagh Armstrong, *If the World Were a Village: A Book about the World's People*, 2nd edn (Bloomsbury, 2011).
67 Richard Sennett has written an elegant account of the importance of this process in *Together: The Rituals, Pleasures and Politics of Cooperation* (Penguin, 2013) – part of his trilogy of works on 'homo faber' and the 'skills people need to sustain everyday life' (p. ix).

Chapter 2: Damaging Humanity

1 John Keegan, *The First World War* (Vintage, 2000), p. 285.
2 Jürgen Habermas, *The Postnational Constellation: Political Essays* (Polity, 2001), p. 45.
3 On dehumanization, see David Livingstone Smith, *Less Than Human: Why We Demean, Enslave, and Exterminate Others* (St Martin's, 2011) and *On Inhumanity: Dehumanization and How to Resist It* (Oxford University Press, 2020).
4 There is already a flood of writing. See Klaus Schwab and Thierry Malleret, *Covid-19: The Great Reset* (World Economic Forum, 2020); Gerard Delanty, ed., *Pandemics, Politics and Society: Critical Perspectives on the Covid Crisis* (De Gruyter, 2021) and J. Michael Ryan, ed., *Covid-19: Volume II: Social Consequences and Cultural Adaptations* (Routledge, 2021).
5 I was inspired to use this term when reading 'Try to Praise the Mutilated World' by Adam Zagajewski, in Joan Murray, ed., *Poems to Live by in Uncertain Times* (Beacon Books, 2001).
6 Italian philosopher Giorgio Agamben gives a sustained and influential discussion of 'bare life' in *Homo Sacer: Sovereign Power and Bare Life* (Stanford University Press, 1998).
7 See World Poverty: https://www.un.org/en/sections/issues-depth/poverty/; Global Report on Food Crisis, 2020: https://www.wfp.org/publications/2020-global-report-food-crises; Water Aid: https://www.wateraid.org/uk/the-crisis/facts-and-statistics; UN Refugee Agency: https://www.unhcr.org/uk/news/press/2020/6/5ee9db2e4/1-cent-humanity-displaced-unhcr-global-trends-report.html.
8 Elizabeth Kolbert, *The Sixth Extinction: An Unnatural History* (Bloomsbury, 2014); Clive Hamilton, *Requiem for a Species: Why We Resist the Truth about Climate Change* (Routledge, 2015).
9 T. N. Khoshoo and John S. Moolakattu, *Mahatma Gandhi and the Environment: Analysing Gandhian Environmental Thought* (TERI Press, 2009), pp. 49, 142.
10 See Global Assessment Report on Biodiversity and Ecosystem Services: https://lp.panda.org/ipbes.
11 David Wallace-Wells, *The Uninhabitable Earth: A Story of the Future* (Allen Lane, 2019), p. 29.
12 See Vandana Shiva, *Earth Democracy: Justice, Sustainability, and Peace* (North Atlantic, 2015). Also see Yifei Li and Judith Shapiro, *China Goes Green: Coercive Environmentalism for a Troubled Planet* (Polity, 2020).
13 See especially Nick Couldry and Ulises A. Mejias *The Costs of Connection: How Data is Colonizing Human Life and Appropriating It for Capitalism* (Stanford University Press, 2019).

14 Shoshana Zuboff, *The Age of Surveillance Capitalism: The Fight for Human Future at the New Frontier of Power* (Profile Books, 2019).

15 Ken Plummer, *Narrative Power: The Struggle for Human Value* (Polity, 2019), p. 99.

16 Marshall Sahlins, *Stone Age Economics* (Routledge, 2017 [1972]), p. 35.

17 See Karl Polanyi, *The Great Transformation: The Political and Economic Origins of Our Time* (Beacon Press, 2001 [1944]).

18 Joan C. Tronto, *Caring Democracy: Markets, Equality, and Justice* (New York University Press, 2013); Michael Sandel, *What Money Can't Buy: The Moral Limits of Markets* (Penguin, 2013); Andrew Sayer, *Why We Can't Afford the Rich* (Policy Press, 2014).

19 Éloi Laurent, *The New Environmental Economics: Sustainability and Justice* (Polity, 2020).

20 The former governor of the Bank of England, Mark Carney, for example suggests the values of solidarity, fairness, responsibility, resilience, sustainability, dynamism and humility. See Mark Carney, *Value(s): Building a Better World for All* (William Collins, 2021). See also a recent work from the director of the London School of Economics, Minouche Shafik: *What We Owe Each Other: A New Social Contract for a Better Society* (Bodley Head, 2021).

21 Kate Raworth, *Doughnut Economics: Seven Ways to Think Like a 21st-Century Economist* (Random House, 2017), p. 10. For a critical overview, see Derek Wall, *Economics After Capitalism: A Guide to the Ruins and a Road to the Future* (Pluto Press, 2015 [2005]). See also Ha-Joon Chang, *23 Things They Don't Tell You About Capitalism* (Penguin, 2011), and *Economics: The User's Guide* (Pelican, 2014); Sandel, *What Money Can't Buy*.

22 Michael Albert, *Realizing Hope: Life Beyond Capitalism* (Zed Books, 2006).

23 Göran Therborn, *The Killing Fields of Inequality* (Polity, 2013), p. 1.

24 See Richard Wilkinson, *The Impact of Inequality: How to Make Sick Societies Healthier* (Routledge, 2005); Richard Wilkinson and Kate Pickett, *The Spirit Level: Why Inequality is Better for Everyone* (Penguin, 2010); Anne Case and Angus Deaton, *Deaths of Despair and the Future of Capitalism* (Princeton University Press, 2020); Branko Milanovic, *The Haves and the Have-Nots* (Basic Books, 2010), and *Global Inequality: A New Approach for the Age of Globalization* (Harvard University Press, 2016). See also *How We Make Poverty?*

New Internationalist, March–April 2020; Göran Therborn, *The World: A Beginner's Guide* (Polity, 2011), pp. 1–4; Amartya Sen, *Inequality Reexamined* (Harvard University Press, 1992), ch. 3, and *The Idea of Justice* (Belknap Press, 2009).

25 Thomas Piketty has written two bestselling blockbusters. The now classic work is his *Capital in the Twenty-First Century* (Harvard University Press, 2014). It is followed by *Capital and Ideology* (Harvard University Press, 2020), which details 'inequality regimes' and ends by discussing a range of futures for a 'participatory socialist' future. See the website attached to his work, The World Inequality Database: https://wid.world/.

26 The 1 per cent/99 per cent divide is now widely known and discussed. The evidence for this comes from many sources, but notably through the work of Piketty (see below) and the annual Oxfam Poverty Reports. Both Forbes and *The Sunday Times* regularly list 'Billionaire' and rich lists. 'We are the 99%' was first used as a slogan by the Occupy movement at Wall Street in September 2011. See Danny Dorling, *Inequality and the 1%*, 3rd edn (Verso, 2019), and Cinzia Arruzza, Tithi Bhattacharya and Nancy Fraser, *Feminism for the 99%: A Manifesto* (Verso, 2019).

27 See Oxfam International policy paper, *Time to Care*, 2020: https://www.oxfam.org/en/research/time-care.

28 For 'facing borders', see the important discussion by Nira Yuval-Davis, Georgie Wemyss and Kathryn Cassidy in *Bordering* (Polity, 2019).

29 See Elizabeth Abbott, *Haiti: A Shattered Nation* (Overlook Duckworth, 2011); Simon Behrman and Avidan Kent, *Climate Refugees: Beyond the Legal Impasse?* (Routledge, 2018). Visually, this is well illustrated in Spike Lee's documentary film about the devastation in New Orleans caused by Hurricane Katrina, *When the Levees Broke: A Requiem in Four Acts* (2006). See also the *Annual Disaster Statistical Review 2016*, produced by the Centre for Research on the Epidemiology of Disasters (CRED), which has been active for more than forty years in the fields of international disaster and conflict health studies: https://www.emdat.be/sites/default/files/adsr_2016.pdf

30 'US Prisons: Outrageously Unjust', *The Globalist*, 9 September 2020: https://www.theglobalist.com/united-states-prison-system-criminal-justice-reform-racism-blacks-minorities/.

31 Saskia Sassen, *Expulsions: Brutality and Complexity in the Global Economy* (Harvard University Press, 2014).

32 Broadly, we are entering the world of locational knowledge and the pluriverse. A broad theoretical frame for this can be derived from Lorraine Code, *Ecological Thinking: The Politics of Epistemic Location* (Oxford University Press, 2006). And Miranda Fricker,

Epistemic Injustice: Power and the Ethics of Knowing (Oxford University Press, 2007). The following books provide a good starting point for thinking about the necessity, importance and meaning of truth: Steve Fuller's *Post Truth: Knowledge as a Power Game* (Anthem, 2018) examines different stances taken; the nature of the post-truth debate is established in Lee McIntyre's *Post-Truth* (MIT Press, 2018) and more polemically in Michiko Kakutani *The Death of Truth* (William Collins, 2018). Three books discuss the nature of truth: Julian Baggini's *A Short History of Truth: Consolations for a Post-Truth World* (Quercus, 2017) is a short and direct account of ten kinds of truth from eternal truths to moral truths; Simon Blackburn provides *Truth: A Guide for the Perplexed* (Penguin, 2006); and John D. Caputo, *Truth: The Search for Wisdom in the Postmodern Age* (Penguin, 2013) soars into a truth for the future. See also Linsey McGoey, *Unknowers: How Strategic Ignorance Rules the World* (Zed Books, 2019).
33 Gil Eyal, *The Crisis of Expertise* (Polity, 2019).
34 Steven Pinker, *The Better Angels of Our Nature: The Decline of Violence in History and Its Causes* (Allen Lane, 2011).
35 See Brad Evans and Henry A. Giroux, *Disposable Futures: The Seduction of Violence in the Age of Spectacle* (City Lights, 2015); Peter Iadicola and Anson Shupe, *Violence, Inequality and Freedom*, 3rd edn (Rowman & Littlefield, 2012); Larry Ray, *Violence and Society*, 2nd edn (Sage, 2018).
36 *See Global Peace Index 2020: Measuring Peace in a Complex World*: http://visionofhumanity.org/app/uploads/2020/06/GPI_2020_web.pdf.
37 Jonahan Holslag, *A Political History of the World: Three Thousand Years of War and Peace* (Pelican, 2018).
38 https://fragilestatesindex.org/.
39 A useful account, even if a little out of date, is Lothar Brock, Hans-Henrik Holm, Georg Sorensen and Michael Stohl, *Fragile States: Violence and the Failure of Intervention* (Polity, 2012).
40 See Anne Applebaum, *Twilight of Democracy: The Failure of Politics and the Power of Friends* (Allen Lane, 2020); Berch Berberoglu, ed., *The Global Rise of Authoritarianism in the 21st Century: Crisis of Neoliberal Globalization and the Nationalist Response* (Routledge, 2020); and Roman Kuhar and David Paternotte, eds, *Anti-Gender Campaigns in Europe: Mobilizing Against Inequality* (Rowman & Littlefield, 2017). See also Jan-Werner Muller, *What Is Populism?* (University of Pennsylvania Press, 2016).
41 https://www.eiu.com/n/campaigns/democracy-index-2020/.
42 See Joshua M. Roose, *The New Demagogues: Religion, Masculinity and the Populist Epoch* (Routledge, 2020).

43 See David Runciman, *How Democracy Ends* (Profile Books, 2018). See also Economist Intelligence Unit, *Democracy Index 2020: In Sickness and in Health?* (EIU, 2020), and Pew Research Center, 'Many Across the Globe are Dissatisfied With How Democracy is Working': https://www.pewresearch.org/global/2019/04/29/many-across-the-globe-are-dissatisfied-with-how-democracy-is-working/.

44 Richard Falk, *On Humane Governance: Toward a New Global Politics* (Polity, 1995).

45 See Nick Srnicek, *Platform Capitalism* (Polity, 2016); Christian Fuchs, *Digital Demagogue: Authoritarian Capitalism in the Age of Trump and Twitter* (Pluto Press, 2018); Martin Moore, *Democracy Hacked: Political Turmoil and Information Warfare in the Digital Age* (Oneworld Publications, 2018). For a more positive view, see Jaimie Susskind, *Future Politics: Living Together in a World Transformed by Tech* (Oxford University Press, 2020).

46 See https://www.washingtonpost.com/politics/2020/07/13/president-trump-has-made-more-than-20000-false-or-misleading-claims/.

47 See Transparency International: https://www.transparency.org/en/. See also Leslie Holmes, *Corruption: A Very Short Introduction* (Oxford University Press, 2015). A whole underworld is described by David C. Korten in *When Corporations Rule the World*, 3rd edn (EDS Publications, 2015 [1995]). See also Guy Standing, *The Corruption of Capitalism: Why Rentiers Thrive and Work Does Not Pay* (Biteback Publishers, 2016).

48 For a good discussion of all this, see Nikolas Rose, *Our Psychiatric Future: The Politics of Mental Health* (Polity, 2019).

49 See Alexander Cooley and Jack Snyder, eds, *Ranking the World: Grading States as a Tool of Governance* (Cambridge University Press, 2015)

Chapter 3: Dividing Humanity

1 Louis MacNeice, 'Snow', in *Collected Poems* (Faber & Faber, 2007), p. 24.

2 Hannah Arendt, *The Human Condition*, 2nd edn (University of Chicago Press, 1998 [1958]), p. 8. For me, Arendt is a key thinker in this area; she can be very difficult to understand because she writes outside and against traditional thinking. A useful guide is Patrick Hayden, *Hannah Arendt: Key Concepts* (Routledge, 2014) and Margarethe von Trotta's 2012 film, *Hannah Arendt*, is wonderfully provocative. See also Richard J. Bernstein's sympathetically critical *Why Read Hannah Arendt Now?* (Polity, 2018).

3 This famous distinction is well presented in Julian Baggini, *How the World Thinks: A Global History of Philosophy* (Granta Books, 2018), Part Three.

4 Cited in Ryszard Kapuściński, *The Other* (Verso, 2008), p. 5. See also Emmanuel Levinas, *Humanism of the Other* (University of Illinois, 2006). See the discussion on multiple meanings of the self by Owen Flanagan in *The Geography of Morals: Varieties of Moral Possibility* (Oxford University Press, 2016), pp. 228 et seq.

5 A cautionary note is needed here. Historian David Cannadine's *The Undivided Past: History Beyond Our Differences* (Penguin, 2014) suggests that history is often driven by a limiting desire to dramatize and exaggerate differences, when in fact cooperation is one of the major features of being human: 'The History of humankind is at least as much about cooperation as it is about conflict, and about kindness to strangers as about the obsession with otherness and alterity' (p. 264). We must see 'beyond our differences'.

6 See Frans de Waal, *The Bonobo and the Atheist: In Search of Humanism Among the Primates* (Norton, 2014), and *The Age of Empathy: Nature's Lessons for a Kinder Society* (Souvenir Press, 2019).

7 Fonna Forman-Barzilai, *Adam Smith and the Circles of Sympathy: Cosmopolitanism and Moral Theory* (Cambridge University Press, 2010), p. 121.

8 Originally, I drafted a chapter on 'Becoming Human' that was framed by the work of Erik Erikson, one of the key analytic thinkers of the twentieth century. He managed to present psychodynamic theory in both a full lifecycle framework and a full historical cultural context: a major achievement. Although there are many problems with Erikson's work, he had the vision to see how this much wider approach to human world development could be done. See Robert Coles, ed., *The Erik Erikson Reader* (Norton, 2000). See also Robert Kegan, *The Evolving Self: Problem and Process in Human Development* (Harvard University Press, 1982), and, more popularly, Thomas Armstrong, *The Human Odyssey: Navigating the Twelve Stages of Life* (Ixia Press, 2019).

9 See particularly David Reich, *Who We Are and How We Got Here: Ancient DNA and the New Science of the Human Past* (Oxford University Press, 2018); Adam Rutherford, *A Brief History of Everyone Who Lived: The Stories in Our Genes* (Weidenfeld and Nicolson, 2017).

10 A very readable account of diverse life forms is described in Colin Tudge, *The Variety of Life: A Survey and a Celebration*

of All the Creatures that Have Ever Lived (Oxford University Press, 2002).

11 Much that I have read in my life has been overwhelmingly and severely limited by the fact it was written in English and came from the Western intellectual tradition. To take one example: Western philosophy. Important as this is, when placed in a world historical context on its own, it immediately becomes a very limited intellectual tradition. There are obviously many great thinkers here. But equally obvious are the limits of such a small group of people (nearly all white Western males). It regularly tries to pass as the only way of thinking seriously, when most of humanity has never ever thought like this. It is riddled with its own myopia. Things are changing: see, for example, Randall Collins's magnificent volume, *The Sociology of Philosophies: A Global Theory of Intellectual Change* (Harvard University Press, 2000). See also Raewyn Connell, *Southern Theory: The Global Dynamics of Knowledge in Social Science* (Polity, 2007); Boaventura de Sousa Santos, *The End of the Cognitive Empire: The Coming of Age of Epistemologies of the South* (Duke University Press, 2018).

12 See Ethnologue: https://www.ethnologue.com/guides/how-many-languages.

13 See: https://en.wikipedia.org/wiki/List_of_indigenous_peoples. For general mappings, see United Nations, Department of Economic and Social Affairs: Indigenous Peoples, *UN Declaration on the Rights of Indigenous Peoples*, 2007: https://www.un.org/development/desa/indigenouspeoples/declaration-on-the-rights-of-indigenous-peoples.html.

14 See Jan Nederveen Pieterse, *Globalization and Culture: Global Mélange*, 4th edn (Rowman & Littlefield, 2019), and Nestor Garcia Canclini, *Hybrid Cultures: Strategies for Entering and Leaving Modernity*, trans. Silvia L. Lopez (University of Minnesota Press, 1995).

15 David Livingstone Smith includes valuable discussions of dehumanization in two of his works: *Less Than Human: Why We Demean, Enslave and Exterminate Others* (St Martins, 2011) and *On Inhumanity: Dehumanization and How to Resist It* (Oxford University Press, 2020).

16 Toni Morrison, *The Origin of Others* (Harvard University Press, 2017), p. 15.

17 Achille Mbembe, 'Necropolitics', *Public Culture*, 15/1 (2003): 11–40; *Necropolitics*, trans. Steven Corcoran (Duke University Press, 2019). This is often linked with Judith Butler's idea of a 'grievable life'; see her *Precarious Life: The Power of Mourning and Violence* (Verso, 2006), pp. 20–35.

18 Catharine A. MacKinnon, *Are Women Human?* (Harvard University Press, 2007), p. 43.

19 ILGA has been publishing its annual *State-Sponsored Homophobia Report* since 2006. See: https://ilga.org/state-sponsored-homophobia-report.

20 Umberto Eco, *Inventing the Enemy* (Vintage, 2013), p. 2.

21 There is an influential school of thought linked with the French historian René Girard that links scapegoating to mimetic desire and rivalry.

22 On all this, see Kwame Anthony Appiah, *The Lies that Bind: Rethinking Identity* (Liveright, 2018); Mary Douglas, *Purity and Danger: An Analysis of Concepts of Pollution and Taboo* (Routledge, 2002 [1966]); Émile Durkheim, *The Rules of Sociological Method*, ed. Steven Lukes, trans. W. E. Halls (Free Press, 1982 [1895]); Emmanuel Levinas (1969) *Totality and Infinity: An Essay on Exteriority*, trans. Alphonso Lingis (Duquesne University Press, 1969); Morrison, *The Origins of Others*.

23 Pankaj Mishra, *Age of Anger: A History of the Present* (Macmillan, 2017).

24 Norman N. Naimark, *Fires of Hatred: Ethnic Cleansing in Twentieth-Century Europe* (Harvard University Press, 2002).

25 Ideas of shame (and guilt), honour and dignity, disgust, anger, resentment, forgiveness and scapegoating weave a deep nexus of emotions, and are often linked to culture and gender. This is discussed by, variously, Kierkegaard, Scheler, Dostoevsky, Nietzsche. See, as illustrative, Martha C. Nussbaum's *Hiding from Humanity: Disgust, Shame and the Law* (Princeton University Press, 2004) and *Anger and Forgiveness: Resentment, Generosity, Justice* (Oxford University Press, 2016).

26 I draw here from Ken Plummer, '"Whose Side Are We On?" Revisited: Narrative Power, Narrative Inequality, and a Politics of Narrative Humanity', *Symbolic Interaction*, 43/1 (2020): 46–71.

27 Paulo Freire, *Pedagogy of the Oppressed* (Penguin, 2017 [1968]); Frantz Fanon, *The Wretched of the Earth* (Penguin, 2001 [1961]).

28 Nancy Hartsock, *The Feminist Standpoint Revisited, and Other Essays* (Westview Press, 1998); Gayatri Chakravorty Spivak, 'Can the Subaltern Speak?' in Cary Nelson and Lawrence C. Grossberg, eds, *Marxism and the Interpretation of Culture* (University of Illinois Press, 1988), pp. 271–313; José Medina, *The Epistemology of Resistance: Gender and Racial Oppression, Epistemic Injustice, and Resistant Imaginations* (Oxford University Press, 2013); Michelle R. Nario-Redmond,

Ableism: The Causes and Consequences of Disability Prejudice
(Wiley-Blackwell, 2019).

29 From Richard Rorty, 'The Moral Purpose of the University: An
Exchange', *The Hedgehog Review*, 2/3 (2000): 106–19; cited
also in Marcus Morgan, *Pragmatic Humanism: On the Nature
and Value of Sociological Knowledge* (Routledge, 2016), p. 118.

30 See the bestselling book by Peter Frankopan, *The Silk Roads:
A New History of the World* (Bloomsbury, 2015); and Maria
Rosa Menocal, *The Ornament of the World: How Muslims,
Jews and Christians Created a Culture of Tolerance in Medieval
Spain* (Little, Brown, 2003).

31 See Siep Stuurman, *The Invention of Humanity: Equality and
Cultural Difference in World History* (Harvard University Press,
2017), pp. 1–2.

32 Stuurman, *The Invention of Humanity*, p. 12.

33 See also Charles King, *The Reinvention of Humanity: How
a Circle of Renegade Anthropologists Remade Race, Sex and
Gender* (Bodley Head, 2019).

34 Martha C. Nussbaum, *Frontiers of Justice: Disability,
Nationality, Species Membership* (Harvard University Press,
2007), p. 324.

35 Mikhail Bakhtin, *Problems of Dostoevsky's Poetics* (University
of Minnesota Press, 1984), p. 293. The works of many sociologists, theologians and philosophers feed into this debate: Hannah
Arendt, Mikhail Bakhtin, Ernest Becker, Seyla Benhabib, David
Bohm, Martin Buber, Kenneth Burke, Arthur Frank, Paulo
Freire, Erich Fromm, Hans-Georg Gadamer, Jürgen Habermas,
George Herbert Mead, Paul Ricœur, Roberto Mangabeira Unger
and Nira Yuval-Davis can all help us to build a deeper under-
standing of this dialogue. Michael Sandel takes his dialogue
on justice around the world, notably to China: see Michael
J. Sandel and Paul J. d'Ambrosio, eds, *Encountering China:
Michael Sandel and Chinese Philosophy* (Harvard University
Press, 2018).

36 I discuss this process more fully in Plummer, *Intimate
Citizenship: Private Decisions and Public Dialogues* (University
of Washington Press, 2003), ch. 6.

37 I discuss empathy in a number of places. In particular see
Plummer, *Cosmopolitan Sexualities: Hope and the Humanist
Imagination* (Polity, 2015), pp. 156–61.

38 See Karen Armstrong, *Twelve Steps to a Compassionate Life*
(Bodley Head, 2011), p. 6. See also https://charterforcompassion.
org/12-steps-compassion-booklet.

39 See the journal *Othering and Belonging*: otheringandbelonging.
org.

40 See Martha C. Nussbaum, *The Cosmopolitan Tradition: A Noble but Flawed Ideal* (Belknap Press, 2019).
41 See Kwame Anthony Appiah, *Cosmopolitanism: Ethics in a World of Strangers* (Allen Lane, 2006), p. xv; Ulrich Beck *Cosmopolitan Vision* (Polity, 2006), p. 7.
42 Donald E. Brown, *Human Universals* (McGraw-Hill, 1991).
43 Edward O. Wilson, *The Origins of Creativity* (Liveright, 2017), p. 1; John Hands, *Cosmo Sapiens: Human Evolution from the Origin of the Universe* (Duckworth Overlook, 2015), p. 539.
44 Almost every thinker in this area will make some claims about essential attributes. His Holiness the Dalai Lama, for example, also has a view: our common humanity is bound up with one another as a shared suffering and search for happiness: things we all share equally. There is for him and many others a 'fundamental equality of humanity'; see his *Beyond Religion: Ethics for a Whole World* (Houghton Mifflin Harcourt, 2011), ch. 2. There is no shortage of items to include. I mention just a few in the text.

Chapter 4: Traumatizing Humanity

1 Todorov has written some forty books, and is seen as 'one of France's most important and respected intellectuals of the past fifty years': see Karine Zbinder, ed., *Tzvetan Todorov: Thinker and Humanist* (Camden House, 2020).
2 On radical evil, see Richard Bernstein, *Radical Evil: A Philosophical Investigation* (Polity, 2002); see also his *The Abuse of Evil: The Corruption of Politics and Religion since 9/11* (Polity, 2005), where he writes: 'Radical evil is making human beings superfluous as human beings', p. 5. This concept is derived from Kant, examined by Arendt and established in Bernstein. The concept of Evil invites us to think and reflect.
3 These terms are derived from the work of Darell J. Fasching; see his *The Ethical Challenge of Auschwitz and Hiroshima: Apocalypse or Utopia?* (State University of New York Press, 1993), and *Comparative Religious Ethics: A Narrative Approach to Global Ethics*, 2nd edn (Wiley-Blackwell, 2011), esp. ch. 2.
4 John K. Roth, *The Failure of Ethics: Confronting the Holocaust, Genocide and Other Mass Atrocities* (Oxford, 2015), pp. 23, 137, 3 italics in original.
5 Elie Wiesel, *Night*, trans. Marion Wiesel (Penguin, 2006), p. xv. This book has a long publishing and translation history, described in the Preface of the 2006 Penguin Classics edition. It was originally published in French, in 1958.

6 Viktor E. Frankl, *Man's Search for Meaning: The Classic Tribute to Hope from the Holocaust* (Rider, 2004 [1959]), pp. 82–3, 85.
7 See Joseph Farrell, *Primo Levi: The Austere Humanist* (Peter Lang, 2004).
8 See Ann Goldstein, ed., *The Complete Works of Primo Levi*, 3 vols (Liveright, 2015).
9 Jeffrey C. Alexander, *Trauma: A Social Theory* (Polity, 2012), ch. 2.
10 Stephen Hopgood, *The Endtimes of Human Rights* (Cornell University Press, 2013), p. 61.
11 See Paul Preston, *The Spanish Holocaust: Inquisition and Extermination in Twentieth-Century Spain* (Norton, 2012); Bohdan Klid and Alexander J. Motyl, eds, *The Holodomor Reader: A Sourcebook on the Famine of 1932–33 in Ukraine* (University of Alberta Press, 2012); Iris Chang, *The Rape of Nanjing: The Forgotten Holocaust of World War II* (Basic Books, 1998).
12 Jean Franco, *Cruel Modernity* (Duke University Press, 2013). See also Oscar Martinez, *A History of Violence: Living and Dying in Central America* (Verso, 2016). Femicide has become a major problem; see: https://www.cepal.org/en/pressreleases/eclac-least-2795-women-were-victims-femicide-23-countries-latin-america-and-caribbean.
13 Robert Muggah and Katherione Aguirre Tobón, *Citizen Security in Latin America*, Igarapé Institute Strategic Paper, April 2018: https://igarape.org.br/wp-content/uploads/2018/04/Citizen-Security-in-Latin-America-Facts-and-Figures.pdf.
14 See Mathew White, *Atrocitology: Humanity's 100 Deadliest Achievements* (Canongate, 2012).
15 See Adam Hochschild, *Bury the Chains: The British Struggle to Abolish Slavery* (Pan, 2012), p. 2.
16 'Cultural trauma occurs when members of a collectivity feel they have been subjected to a horrendous event that leaves indelible marks upon their group consciousness, marking their memories forever and changing their future identity in fundamental and irrevocable ways': Alexander, *Trauma*, p. 6. The term is applied and extended in many works: notably Jeffrey C. Alexander, Ron Eyerman, Bernhard Giesen, Neil J. Smelser and Piotr Sztompka, *Cultural Trauma and Collective Identity* (University of California Press, 2004); Ron Eyerman, *Cultural Trauma: Slavery and the Formation of African American Identity* (Cambridge University Press, 2001), and *Is this America? Katrina as Cultural Trauma* (University of Texas Press, 2015); Ron Eyerman and Giuseppe Sciortino, eds,

The Cultural Trauma of Decolonization: Colonial Returnees
in the National Imagination (Palgrave Macmillan, 2019); Ron
Eyerman, Jeffrey C. Alexander and Elizabeth Butler Breese,
Narrating Trauma: On the Impact of Collective Suffering
(Paradigm Publishers, 2001).

17 'Violent ignorance is a name for the action of turning away
from painful knowledge and for the further violence this can
bring': Hannah Jones, *Violent Ignorance: Confronting Racism
and Migration Control* (Zed Books, 2021), p. ix.

18 Thomas Pakenham, *The Scramble for Africa* (Abacus, 1992).

19 Lorraine V. Aragon, 'Uncovering the Trauma of Indonesia's
Cold War Killing Fields' (Review of Lemelson's documentary
film, *40 Years of Silence: An Indonesian Tragedy*), *Current
Anthropology*, 55/4 (August 2014): 493–94. See also Joshua
Oppenheimer's documentary film *The Act of Killing* (2012),
which is an eye-opener on these events.

20 An estimated 36 million Chinese men, women and children
starved to death during China's Great Leap Forward in the
late 1950s and early 1960s. See Yang Jisheng, *Tombstone: The
Great Chinese Famine 1958–62* (Farrar-Strauss, 2013). See also
Frank Diketter, *The Cultural Revolution: A People's History*
(Bloomsbury, 2017).

21 See Ibram X. Kendi, *Stamped from the Beginning: The Definitive
History of Racist Ideas in America* (Bodley Head, 2016); see
also his *How to Be an Antiracist* (Bodley Head, 2019).

22 Christopher Lebron, *The Making of Black Lives Matter: A Brief
History of an Idea* (Oxford University Press, 2017).

23 On colonization, see Robert Gildea, *Empires of the Mind:
The Colonial Past and the Politics of the Present* (Cambridge
University Press, 2019); Sathnam Sanghera, *Empireland: How
Imperialism Has Shaped Modern Britain* (Viking, 2021); Shashi
Tharoor, *Inglorious Empire: What the British Did to India*
(Hurst, 2017); David Olusoga, *Black and British: A Forgotten
History* (Pan, 2017); Philip Dwyer and Amanda Nettelbeck,
eds, *Violence, Colonialism and Empire in the Modern World*
(Palgrave Macmillan, 2017). All of which needs contrasting
with Nial Ferguson's *Empire: How Britain Made the Modern
World* (Penguin, 2018).

24 Carlos Gigoux and Colin Samson, *Indigenous Peoples and
Colonialism: Global Perspectives* (Polity, 2016).

25 See Dwyer and Nettlebeck, eds, *Violence, Colonialism and
Empire in the Modern World*.

26 See, for example, Beverly Allen, *Rape Warfare: The Hidden
Genocide in Bosnia-Herzegovina and Croatia* (University of
Minnesota Press, 1996); Sara Sharratt, *Gender, Shame and*

Sexual Violence: The Voices of Witnesses and Court Members at War Crimes Tribunals (Ashgate, 2011); Janie L. Leatherman, *Sexual Violence and Armed Conflict* (Polity, 2011).

27 See UN Women: https://www.unwomen.org/en/what-we-do/ending-violence-against-women/facts-and-figures. and, more recently: https://www.who.int/news/item/09-03-2021-devastatingly-pervasive-1-in-3-women-globally-experience-violence.

28 See Genocide Watch: https://www.genocidewatch.com/countries-at-risk

29 See Walk Free: https://www.walkfree.org/. Anti-Slavery International estimates range from 21 million to 46 million people. See also International Centre for Transitional Justice: https://www.ictj.org/sites/default/files/ICTJ-Global-Transitional-Justice-2009-English.pdf.

30 See 'Violence against Women and Girls: The Shadow Pandemic', UN Women, 6 April 2020: https://www.unwomen.org/en/news/stories/2020/4/statement-ed-phumzile-violence-against-women-during-pandemic.

31 For an extremely valuable account of the kinds of issues this raises, see Michael Newman, *Transitional Justice: Contending with the Past* (Polity, 2019). Transitional justice looks at the mechanisms through which societies overcome traumatic pasts, often after civil wars or brutal dictatorships. See also https://www.ictj.org/about.

32 Desmond and Mpho Tutu, *The Book of Forgiving: The Fourfold Path for Healing Ourselves and Our World* (HarperCollins, 2014).

33 See Howard Zehr, with Ali Gohar, *The Little Book of Restorative Justice*: https://www.unicef.org/tdad/littlebookrjpakaf.pdf.

34 The classic overview work on truth commissions is Priscilla B. Hayner, *Unspeakable Truths: Facing Challenge of Truth Commissions* (Routledge, 2010), which looks at many commissions and gives a focus to sixteen of them, including in Argentina, Chile, El Salvador, South Africa and Guatemala. See also Onure Bakiner, *Truth Commissions: Memory, Power, and Legitimacy* (University of Pennsylvania Press, 2016). For a list of such commissions, see Wikipedia: https://en.wikipedia.org/wiki/List_of_truth_and_reconciliation_commissions.

35 Viet Thanh Nguyen. *Nothing Ever Dies: Vietnam and the Memory of War* (Harvard University Press, 2016), p. 4.

36 See Susan Neiman, *Learning from the Germans: Confronting Race and the Memory of Evil* (Allen Lane, 2019).

37 For an account of this, see Hannibal Travis, *Genocide, Ethnonationalism and the United Nations: Exploring the Causes of Mass Killing since 1945* (Routledge, 2013).

38 Catherin Lu, *Justice and Reconciliation in World Politics* (Cambridge University Press, 2017), p. 19.

Part III: Humanizing the World: Flourishing Humanity

1 Alasdair MacIntyre, *After Virtue* (2014), p. 250.

Chapter 5: Narrating Humanity

1 Ken Plummer, *Narrative Power: The Struggle for Human Value* (Polity, 2019), p. 23.
2 Rens Bod, *A New History of the Humanities: The Search for Principles and Patterns from Antiquity to the Present* (Oxford, 2013), p. 1.
3 For discussions of this, see Jean Clottes, *What Is Paleolithic Art? Cave Paintings and the Dawn of Human Creativity*, trans. Oliver Y. Martin and Robert D. Martin (University of Chicago Press, 2016), and David Lewis-Williams, *The Mind in the Cave: Consciousness and the Origins of Art* (Thames & Hudson, 2004).
4 There have been many classifications of stories; see, for example, Langdon Elbsbree, *Rituals of Life: Patterns in Narratives* (Kennikat Press, 1982).
5 On this attentive role in the evolution of stories, see Brian Boyd, *On the Origin of Stories: Evolution, Cognition, and Fiction* (Harvard University Press, 2009).
6 See Stanford Humanities Centre: https://shc.stanford.edu/what-are-the-humanities.
7 Mikhail Epstein, *The Transformative Humanities: A Manifesto* (Bloomsbury, 2012), p. 7 (my italics).
8 See the The Scholar's Page website for a shock about how ignorant you may well be. I was! https://scholars-stage.blogspot.com/2019/10/a-non-western-canon-what-would-list-of.html.
9 Plummer, *Narrative Power*, p. 80.
10 For a fuller discussion, see Plummer, *Narrative Power*, ch. 5.
11 Rachel Carson, *The Sea Around Us* (1951), cited in Simon L. Lewis and Mark A. Maslin, *The Human Planet: How We Created the Anthropocene* (Penguin Books, 2018), p. 44. This is a very useful book on the history of the planet.
12 See David A. Leeming, *Creation Myths of the World: An Encyclopedia*, 2nd edn (ABC-CLIO, 2010). Today, Christians in the USA have their own creation museum: The Museum of the Bible. See Susan L. Trollinger and William Vance Trollinger,

234 Notes to pp. 110–14

Jr., *Righting America at the Creation Museum* (John Hopkins University Press, 2016).

13 David Christian's most popular book is *Origin Story: A Big History of Everything* (Penguin, 2018). Christian co-founded, with Bill Gates, the Big History Project, a linked scholarly organization.

14 Sources include Christian *Origin Story*; John Hands, *Cosmo Sapiens: Human Evolution from the Origin of the Universe* (Duckworth Overlook, 2015); Alexander Harcourt, *Humankind: How Biology and Geography Shape Human Diversity* (Pegasus, 2015); Alice Roberts, *The Incredible Human Journey: The Story of How We Colonised the Planet* (Bloomsbury, 2010); Lewis and Maslin, *The Human Planet*; Yuval Noah Harari, *Sapiens: A Brief History of Humankind* (Vintage, 2011); Steven Mithen, *The Prehistory of the Mind: A Search for the Origins of Art, Religion and Science* (Thames & Hudson, 1996), and *After the Ice: A Global Human History, 20,000–5000 BC* (Weidenfeld & Nicholson, 2003).

15 On Neanderthals, see Rebecca Wragg Sykes, *Kindred: Neanderthal Life, Love, Death and Art* (Bloomsbury, 2020).

16 See Peter Burke, *Cultural Hybridity* (Polity, 2009); Nestor Garcia Canclini, *Hybrid Cultures: Strategies for Entering and Leaving Modernity*, trans. Silvia L. Lopez (University of Minnesota Press, 1995).

17 Bod, *A New History of the Humanities*.

18 See Karl Jaspers, *Way to Wisdom: An Introduction to Philosophy*, 2nd edn (Yale University Press, 2003 [1951]), p. 100. For a valuable discussion, see also Robert N. Bellah and Hans Joas, eds, *The Axial Age and Its Consequences* (Harvard University Press, 2012).

19 See, in particular, the very different account given by the Brazilian philosopher Roberto Mangabeira Unger, *The Religion of the Future* (Harvard University Press, 2014).

20 On power, religion and the meta narrative, see James W. Laine, *Meta-Religion: Religion and Power in World History* (University of California Press, 2014).

21 Robert N. Bellah, *Religion in Human Evolution: From the Paleolithic to the Axial Age* (Belknap, 2013), p. 269.

22 See Darrell J. Fasching, Dell deChant and David M. Lantigua, *Comparative Religious Ethics: A Narrative Approach to Global Ethics*, 2nd edn (Wiley-Blackwell, 2011). Although marketed as a textbook, this is a stimulating work that I have found to be very valuable, linking religion to narrative as it does.

23 Shmuel N. Eisenstadt, ed., *Multiple Modernities* (Routledge, 2017).

24 Sociologist Kent Augustson has argued that these major civiliza-
    tions over the past nine hundred years are vital: 'Accounting for
    up to 85 percent of the world's population, to know their story,
    even in relief, is to know the world.' See *Our Axial Age: Putting
    Our World in Perspective* (CreateSpace, 2016), p. xiii.
25 For a general account, see Ken S. Coates, *A Global History of
    Indigenous Peoples: Struggle and Survival* (Palgrave Macmillan,
    2004). For a more focused account, see Elizabeth Marshall-
    Thomas, *The Old Way: A Story of the First People* (St Martin's
    Press, 2007). James C. Scott's *Against the Grain: A Deep
    History of the Earliest States* (Yale University Press, 2017)
    provides a new account of our past.
26 Vaclav Smil, *Transforming the Twentieth Century: Technical
    Innovations and Their Consequences* (Oxford University Press,
    2006).
27 UN Department of Economic and Social Affairs, Population
    Division (2018), *The World's Cities in 2018*: https://www.un.org/
    en/events/citiesday/assets/pdf/the_worlds_cities_in_2018_data_
    booklet.pdf.
28 And leading to a change in feeling: see Paul Gilroy, *Postcolonial
    Melancholia* (Columbia University Press, 2008) on the aftermath
    of colonization and slavery.
29 See, for examples, Peter N. Stearns, *World History: The Basics*
    (Routledge, 2010); Tim Marshall, *Prisoners of Geography:
    Ten Maps that Tell You Everything You Need to Know about
    Global Politics* (Elliott and Thompson, 2016); Neil MacGregor,
    A History of the World in 100 Objects (Penguin, 2012); John
    Burrow, *A History of Histories: Epics, Chronicles, Romances
    and Inquiries from Herodotus and Thucydides to the Twentieth
    Century* (Penguin, 2009).
30 These ideas are derived in part from Andrew Chadwick, *The
    Hybrid Media System: Politics and Power*, 2nd edn (Oxford
    University Press, 2017); and Nick Couldry and Andreas Hepp,
    The Mediated Construction of Reality (Polity, 2017).
31 Klaus Schwab's *Shaping the Future of the Fourth Industrial
    Revolution: A Guide to Building a Better World* (Penguin,
    2018) is very much a business handbook for dealing with the
    fourth revolution. It is very uncritical.
32 See Shoshana Zuboff, *The Age of Surveillance Capitalism:
    The Fight for Human Future at the New Frontier of Power*
    (Profile Books, 2019), pp. 11–12. For a major discussion of the
    colonizing of human life though digitalism, see Nick Couldry
    and Ulises A. Mejias, *The Costs of Connection: How Data is
    Colonizing Human Life and Appropriating It for Capitalism*
    (Stanford University Press, 2019).

33 See Yuval Noah Harari, *Homo Deus: A Brief History of Tomorrow* (Vintage Books, 2015).

34 See J. Baird Callicott, *Thinking Like a Planet: The Land Ethic and the Earth Ethic* (Oxford University Press, 2014). This is an extensive philosophical treatise about our duties and responsibilities to the earth. Others have used the term more metaphorically, as I do here.

35 Ella Myers introduces these ideas in *Worldly Ethics: Democratic Politics and Care for the World* (Duke University Press, 2013).

36 Michael Barnett, *Empire of Humanity: A History of Humanitarianism* (Cornell University Press, 2011), and Thomas Davies, *NGOs: A New History of Transnational Civil Society* (Hurst, 2013) both trace three phases, starting in the eighteenth century and speeding up in the twentieth.

37 See Bruce Mazlish, *The Idea of Humanity in a Global Era* (Palgrave Macmillan, 2009).

38 See Fredrick Douglass, *My Bondage and My Freedom* (1855): https://www.gutenberg.org/files/202/202-h/202-h.htm; Joel Quirk, *The Anti-Slavery Project: From the Slave Trade to Human Trafficking* (University of Pennsylvania Press, 2014).

39 See Ruth Henig, *The Peace that Never Was: A History of the League of Nations* (Haus Publishing, 2019).

40 Paul Kurtz, *Humanist Manifesto 2000: A Call for New Planetary Humanism* (Prometheus Books, 2000). There is a useful summary of the manifestos in Wikipedia (https://en.wikipedia.org/wiki/Humanist_Manifesto).

41 Lynn Meskell, *A Future in Ruins: UNESCO, World Heritage, and the Dream of Peace* (Oxford University Press, 2018).

42 Seng Tan and Amitav Acharya, eds, *Bandung Revisited: The Legacy of the 1955 Asian-African Conference for International Order* (NUS Press, 2008).

43 On the importance of the idea of Crimes Against Humanity, see Norman Geras, *Crimes Against Humanity: Birth of a Concept* (Manchester University Press, 2011) which provides a critical (Marxist) overview. See also M. Cherif Bassiouni, *Crimes Against Humanity: Historical Evolution and Contemporary Application* (Cambridge University Press, 2014) for a detailed and technical account

44 See Thomas G. Weiss and Rorden Wilkinson, *Rethinking Global Governance* (Polity, 2019). A valuable history of the emergence of global governance can be found in Mark Mazower's *Governing the World: The History of an Idea* (Penguin, 2012). The standard critical commentary is Thomas G. Weiss, *What's Wrong with the United Nations and How to Fix It*, 3rd edn (Polity, 2016).

Chapter 6: Valuing Humanity

1 Important here are Andrew Sayer, *Why Things Matter to People: Social Science, Values and Ethical Life* (Cambridge University Press, 2011); Hans Joas, *The Genesis of Values* (Polity, 2000).

2 Frans de Waal, *The Bonobo and the Atheist: In Search of Humanism Among the Primates* (Norton, 2014); primates show signs of cooperation, empathy and feelings for each other. See also Donna J. Haraway, *The Companion Species Manifesto: Dogs, People, and Significant Otherness*, 2nd edn (University of Chicago Press, 2003).

3 This is the position that is strongly claimed by Christian Smith in *Moral, Believing Animals: Human Personhood and Culture* (Oxford University Press, 2003).

4 Michael Ignatieff, *The Ordinary Virtues: Moral Order in a Divided World* (Harvard University Press, 2017); this was a three-year Carnegie Centennial Project, observing 'ethics in action' in seven cities in six major world settings.

5 Nancy Scheper-Hughes, *Death Without Weeping: The Violence of Everyday Life in Brazil* (University of California Press, 1993). See also the studies in Veena Das, Arthur Kleinman, Margaret Lock, Mamphela Ramphele and Pamela Reynolds, eds, *Remaking a World: Violence, Social Suffering, and Recovery* (University of California Press, 2001) (one of three volumes on this subject); Cheryl Mattingly, *Moral Laboratories: Family Peril and the Struggle for the Good Life* (University of California Press, 2014); George W. Noblit and Van O. Dempsey, *The Social Construction of Virtue: The Moral Life of Schools* (State University of New York Press, 1996). There are also many medical studies that get close to everyday values.

6 This is the hub of John Dewey's account of human experience. See his 'Morality is Social', in John J. McDermott, ed., *The Philosophy of John Dewey* (University of Chicago Press, 1981), pp. 712–22. See also Philip Kitcher, *The Ethical Project* (Harvard University Press, 2011).

7 Ignatieff, *The Ordinary Virtues*, p. 52.

8 Isaiah Berlin quotes Kant in an opening epigraph in *The Crooked Timber of Humanity: Chapters in the History of Ideas* (Pimlico, 2003). I draw on Berlin's idea of pluralism throughout: 'the conception that there are many different ends that men may seek and still be fully rational ... capable of understanding each other and sympathizing and deriving light from each other': p. 11. That said, with hindsight, Berlin's stance was seeped in the narrowness of Western thought.

9 Jonathan Haidt's *The Righteous Mind: Why Good People Are Divided by Politics and Religion* (Penguin, 2012) highlights irrational foundations. Emotions are central to much of Nussbaum's writings: see, for example, her *Upheavals of Thought: The Intelligence of Emotions* (Cambridge University Press, 2001) and *Political Emotions: Why Love Matters for Justice* (Harvard University Press, 2013).

10 For a fascinating account, see Shawn R. Tucker, *The Virtues and Vices in the Arts* (Cascade Books, 2015).

11 Kitcher *The Ethical Project*, p. 2.

12 Values work on many levels. On the links with animals, see the work of Frans de Waal – e.g., *The Age of Empathy: Nature's Lessons for a Kinder Society* (Souvenir Press, 2019)); on steps in moral development, see Michael Tomasello, *A Natural History of Human Morality* (Harvard University Press, 2016); on the evolution of human consciousness, see Daniel C. Dennett, *From Bacteria to Bach and Back: The Evolution of Minds* (Penguin, 2018). Jonathan Haidt provides an integrative psychological approach in *The Righteous Mind*, as does Webb Keane in *Ethical Life: Its Natural and Social Histories* (Princeton University Press, 2015). Sociologist and social theorist Hans Joas traces the historical genealogy of individualism in *The Sacredness of the Person: A New Genealogy of Human Rights* (Georgetown University Press, 2013). For a sweeping view, see Michael Shermer, *The Moral Arc: How Science and Reason Lead Humanity Toward Truth, Justice, and Freedom* (Henry Holt, 2015).

13 See Richard E. Nisbett, *The Geography of Thought: How Asians and Westerners Think Differently – And Why* (Nicholas Brealey, 2005). See also Owen Flanagan, *The Geography of Morals: Varieties of Moral Possibility* (Oxford University Press, 2019); there are some wonderful biographical and bibliographical essays in this book.

14 See Jared Diamond, *The Third Chimpanzee: The Evolution and Future of the Human Animal* (HarperCollins, 1992).

15 I draw here from the very useful account provided by Göran Therborn in *The World: A Beginner's Guide* (Polity, 2011), pp. 7ff.

16 See de Waal, *Age of Empathy*.

17 See Steven Mithen, *The Prehistory of the Mind: A Search for the Origins of Art, Religion and Science* (Thames & Hudson, 1996) and *After the Ice: A Global Human History, 20,000–5000 BC* (Weidenfeld & Nicholson, 2003). See also Daniel C. Dennett, *From Bacteria to Bach and Back: The Evolution of Minds* (Penguin, 2018); Merlin Donald, *Origins of the Modern Mind: Three Stages in the Evolution of Culture and Cognition* (Harvard

University Press, 1991); and Colin Renfrew, *Prehistory: Making of the Human Mind* (Weidenfeld & Nicolson, 2012). My title is a composite of these similar sounding books

18 See, for example, Amy Olberding, *Moral Exemplars in the Analects: The Good Person Is* That (Routledge, 2017).

19 Martin Luther King, 'Why I am Opposed to the War in Vietnam'; speech given on 30 April 1967, at Riverside Church, New York: https://beyondcapitalismnow.wordpress.com/2013/08/08/martin-luther-king-why-i-am-opposed-to-the-war-in-vietnam-april-30-1967-riverside-church-new-york/).

20 Norbert Elias, *The Civilizing Process* (Oxford, 1939); Michel Foucault, *Discipline and Punish: The Birth of the Prison*, trans. Alan Sheridan (Penguin, 1991 [1975]).

21 Neil Postman, *Amusing Ourselves to Death: Public Discourse in the Age of Show Business* (Penguin Books, 1965).

22 See World Economic Forum: https://www.weforum.org/agenda/2019/02/how-should-faith-communities-halt-the-rise-in-religious-violence/.

23 Dalai Lama, *Beyond Religion: Ethics for a Whole World* (Boston, MA: Houghton Mifflin Harcourt, 2011).

24 See Religion for Peace: https://rfp.org/who-we-are/. For further examples, see Anthony Carroll and Richard Norman, eds, *Religion and Atheism: Beyond the Divide* (Routledge, 2017); Sami Zubaida, *Beyond Islam: A New Understanding of the Middle East* (I. B. Tauris, 2010); Stephen Batchelor, *After Buddhism: Rethinking the Dharma for a Secular Age* (Yale University Press, 2016). See also Ulrich Beck, *A God of One's Own: Religion's Capacity for Peace and Potential for Violence* (Polity, 2010).

25 Old French *vital*, from Latin *vitalis* ('of life, life-giving').

26 A good statement on fallibility can be found in Richard J. Bernstein, *The Abuse of Evil: The Corruption of Politics and Religion since 9/11* (Polity, 2005).

27 A significant introduction to the fragility of values can be found in Zygmunt Bauman, *Postmodern Ethics* (Blackwell, 1993). As he says, 'morality' is ambivalent, 'non-rational', and 'incurably *aporetic*' (pp. 10–11).

28 I use these as major examples. Others could be added – such as nonviolence, the history of which has been well traced by Mark Kurlansky in *Non-Violence: The History of a Dangerous Idea* (Jonathan Cape, 2006).

29 Harry J. Gensler, *Ethics and the Golden Rule* (Routledge, 2013), pp. 76–107.

30 This moral sensibility is raised by Adam Smith. More recently we find it in the self of George Herbert Mead, the I–Thou duality of

Martin Buber, the dialogic communicative ethical tradition and the ethics of intersubjectivity and care: see Ronald C. Arnett, Janie M. Harden Fritz and Leeanne M. Bell, *Communication Ethics Literacy: Dialogue and Difference* (Sage, 2009). Most recently, see Stephen Darwall, *Second-Person Standpoint: Morality, Respect, and Accountability* (Harvard University Press, 2009); see also Judith Andre, *Worldly Virtue: Moral Ideas and Contemporary Life* (Lexington Books, 2019); Joan C. Tronto, *Caring Democracy: Markets, Equality, and Justice* (New York University Press, 2013).

31 So-called 'natural ends', 'human goods' and 'motivations' are often the hidden tacit ideas behind what is now often called virtue theory.

32 For example, Kwame Gyekye, 'African Ethics', in Edward N. Zalta, ed., *The Stanford Encyclopedia of Philosophy*: https://plato.stanford.edu/archives/fall2011/entries/african-ethics/.

33 Christian Smith, *To Flourish or Destruct: A Personalist Theory of Human Goods, Motivations, Failure and Evil* (University of Chicago Press, 2015), esp. ch. 5.

34 Abraham Maslow, *Motivation and Personality*, 3rd edn (Harper and Row, 1970 [1954]), p. 165.

35 Martha C. Nussbaum, *Creating Capabilities: The Human Development Approach* (Harvard University Press, 2011), p. 18.

36 See also Martha C. Nussbaum, *Cultivating Humanity: A Classical Defense of Reform in Liberal Education* (Harvard University Press, 1997).

37 An influential work, often credited with this renewed interest, is Alasdair Macintyre, *After Virtue: A Study in Moral Theory*, 3rd edn (University of Notre Dame Press, 2007 [1981]).

38 Christopher Peterson and Martin Seligman, *Character Strength and Virtues: A Handbook and* Classification (Oxford University Press, 2004); Andre, *Worldly Virtue*; Michael S. Brady *Suffering and Virtue* (Oxford University Press, 2018).

39 See Lynn Hunt, *Inventing Human Rights: A History* (Norton, 2006); Micheline R. Ishay, *The History of Human Rights: From Ancient Times to the Globalization Era*, 2nd rev. edn (University of California Press, 2008).

40 See Bruce Friesen, *Moral Systems and the Evolution of Human Rights* (Springer, 2014); he argues that human rights are the first 'global indigenous' moral system. See also Joas, *The Sacredness of the Person*; Alison Brysk, *The Future of Human Rights* (Polity, 2018).

41 Rodrique Tremblay, *The Code for Global Ethics: Toward a Humanist Civilization* (Trafford Publishing, 2009), p. 17.

42 See Heather Widdows, *Global Ethics: An Introduction* (Routledge, 2011); Kimberly Hutchings, *Global Ethics: An Introduction*, 2nd edn (Polity, 2018); see also Nigel Dower, *World Ethics: The New Agenda*, 2nd edn (Edinburgh University Press, 2007).

43 There is a vast literature on justice. See, for example, Amartya Sen, *The Idea of Justice* (Belknap Press, 2009) and Michael J. Sandel, *Justice: What's the Right Thing to Do?* (Farrar Straus Giroux, 2009).

44 See Brian Cox and Andrew Cohen, *Human Universe* (HarperCollins, 2014).

Chapter 7: Transforming Humanity

1 Arturo Escobar, *Pluriversal Politics: The Real and the Possible* (Duke University Press, 2020).

2 Yuval Noah Harari, *Homo Deus: A Brief History of Tomorrow* (Vintage Books, 2017), p. 67.

3 With irony, three major world sociologists have written about the future in their last published books. In *What is the Future?* (Polity, 2016), John Urry (d. 2016), developed an important account of what it is to study the future, raising many of the problems of theorizing the complexities of time as well as drafting out some scenarios for 'the future of futures'. Chapter 3, 'New Catastrophic Futures', provides an extraordinary listing of works that predict the collapse, the end times and catastrophic cascades. See also the ideas of Ulrich Beck (d. 2015) on risk society: his last major work was *The Metamorphosis of the World: How Climate Change is Transforming Our Concept of the World* (Polity, 2016). And see Zygmunt Bauman (d. 2017), *Retrotopia* (Polity, 2017); he was a long-time observer of the widespread disenchantment of the world; this book suggests how we look to the past to rectify the failings of the present human condition.

4 See Heinrich Geiselberger, ed., *The Great Regression* (Polity, 2017); Edward Luce, *The Retreat of Western Liberalism* (Little, Brown, 2017); Sylvia Walby, *Crisis* (Polity, 2015).

5 There are indeed many contrasting accounts of the future. For one set of visions, see Peter Frase, *Four Futures: Life After Capitalism* (Verso, 2016). For Frase, the future lies in communism, socialism, rentism or exterminism. See, more widely, Nick Bostrom, 'The Future of Humanity', in Jan Kyrre Berg Olsen, Evan Selinger and Soren Riis, eds, *New Waves in Philosophy of Technology* (Palgrave Macmillan, 2009), pp. 186–215.

6 A valuable study on all this is Toby Ord's *The Precipice: Existential Risk and the Future of Humanity* (Bloomsbury, 2020).

7 *Apocalypse Now* (1979), dir. Francis Ford Coppola.

8 See Rob Nixon, *Slow Violence and the Environmentalism of the Poor* (Harvard University Press, 2011); Amitav Ghosh, *The Great Derangement: Climate Change and the Unthinkable* (University of Chicago Press, 2016).

9 Urry, *What is the Future?*, pp. 36–7.

10 David Wallace-Wells, *The Uninhabitable Earth: A Story of the Future* (Allen Lane, 2019).

11 David Christian, *Origin Story: A Big History of Everything* (Penguin, 2018), p. 263.

12 Ord, *The Precipice*, p. 33.

13 See Jared Diamond, *Collapse: How Societies Choose to Fail or Survive*, 2nd edn (Penguin, 2011).

14 Max Tegmark, *Life 3.0: Being Human in the Age of Artificial Intelligence* (Allen Lane, 2017), pp. 161–203. The quote is from the Future of Life Institute, quoted by Tegmark on p. 22.

15 Ray Kurzweil, *The Singularity Is Near: When Humans Transend Biology* (Duckworth, 2006). Kurzweil is a prime example of a transhumanist futurist; he argues that we will live forever. *The Singularity is Near* was also made into film, released in 2012: see http://singularity.com.

16 Michio Kaku is a physicist; see his *The Future of Humanity: Terraforming Mars, Interstellar Travel, Immortality and Our Destiny Beyond Earth* (Penguin, 2019).

17 Steven Pinker, *Enlightenment Now: The Case for Reason, Science, Humanism and Progress* (Allen Lane, 2018).

18 See Angus Deaton, *The Great Escape: Health, Wealth and the Origins of Inequality* (Princeton University Press, 2013).

19 Hans Rosling, a Swedish physician, academic, public speaker and co-founder of the Gapminder Foundation, shows just how ignorant people are of these advances that have been made. Even the cleverest of people have little idea of the evidence for human progress and tend to hold negative views on most of these issues. And yet, in *Factfulness: Ten Reasons We're Wrong about the World – and Why Things Are Better Than You Think* (Sceptre, 2018), Rosling shows some thirty-two clear areas of improvement, from the containment of HIV infection and the regulation of smallpox, to the escalation of new feature films each year, and the rise in scholarship and publications. Living in a time of coronavirus is not the same as living in the time of the Black Death.

20 See the discussions in Felix Dodds, David Donoghue and Jimena Leiva Roesch, *Negotiating the Sustainable Development Goals:*

A Transformational Agenda for an Insecure World (Routledge, 2016).

21 The Sustainable Development Goals are updated regularly; see: https://www.undp.org/content/undp/en/home/sustainable-development-goals.html. See also 'Will the Covid-19 Pandemic Threaten the SDGs?', *The Lancet*, September 2020: https://www.ncbi.nlm.nih.gov/pmc/articles/PMC7462553/.

22 Rebecca Solnit, *Hope in the Dark: Untold Histories, Wild Possibilities* (Haymarket Books, 2016), p. xv.

23 *Earth from Space* is a four-part documentary film screened first in 2019. It powerfully illustrates the movement from planet to person.

24 Jeffrey C. Goldfarb, *The Politics of Small Things: The Power of the Powerless in Dark Times* (University of Chicago Press, 2007).

25 Sociology has long taken action and structure as central theoretical problems. I sense with the technology of Google Earth a technical facility for moving between big worlds and little worlds, agency and structure.

26 See also Thomas Davies, *NGOs: A New History of Transnational Civil Society* (Hurst, 2013).

27 Rickie Solinger, Madeline Fox and Kayhan Irani, eds, *Telling Stories to Change the World: Global Voices on the Power of Narrative to Build Community and Make Social Justice Claims* (Routledge, 2008), p. 11.

28 Peter Weibel, ed., *Global Activism: Art and Conflict in the 21st Century* (MIT Press, 2014).

29 Ashish Kothari, Ariel Salleh, Arturo Escobar, Federico Demaria and Alberto Acosta, eds, *Pluriverse: A Post-Development Dictionary* (Tulika Books, 2019); Global Tapestry of Alternatives (GTA): https://globaltapestryofalternatives.org.

30 Nicholas D. Kristof and Sheryl Wudunn, *Half the Sky: How to Change the World* (Virago, 2009).

31 Joe Willis, *Contesting World Order? Socioeconomic Rights and Global Justice Movements* (Cambridge University Press, 2017), p. 10.

32 Davies, *NGOs: A New History of Transnational Civil Society*.

33 Raewyn Connell looks at the world history of ideas and suggests the need for a mosaic epistemology in 'Meeting at the Edge of Fear: Theory on a World Scale', *Feminist Theory* 16/1 (2015): 49–66. See also Walter Mignolo, 'On Pluriversality and Multipolar World Order: Decoloniality after Decolonization: Dewesternization after the Cold War', in Bernd Reiter, ed., *Constructing the Pluriverse: The Geopolitics of Knowledge* (Duke University Press, 2018), pp. 90–116.

34 See Kothari et al., *Pluriverse: A Post-Development Dictionary*.

35 On the diversity of these politics, see Ken Plummer, *Narrative Power* (Polity, 2019), p. 78, Table 4.2.

36 See Erik Olin Wright, *Envisioning Real Utopias* (Verso, 2010); and Ruth Levitas, *Utopia as Method: The Imaginary Reconstitution of Society* (Palgrave Macmillan, 2013).

37 See Roger Scruton, *The Uses of Pessimism and the Danger of False Hope* (Atlantic Books, 2010).

38 See Terry Eagleton, *Hope Without Optimism* (Yale University Press, 2019).

39 Lauren Berlant, *Cruel Optimism* (Duke University Press, 2011).

40 For instances of such failures, like collectivization in Russia, the Great Leap in China, see James C. Scott, *Seeing Like A State: How Certain Schemes to Improve the Human Condition Have Failed* (Yale University Press, 2020).

41 I have explored both hope and utopian thought before: as part of the humanist imagination, as 'the little grounded everyday "utopian" processes of global hope', in *Cosmopolitan Sexualities: Hope and the Humanist Imagination* (Polity, 2015), pp. 183–7; as a tool for doing sociology, in *Sociology: The Basics*, 2nd edn (Routledge, 2016); and as 'acts of narrative hope' in *Narrative Power: The Struggle for Human Value* (Polity, 2019), p. 150. .

42 Ernst Bloch, *The Principle of Hope*, 3 vols (MIT Press, 1954, 1955, 1959).

43 Hans Jonas, *The Imperative of Responsibility: In Search of an Ethics for the Technological Age* (Chicago University Press, 1984 [1979]).

44 See Charles Tilly and his idea of 'contentious claims' in *Social Movements 1768–2004* (Routledge, 2004).

45 See: https://www.npr.org/2019/09/23/763452863/transcript-greta-thunbergs-speech-at-the-u-n-climate-action-summit. Also see Greta Thunberg, *No One is Too Small to Make a Difference* (Penguin, 2019); and Extinction Rebellion, *This is Not a Drill: An Extinction Rebellion Handbook* (Penguin, 2019).

Chapter 8: A Manifesto for the Twenty-First Century

1 Parag Khanna, *The Future is Asian: Commerce, Conflict, and Culture in the 21st Century* (Simon and Schuster, 2019), p. 2.

2 Edward Luce, *The Retreat of Western Liberalism* (Abacus, 2018), p. 200.

3 The speech can be listened to at: http://okra.stanford.edu/media/audio/1967_04_04_beyond_vietnam.mp3. It is not unfortunately included in the fine collection of writings, *Testament of*

Hope: The Essential Writings and Speeches of Martin Luther King, Jr., edited by James M. Washington (HarperCollins, 1986).

4 See John Rawls, *A Theory of Justice* (Harvard University Press, 1971).

5 Shoshana Zuboff, *The Age of Surveillance Capitalism: The Fight for a Human Future at the New Frontier of Power* (Profile Books, 2019), p. 522.

6 Such ideas can be followed up in many places: for example, the UN Report, *The Right to Privacy in the Digital Age* (2018): https://www.ohchr.org/EN/Issues/DigitalAge/Pages/ ReportDigitalAge.aspx. Others have been making claims for developing a broad framework of digital citizenship to be taught in schools and developed more widely to make people think about both the risks of being online, and the etiquette and civility needed for it to work well. Human digitalism, based on shared cosmopolitan human values, is being taught in some schools. See Engin Isin and Evelyn Ruppert, *Being Digital Citizens* (Rowman & Littlefield, 2015); Karen Mossberger, Caroline J. Tolbert and Ramona S. McNeal, *Digital Citizenship: The Internet, Society, and Participation* (MIT Press, 2007). See also Kevin Healey and Robert H. Woods, *Ethics and Religion in the Age of Social Media: Digital Proverbs for Responsible Citizens* (Routledge, 2019).

7 https://vikalpsangam.org/about/the-search-for-alternatives-key-aspects-and-principles/.

Epilogue: On Being Well in the World – The Joys of Living

1 An earlier draft of this book included a full chapter on 'happiness', humanity and the rise of the 'happiness industry'. In a short book like this, many issues were not able to be included. But this epilogue gives a sense of the small ways in which lives find some contentment in the world. For two recent, critical discussions of the happiness industry, see Edgar Cabanas and Eva Illouz, *Manufacturing Happy Citizens: How the Science and Industry of Happiness Control our Lives* (Polity, 2019), and Daniel Nehring, Ole Jacob Madsen, Edgar Cabanas, China Mills and Dylan Kerrigan, eds, *The Routledge International Handbook of Global Therapeutic Cultures* (Routledge, 2020).

Index

environmental damage, 2,
47–9, 63, 174, 180
apocalyptic futures, 150
expulsion by, 56
harm reduction, 181
narratives, 118–19
prevention, 164
Epicurus, 142, 204
epistemology, *see* knowledge
Epstein, Mikhail, 107
equality, 6, 80
democracy, 61–2
digitalism, 196
dignity, 29, 30
gender, 20, 154, 155, 156
rights, 26, 27
social justice, 147
values, 193, 194
see also inequalities
equity, 54
Erikson, Erik, 225n8
Escobar, Arturo, 18, 45, 149,
212n4
essentialism, 4, 12, 29–30, 32,
34, 218n54
Estonia, 136
ethics
collective responsibility,
166
critical science, 24
earthly values, 146
failure of, 88
global, 15, 140, 144–5, 194
globalization, 138
Islamic, 161
as a project, 130–1
values connected to, 127
see also morality
Ethiopia, 56, 61
ethnic cleansing, 2, 73–4, 76
ethnicity, 2–3
colonization, 73
dehumanization, 33, 77
fear, 74
hierarchies, 76

inequalities, 54
populist hate, 61
rights, 28
transformative politics, 162
violence against women, 95
see also race; racialization;
racism
ethnocentrism, 80, 132, 139,
183
ethno-nationalism, 64
eugenics, 23
Europe, 55, 94, 136, 137
European Union, 117
evil, 86, 88, 127, 133, 229n2
evolution, 21–2, 110, 119, 152,
216n31
exclusion, 34–5, 46, 55–7, 63,
73, 174
circle of humanity, 187
damaged humanity, 185
harm reduction, 181
monitoring resources, 65
narratives of worldly care,
190–1
paradox of humanity, 81,
185
resistance, 194
existential humans, 38–9, 70
existential risks, 150–1, 174
existential values, 146, 196
experts, 58
Extinction Rebellion, 49,
167–8
extinctions, 151
extremism, 19–20

fairness, 141, 180, 192
'fake news', 62, 180, 196
fallacy of the end times, 33
famine, 2, 90
Fanon, Frantz, 16, 18, 78
Fasching, Darrell J., 114
Fassin, Didier, 25–6
fear, 74, 76
femicide, 4, 46, 86, 90